The
Yes, you can
of Invacare Corporation

The Yes, you can
of Invacare Corporation

JEFFREY L. RODENGEN *&* **ANTHONY L. WALL**

Edited by Heather G. Cohn
Design and layout by Dennis Shockley and Joey Henderson

For Randy Cierly-Sterling, a friend.
Few possess his talent, fewer still his resolve.

WRITE STUFF

Write Stuff Enterprises, Inc.
1001 South Andrews Avenue, Second Floor
Fort Lauderdale, FL 33316
1-800-900-Book (1-800-900-2665)
(954) 462-6657
www.writestuffbooks.com

Publisher's Cataloging in Publication

Rodengen, Jeffrey L.
  The yes you can of Invacare corporation/Jeffrey
L. Rodengen, Anthony L. Wall. – 1st ed.
  p. cm.
  Includes bibliographical references and index.
  ISBN 0-945903-72-3

  1. INVACARE Corporation (Elyria, Ohio) 2.
Wheelchair industry – Ohio – History. 3. Medical
instruments and apparatus industry – Ohio –
History. I. Wall, Anthony L. II. Title.

  HD9995.W544.I58R64 2000   338.4761703'09771
                               QBI00-544

Library of Congress
Catalog Card Number 00-133759

ISBN 0-945903-72-3

Completely produced in the
United States of America
10 9 8 7 6 5 4 3 2 1

Also by Jeffrey L. Rodengen

The Legend of Chris-Craft

*IRON FIST: The Lives
of Carl Kiekhaefer*

*Evinrude-Johnson and
The Legend of OMC*

*Serving the Silent Service:
The Legend of Electric Boat*

*The Legend of
Dr Pepper/Seven-Up*

The Legend of Honeywell

*The Legend of
Briggs & Stratton*

The Legend of Ingersoll-Rand

*The Legend of Stanley:
150 Years of The Stanley Works*

The MicroAge Way

The Legend of Halliburton

*The Legend of
York International*

*The Legend of
Nucor Corporation*

*The Legend of Goodyear:
The First 100 Years*

The Legend of AMP

The Legend of Cessna

The Legend of VF Corporation

The Spirit of AMD

*New Horizons:
The Story of Ashland Inc.*

The Legend of Rowan

*The History of
American Standard*

The Legend of Mercury Marine

The Legend of Federal-Mogul

*Against the Odds:
Inter-Tel—The First 30 Years*

The Legend of Pfizer

*State of the Heart:
The Practical Guide to
Your Heart and Heart Surgery*
with Larry W. Stephenson, M.D.

*The Legend of
Worthington Industries*

*The Legend of
Trinity Industries, Inc.*

The Legend of IBP, Inc.

*The Legend of
Cornelius Vanderbilt Whitney*

The Legend of Amdahl

The Legend of Litton Industries

The Legend of Bertram
with David A. Patten

The Legend of ALLTEL
with David A. Patten

The Legend of Gulfstream

*The Legend of
Ritchie Bros. Auctioneers*

TABLE OF CONTENTS

FOREWORD

by
Bernadine P. Healy, M.D.

THIS BOOK CELEBRATES the history of Invacare. It is the story of one of America's great, innovative companies— a story of vision, entrepreneurialism, creative management, dedication, and humanism.

Since the company's inception, Invacare Corporation has been influenced by a strong sense of social responsibility to people with disabilities and those who care for them, and also to the various communities where Invacare's facilities are located.

Invacare develops vital products and technologies that improve the quality of life of those with short- or long-term disabilities. The company further emphasizes its commitment to those it serves through participation in and sponsorship of Easter Seals, the Paralyzed Veterans of America's National Veterans Wheelchair Games, wheelchair basketball and quad-rugby teams, and events sponsored by the Cleveland Clinic Mellen Center for multiple sclerosis treatment and research. In association with Easter Seals camps throughout the country, Invacare sponsors wheelchair athletes who lead the camps and serve as valuable role models for children with disabilities. Without the opportunity to participate in these "Invacare Days" camps, many of these children would never experience firsthand the satisfaction of participating in recreation and sporting activities. Such hands-on involvement

exemplifies the company's caring and compassionate approach toward helping the disabled deal with their challenges.

Many countries relegate people with disabilities to background roles. All too often, the disabled are not visible in society and the workplace. Even in many developed countries, the image of a wheelchair conjures thoughts of people on the fringes of society, somehow not participating to the fullest. We have made great strides in integrating those with disabilities in this country, and companies like Invacare make this possible through their enabling technologies.

Invacare's commitment to research and development has contributed greatly to the evolution of the wheelchair, from the early days of the simple attendant-pushed models to today's highly sophisticated all-power vehicles using state-of-the-art technologies, allowing even quadriplegics the sort of mobility that could only have been dreamed of years ago.

One such example is Invacare's development of a gearless-brushless motor, which utilizes the principle of electromagnetism to achieve a true breakthrough in motor design and operation. The result is a quiet motor that is easy to operate and service.

Another product that contributes directly to an improvement in the quality of life is an oxygen system that enables patients dependent upon inhaled oxygen to refill their own oxygen cylinders with a concentrator at home. These and other Invacare-led innovations enhance a sense of freedom and convenience for patients.

The needs of patients with acute or long-term disabilities will only increase as our population ages. In addition, we must focus not only on the independence and dignity of those facing such afflictions, but also on their caregivers. Technological developments such as an electric, elevating bed or a wheelchair designed for ease of operation make life easier on the loved ones rendering home care to the disabled.

As we look to the future, I believe that we need to continue to respond to the changing nature of the patients we serve and the illnesses and disabilities they are confronting. Helping those with chronic disabilities who face long-term, lingering illnesses will likely prove to be modern medicine's biggest test. I think that this will continue to be a challenge, not only because people are living longer and want the most from their quality of life, but because people of all ages are surviving illnesses that in another time would have been fatal.

The key elements are quality of life considerations as well as responsiveness to the physiological needs of the disabled, whether their disabilities are skeletal or neurological.

I am proud to have been a part of Invacare. In addition to its outstanding success in the field of technical innovation, it is also a company that has always been driven by humanitarian purposes. Invacare is about compassion and empowerment and maximizing the value of every person, one by one, whatever the illness or disability might be.

Bernadine P. Healy, M.D.
Director, Invacare Corporation

Dr. Healy, a physician and educator, has a long career of leadership in public service at the local and national levels.

ACKNOWLEDGMENTS

RESEARCHING, WRITING, and publishing *The Yes, You Can of Invacare Corporation* would not have been possible without the effort and guidance of a great many individuals, both inside and outside Invacare.

Special thanks go to Mal Mixon; Lou Slangen, senior vice president, sales and marketing; and Dr. Bernadine P. Healy. Very special thanks go to Susan Elder, director of marketing communications, and her assistant, Judy Maynard, without whose generous assistance, professionalism, and responsiveness this book would have been impossible to produce. We are indebted to Susan for her tireless help and suggestions at all phases of the manuscript. Her involvement was crucial in enabling us to capture the story of Invacare, and her patience with a multitude of requests, many made on short notice, was greatly appreciated.

We are also grateful to Gil Haury, retired director of Invacare's corporate test lab; Dawn Orsik, graphic designer; Mary Carol Peterson, product manager, Invacare Top End; Lee Sheffield, lead technician; Ron Thomas, director of facilities; and Nyal Yost, retired vice president, for their help in rounding up images.

This project would not have been possible without the assistance of our hard-working team of editors, particularly Executive Editor Jon VanZile and Associate Editor Heather G. Cohn, and our industrious team of research assistants, Jay Miller and Chrissy Kadleck. The principal research and narrative timeline were accomplished by Jay; Chrissy provided the narrative timeline for the history of the wheelchair and sought out and organized the art that illustrates this volume. The art was skillfully integrated with text by our award-winning art team, especially Art Director Dennis Shockley and former Art Director Joey Henderson.

Thanks are also extended to the many past and present employees of Invacare who lent their time, expertise, and knowledge, including Gerry Blouch, president and board member; Tom Buckley, former senior vice president, marketing; Bill Corcoran, vice president, Invacare Credit Corporation; Neal Curran, vice president, engineering and product development; Michael Devlin, former director, home care professional marketing; John Dmytriw, senior operations director; Jim Dowdell, human resources generalist; Lou Hyster, senior managing engineer; Dave Johnson, vice president, operations and logistics; Judy Kovacs, vice president, customer services and product support; Kathy Leneghan, corporate controller; Libbie Lockard, former manager of trade shows and special events; Jan Lovelace, director, human resources; Darrel Lowery, vice president, supply chain management; Tom Miklich, CFO and general counsel; Pat Nalley, retired vice president of sales and marketing/assistant to the president; Dale Nash, director, national distributor accounts; Steven Neese, vice president of e-commerce; Mike Parsons, vice president of North American sales; Mike Perry, vice president of distributed products; Dave Pessel, former chief corporate information officer; Dave Piersma, director, distribution; Hymie Pogir, vice president and product manager, Invacare technologies; Edith Powers, retired executive assistant to Mal Mixon; J. B. Richey, senior vice president, electronic and design engineering; Otmar Sackerlotzky, retired vice president, quality; Lou Slangen, senior vice president, sales and marketing; Ken Sparrow, managing director, Australasian operations; Larry Steward, former vice president, human resources; Lou Tabickman, president, European operations; Ron Thomas, director of facilities; Debbie Warden, assistant to Mal Mixon; Tom Wiegand, former director, corporate pricing and sales administrative services; Dave Williams, director of government relations.

In addition, we would like to thank Joe Callahan, former board member; Bill Jones, former board chairman and member; Dale LaPorte, general counsel (Calfee, Halter & Griswold, LLP); Ernie Mansour, Invacare litigation attorney, Mansour, Gavin, Gerlack & Manos Company, L.P.A.; Dan Moore, board member; and Jim Williams, president and CEO, Easter Seals.

And, as always, the authors extend a very special word of thanks to the dedicated staff at Write Stuff. Proofreader Bonnie Freeman and transcriptionist Mary Aaron worked quickly and efficiently; Erika Orloff assembled the comprehensive index. Particular gratitude goes to Executive Author David A. Patten; former Executive Author Tony Wall; Executive Author Rich Hubbard; Senior Editor Melody Maysonet; Senior Art Director Sandy Cruz, and Rachelle Donley and Wendy Iverson, art directors; Office Manager Marianne Roberts; Production Manager Bruce Borich, former Production Manager Gary Pulliam; Executive Assistant Nancy Rackear; former Executive Assistant Amanda Fowler; Manager of Sales and Promotions Grace Kurotori; Director of Marketing Sheryl Herdsman; former Director of Marketing Bonnie Bratton; Distribution Supervisor Rory Schmer; former Logistics Specialist Rafael Santiago; Administrative Assistant Elisa Leal, and Project Coordinator Karine Rodengen.

This 1850 painting by artist Henry Alken shows a person with a disability in what is literally a chair on wheels. Although the chair itself looks somewhat comfortable, the device is large and cumbersome and was no doubt difficult for the occupant to propel by himself due to the high chair arms. It was most likely intended for use inside the home, with the occupant being pushed by an attendant, as shown. *(Photo courtesy National Library of Medicine, History of Medicine Division.)*

CHAPTER ONE

THE HISTORY OF THE WHEELCHAIR

SIXTH CENTURY TO THE PRESENT DAY

People with disabilities want more than wheelchair mobility. What they really want is access, integration, and jobs—they want to do all the same things able-bodied people want to do.

—A. Malachi Mixon, III, chairman and CEO, Invacare, 2000

I T TOOK THOUSANDS OF YEARS for humankind to combine two of its more useful inventions—the wheel and the chair—into a single vehicle designed to provide mobility for the disabled.

And, although the first, rudimentary wheelchairs can be traced to the sixth century, the history of this device is still being written as social awareness, medical science, and technological advancements further the development of rehabilitative medicine.[1]

Hailed by some as the most therapeutic device in rehabilitative medicine,[2] the wheelchair today is used by close to 1.4 million Americans, according to the 1990 U.S. Bureau of the Census. Yet only in the last twenty years has the wheelchair industry—itself relatively young—become truly responsive to the needs of chair users and their desire for autonomous, active living. Today's wheelchairs are sleek, sporty, and colorful, sending a bold message of confidence and capability. In addition, the wheelchairs available today have been designed with multiple user needs in mind. These vehicles are a far cry from their unwieldy ancestors,[3] which in many ways segregated their users from society rather than integrating them.[4]

Today's multifunctional and attractive chairs are causing people to view wheelchairs and other rehabilitative products as enabling rather than

Wheel Chair 1920s
8.4 USA
Nonprofit

stigmatizing. "As the cultural thinking shifts to, 'It's all right to use these products,' more people are going to use them," said Neal Curran, vice president of engineering and product development for Invacare Corporation, the world's largest producer of wheelchairs. "As wheelchairs become more visible, they're more attractive and less medical in nature."[5]

Thanks to technological advances and legislation such as the 1990 Americans with Disabilities Act (ADA), it is more feasible than ever for a person with a disability to maintain a mobile lifestyle. But this wasn't always the case: the modern wheelchair was a long time in coming.

Beginning with the Wheel

The earliest evidence of wheeled vehicles dates back to 3500 B.C. and a Sumerian stone carving of a two-wheeled cart. From Assyria in 3000 B.C. and the Indus Valley in 2500 B.C., there is evidence of still other wheeled vehicles. However, these

---

This U.S. postage stamp shows a 1920-model Colson wheelchair, which was propelled by hand levers. It probably allowed its user only a modicum of mobility and independence because of its size and weight. (©United States Postal Service 1988.)

early inventions—including spoke-wheeled chariots around 2000 B.C. in Asia Minor[6]—are not believed to have been used to transport the disabled.[7]

Instead, the litter—a lightweight, simple structure that was easily carried by friends, family, slaves, or servants—was the preferred mode of travel for the sick and wounded. In fact, even those who could afford more elaborate means of transportation, such as chariots, elephants, or horses, often preferred to travel in covered litters called palanquins.[8]

Possibly the earliest record of a chair on wheels is found on a Chinese sarcophagus dated at around A.D. 525 that depicts three scenes from the *Confucian Stories of Filial Piety*.[9] In them, a youth holds a three-wheeled chair for his grandfather, a chair that is remarkably similar to the wheeled, wooden garden chairs of a later era.[10]

In the Middle Ages, the litter was replaced by a more practical and efficient means of travel credited to the Chinese Jugo Lyang in the third century: the wheelbarrow. Although it was a less glamorous mode of transportation than a litter and still required the aid of another person to operate, the wheelbarrow quickly gained in popularity.[11]

Introduced in Europe in the twelfth century, the wheelbarrow, or "barrow," was used for carrying loads of all kinds, including the sick and the dead. According to Dr. Herman Kamenetz in his book *The Wheelchair Book: Mobility for the Disabled*:

> *Pictures of the sixteenth century show the old and disabled coming to the magical Fountain of Youth, wheeled in barrows, horse-drawn in carriages, carried in litters or on a man's shoulders and walking away leaving Fountain, litters, barrows and old age behind.*[12]

Moving Forward

In 1588, Balthasar Hacker built the first model wheelchair in Nuremberg, Germany. It was a chair on wheels that doubled as a bed but could also be used as a commode.[13] It was generally used by people with gout.[14] Hacker's innovative design would eventually—by a long, circuitous route—give birth to a $1 billion industry in the United States.

The first high-profile chair was made in 1595 for King Philip II of Spain, who suffered from gout, by Flemish nobleman Jehan Lhermite. The overstuffed armchair was upholstered in horsehair, had movable leg rests and a backrest, and moved on four small wheels.[15] Said Lhermite of the chair:

Sixth century—One of the earliest wheeled chairs on record can be found in a drawing on a Chinese sarcophagus dated at around A.D. 525.

1595—Gout sufferer King Philip II of Spain has a special chair designed for himself which may have somewhat resembled the wooden chair at right.

Middle Ages—The wheelbarrow, or "barrow," is used in Europe to transport the sick and the dead.

1750—James Heath of Bath, England, creates the "Bath chair," a three-wheeled chair typically used by the disabled and women.

"Though it was of wood, leather and ordinary iron, [it] was worth ten times its weight in gold and silver for his Majesty's comfort."[16]

As early as the seventeenth century, there were reports of other one-of-a-kind wheelchairs tailor-made for specific individuals.[17] But these and later versions tended to be heavy and cumbersome and usually required either great strength or a full-time attendant to push them. Thus many of the disabled continued to be confined to immobility in institutions or their homes and were totally dependent on others.[18] By the end of the Renaissance, the rolling chair was still developing.

The first known inventor of the self-propelled chair appears to have been Johann Hautsch, who in 1640 built a chair that could be operated with two cranks. About fifteen years later in Altdorf, a town close to Nuremberg, a paraplegic watchmaker named Stephan Farfler built a low chair for himself with three small wheels—two in the back, one in the front—that he could use outside the home. The single front wheel was propelled by two rotary handles on each side of the chair.[19]

The wheelchair as we would recognize it today first appeared in the early eighteenth century. Styled like an armchair, it was equipped with two large wooden wheels in front with hand rims for propulsion and one smaller wheel in back for balance. Although this chair was a vast improvement over its predecessors, it remained heavy, ornate, and difficult to propel and failed to offer any real independence to its user.[20]

The Eighteenth Century: A Transitional Time

Although the chairs of the eighteenth century didn't truly allow their users to get around independently, designers did begin to consider comfort. One such designer/inventor, John Joseph Merlin, created the Merlin chair, which had full-size wheels and a smaller, lighter outer wheel that enabled users to control the vehicle without getting their hands dirty.[21]

Around 1750, James Heath of Bath, England, created the "Bath chair" for outside use.[22] His invention remained popular through Victorian times. Typically used by women and the disabled, the Bath chair had two large rear wheels joined by an axle and a smaller, pivoting wheel in the front. A horizontal bar was placed on the back of the chair to allow an attendant to push, while the person

1800s—The development of the bicycle influences wheelchair design, which begins to develop in response to the Civil War's returning veterans.

1948—An English doctor develops wheelchair sports for recuperating veterans. Twelve years later, disabled athletes compete for the first time in the Olympics. The needs of these athletes continue to drive wheelchair innovation over the next fifty years.

1930s—Herbert Everest and Harry Jennings create the first foldable, "lightweight" wheelchair. It weighs fifty pounds.

2000—Wheelchair users can choose from a variety of manual and motorized chairs geared to many different needs. Technological advances enable even the most disabled users to control their chairs by the merest movement of the head or tongue, and even by inhaling or exhaling.

seated used a steering handle connected with the front wheel to guide the chair.[23] Later variations of the Bath chair may be credited to John Dawson, who proclaimed himself a "wheel-chair maker" in 1798.[24]

Several drawings by Thomas Rowaldson, dated between 1792 and 1798, may provide the link between King Philip's gout chair and the wooden wheelchair used in hospitals during the twentieth century. The drawings show a wooden wheelchair being pushed by an attendant; its wheels were each made of one piece of wood seemingly large enough for self propulsion and a small third wheel tucked under the footboard.[25]

Many of the rolling chairs used in Bath in the late 1800s were the work of two brothers—John and Alfred Carter. In their 1881 catalog, they offered a wide variety of indoor and outdoor chairs and several models that could be self-propelled.[26]

These same kinds of wheelchairs first appeared in the United States around the time of the Civil War (1861–65). In the North alone, 281,881 men returned home with injuries.[27] Some were missing limbs or were otherwise unable to get around on

Above: The Bath chair, first developed in 1750, remained popular through Victorian times. Wire-spoked wheels on this Bath chair indicate that it is a post-1890s model—probably from the 1920s or 1930s. *(Photo courtesy Bath & North East Somerset Libraries, Arts & Archives Service, Bath Central Library.)*

Left: King Philip of Spain's gout chair may have somewhat resembled this 1798 wheelchair. Although it lacks a handle for pushing and its arms look low enough to allow for self-propulsion, it appears intended more for sitting than for getting around. *(Photo courtesy National Library of Medicine, History of Medicine Division.)*

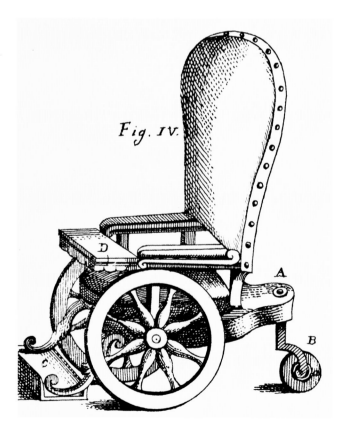

Fig. IV.

their own. The survival rate for the severely disabled was not promising at the time of the Civil War, or even following World War I, which may be one reason the chairs were slow in developing. Said Joseph Shapiro in his book *No Pity*:

> *Quadriplegics almost never lived in those days between the world wars. Rehabilitative medicine was just developing in a crude form in response to the return of paralyzed war veterans.[28]*

Although a few self-propelled models may have been available, the occupants of Civil War–era wheelchairs were often pushed by an attendant. Because the chairs were still large and awkward, they afforded their users only a modicum of independence.

The wood-and-wicker wheelchairs then were rigid and rectangular with high backs. They were too wide to get through most doors, a reflection of the fact that most disabled people then were considered useless members of society. Wheelchairs were made for people who were closeted at home or who lived in institutions.[29]

Bicycle Benefits

The development of the bicycle, which began in Europe in the 1800s and quickly spread to the United States, had a significant impact on the wheelchair. Bicycle technology—and thus wheelchairs—took a tremendous leap forward when the wheels evolved from wood to iron, hollow rubber tires were added, and sizes were standardized. Borrowing from the success of the bicycle, Peter Gendron was the first in the United States to add a wire-spoked wheel to a wheelchair in 1890.[30]

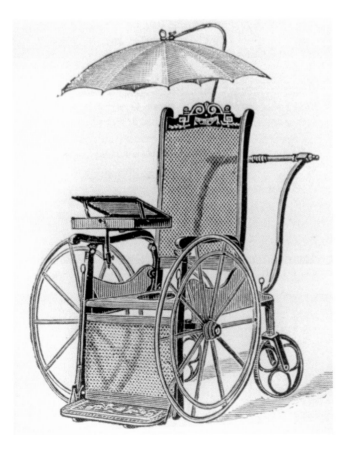

In the late 1800s, most wheelchairs were produced without hand rims, though their wheels were large enough for self-propulsion. The chairs made during this time had caned seats and backs, and while their design had improved slightly, they were still being fashioned "one size fits all" for invalids—not for those who wanted to be active once again. More than seventy years would pass before a wheelchair was tailored to allow any real mobility, and eighty years before the field of rehabilitative medicine prompted further advances.[31]

According to one catalog, collapsible (front to back) wheelchairs were available in America around 1910. However, in the early 1900s, there was still no folding chair that would enable the disabled to travel on their own, except for one model whose back folded down. Around 1914, a self-propelled chair with bicycle wheels became available. It folded from front to back and weighed seventy pounds.[32]

Among these early wheelchair manufacturers was The Worthington Company, which itself evolved from the Fay Manufacturing Company, an early tricycle manufacturer. These two companies would ultimately evolve to become Invacare Corporation.

Changes Come Slowly

The birth of the modern wheelchair was prompted by an increase in the number of people left permanently disabled by World War I, as well as by an increase in traffic and industrial accidents.[33] In these years, the prognosis for those with spinal cord injuries was not favorable, and many did not survive their injuries. Thanks to medical advancements, however, by World War II (1939–45) the survival rate had increased dramatically, creating a new population of disabled veterans.[34] According to Shapiro:

In World War I, only four hundred men survived with wounds that paralyzed them from the waist

This wheelchair from the late 1800s or early 1900s had a writing desk, a sunshade, and possibly a commode. The hand rims suggest that users could have propelled themselves. The wheelchair also appears to have had a brake mechanism. *(Photo courtesy National Library of Medicine, History of Medicine Division.)*

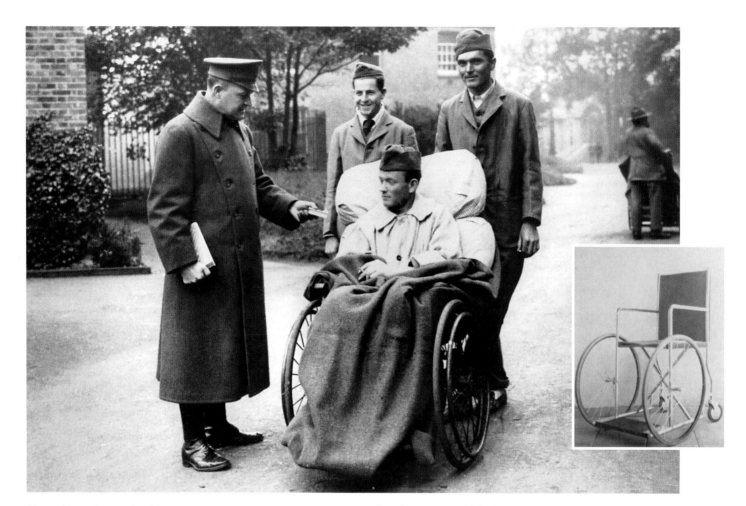

Above: Up until the mid-1900s, the initial survival rate for veterans with debilitating medical problems such as spinal cord injuries was not promising. However, by World War II, more than 85 percent would survive their injuries, thus creating an increased need for rehabilitative products such as the wheelchair this English soldier is sitting in. *(Photo courtesy National Library of Medicine, History of Medicine Division.)*

Inset: This wheelchair, notably slimmer than its forerunners, was created by Herbert Everest and Harry Jennings. The pair would later go into business to market the revolutionary chairs. *(Photo courtesy E&J.)*

down, and 90 percent of them died before they reached home. But, in World War II, two thousand paraplegic soldiers survived, and over 85 percent of them were still alive in the late 1960s. The development of antibiotic drugs and new medical procedures improved the odds. As recently as the 1950s,

death remained likely in the very early stages of a spinal cord injury as a result of respiratory, bladder and other health complications.[35]

Although the life expectancy of paraplegics and quadriplegics was improving, the same could not be said of wheelchair design. In nearly a century, the only major refinement made to the wheelchair was the material used to make its wheels. It wasn't until after 1932, when Californians Herbert Everest, a paraplegic, and his mechanical engineer friend, Harry Jennings Sr., created a foldable, lightweight chair, that the wheelchair changed significantly.

Frustrated with the clumsy wooden chair he had to attach to the trunk of his car when he traveled, Everest longed for a more versatile, user-friendly chair.[36] Said Everest:

In the years before 1935, anyone wishing to buy a wheelchair had a choice of a restricted few. In fact he [sic] took what the dealer had or went without. These chairs, which were 28 inches wide, weighed from 75 lbs. to 90 lbs. The slightly smaller, non-self-propelled chairs reduced the occupant to complete dependence upon an attendant. Nearly all chairs were too wide to go through doors, and they could not go up and down steps.[37]

Everest's complaints echoed those of many wheelchair users. His and Jennings's new chair weighed a spritely fifty pounds compared with turn-of-the-century chairs, some of which weighed as much as ninety pounds.[38] The pair went into business as Everest & Jennings (E&J) to market the revolutionary wheelchairs.

Unbeknownst to E&J, another folding chair was being designed and marketed by an American named Sam Duke around the same time.[39] In 1919, Duke started his own catering and party rental supply business in Chicago. However, as the growing need for wheelchairs, walkers, and hospital beds became apparent, Duke focused his entre-preneurial efforts on creating the American Wheelchair Company.[40]

In 1931, Duke made his folding wheelchair by taking a wooden garden chair and adding two large wheels (wagon wheels) in the back, two smaller wheels (bicycle wheels) in front, and handles on the back. He also painted the chair and gave it a heavy channel seat.[41]

One year later, Everest & Jennings developed their wheelchair—the world's first folding, tubular-steel wheelchair. The company would dominate the wheelchair industry for the next fifty years.[42] Everest became a rolling advertisement for E&J and drew attention wherever he traveled in his innovative chair[43]—as did other famous clients.

These amputees from around 1900 are said to have raced in their wheelchairs. *(Photo courtesy National Library of Medicine, History of Medicine Division.)*

KEEPING THE SPINE ALIGNED

IMAGINE SITTING ALL DAY IN A WHEEL-chair that was too big or too small for you. That's what many early wheelchair users had to do. Although some of these chairs were custom made, most did not provide a custom fit or take user comfort into account. Consequently, an individual might lean to one side or another in order to compensate.

After a period of time, the body would "learn" this posture as the muscles, bones, and ligaments adapted. The end result was an unnatural curvature of the spine called scoliosis, which could result in back pain as the muscles took over the spine's structural support duties.

Although scoliosis can develop from a variety of causes, those with disabilities such as spinal cord injuries, cerebral palsy, and muscular dystrophy—particularly wheelchair users—are more prone to it and other abnormal curvatures of the spine. Depending on the severity of the scoliosis, it may be treated with better back support and posture. In severe cases, wearing a brace or a body cast and/or fusing the spine back into alignment may be necessary in order to correct the problem.

Today, wheelchair users can choose from a variety of sophisticated seating and positioning options that help prevent the onset of scoliosis.

In 1943, E&J built a custom folding wheelchair for President Franklin D. Roosevelt to use on his airplane. Roosevelt had been in a wheelchair since a bout with polio in 1931. Polio was another major factor in the increasing demand for wheelchairs; in the United States, the worst epidemic of the disease occurred from 1942 to 1953 (with 33,344 recorded cases in 1950 alone).[44]

Because he felt that his disability would diminish his image, Roosevelt asked that he not be pictured in his wheelchair.[45] This telling historical footnote reflects much about public perceptions of disabilities and the disabled. Both the media and the White House respected his wishes and rarely showed Roosevelt's wheelchair in photographs.[46]

Game for Change

Toward the end of World War II, many veterans were given a standard chrome E&J-model wheelchair with an eighteen-inch seat.[47] But, because they were not tailored to individual body shape and arm length, these vehicles often fell woefully short of providing a comfortable, custom fit.[48] As a result, many wheelchair users suffered bruised elbows and upper arms; others even developed scoliosis when

their poorly fitting wheelchairs caused them to lean to one side.[49]

However, change was coming. After World War II, Sir Ludwig Guttmann and his colleagues at Stoke Mandeville Hospital in England began using wheelchair sports as a form of exercise and rehabilitation for recuperating veterans.[50] Their successful program soon spread through Europe and overseas to the United States.[51]

In 1948, Guttman organized more formal "games" for disabled British veterans. Four years later, these games expanded into the first international competition for people with physical disabilities, with participants from the Netherlands, Germany, Sweden, Norway, and Israel.[52]

It was another war—this time the Vietnam conflict—that brought about dynamic changes in the lives of wheelchair users and in wheelchair design.[53] By the 1970s, paraplegics could live another thirty to forty years after their injuries. Social attitudes were changing too.[54] As efforts were made to restore self-esteem and independence to the disabled, advocacy groups grew in strength, and the issue of civil rights for people with disabilities gained precedence.[55]

Even Hollywood joined in the crusade, creating the 1970s film *Coming Home*, which featured a love scene between Jane Fonda and Jon Voight, whose character was a paraplegic.[56]

Wheelchair sports were growing in popularity even before the Vietnam War. In Rome in 1960, disabled athletes competed in the same venues as Olympic athletes for the first time. The term "Paralympics" was introduced at the games of 1964 in Tokyo, and the event has been held every four years ever since, except in 1980 and 1984.[57]

Many disabled athletes, such as wheelchair racing pioneer Bob Hall, believe that recent wheelchair innovation stems from sports,[58] which prompted the creation of lighter, more compact, faster, and more easily maneuverable models.[59] Wheelchair athletes, in search of lighter models and better racing times, made modifications to their chairs with saws and welding equipment in their own garages. Among these early innovators was a machinist and polio survivor named Bud Rumpel, who built himself a custom wheelchair in the 1960s.[60] These home-made alterations to Everest & Jennings's standard models led to a new concept in wheelchair design: the sports chair.[61]

The Sports Wheelchair

By these means, the standard fifty-pound wheelchair was trimmed down to somewhere around twenty pounds. Some wheelchair athletes who altered their chairs went on to form companies that have revolutionized the wheelchair industry.[62] Two such sports wheelchair pioneers were George Murray, who with Chris

Peterson and Mary Carol Peterson formed Top End in 1986, and Marilyn Hamilton, who with the help of two hang-gliding friends built an ultralightweight wheelchair and formed Quickie Designs.[63]

Consumers, whose choices had been lacking, were eager for the stylish, lightweight wheelchairs that did not carry the institutional stigma of previous models.[64] Hall, like many in the disabled community, saw the introduction of the sports wheelchair as enabling the disabled to have "a more evolved attitude about what kind of life was possible with a disability."[65]

Said Shapiro:

> For one thing, there were more wheelchair users, up from half a million in 1960 to 1.2 million by 1980, most of whom were no longer living in nursing homes or institutions as they had been just a couple of decades before. This new generation of wheelchair users was newly politicized and wanted maximum independence. They were demanding curb cuts, lifts on buses, and handicapped parking spaces. They had come to expect that they would go to college, take jobs, get married and sometimes even start families.[66]

A far cry from the three-wheeled Bath chair, today's modern racing wheelchairs, such as this Invacare chair, are sleek, aerodynamic, and built for speed. Using arms instead of legs, wheelchair racers often best the times of runners. These chairs go beyond granting day-to-day mobility, allowing their users to compete as athletes.

A Chain Reaction

In 1975—four years prior to the commercial development of sports wheelchairs—Hall became the first person to compete in the Boston Marathon in a wheelchair, paving the way for many future road racers.[67] Within a few years, several recognized U.S. road races launched wheelchair divisions, and more people with disabilities began to train for these races than had ever been anticipated.[68]

The movement received so much participation that the government began to fund research into how wheelchair users interacted with their chairs. As a result, performance, durability, comfort, and appearance truly became considerations in the design of wheelchairs.

The demand for improved performance and lighter weight was great enough to support an industry for ultralight wheelchairs—high-performance manual wheelchairs weighing less than twenty-five pounds and designed for daily use.[69]

Industry Shift

In spite of the popularity of wheelchair sports and racing, the largest wheelchair manufacturers were painfully slow in recognizing the changing marketplace, leaving the door open for new players.[70] Companies like Invacare Corporation took advantage of the opening and began developing new products tailored to the everyday wheelchair user. In the early 1980s, Invacare and other companies quickly began seizing market share that had been held almost entirely by Everest & Jennings, which was busy protecting its early patents. And, in 1982, when Invacare introduced the industry's first computer-controlled power wheelchair—a precursor of today's sophisticated power chairs—it took the first step

toward surpassing E&J as the world's premier wheelchair manufacturer.

Years later, Invacare acquired companies specializing in the ultralight wheelchair market, such as Top End, which developed the industry standard for tennis chairs.

The Evolution of the Power Wheelchair

While the manual chair underwent a rapid evolution because of wheelchair sports, a new kind of chair developed because of a different kind of advance: the development of small motors that allowed for power wheelchairs. Interestingly, the electronically powered wheelchair had its beginnings during World War I, but like its manually powered cousin, it too was slow to develop.[71]

During the 1940s, automobile batteries and starter motors were used to make simple power wheelchairs, which operated at a single speed. Later, the addition of a slip clutch mechanism enabled users to somewhat control the speed of their chairs. The mechanical relay was subsequently used to provide limited electronic speed control.[72]

Because of their limited control, these early electric wheelchairs were often unreliable and sometimes even dangerous. Maintenance was a constant problem, as were operational difficulties.[73] Improvements in electronic technology led to the development of

Opposite: Invacare-sponsored racer James Briggs tears up the track in his Top End by Action wheelchair. *(Photo by M. C. Peterson.)*

Right: Manual wheelchairs, such as this Invacare MVP, have improved considerably since the first unwieldy models appeared. Wheelchairs have continued to develop to grant mobility to an even larger population of consumers with more severe disabilities.

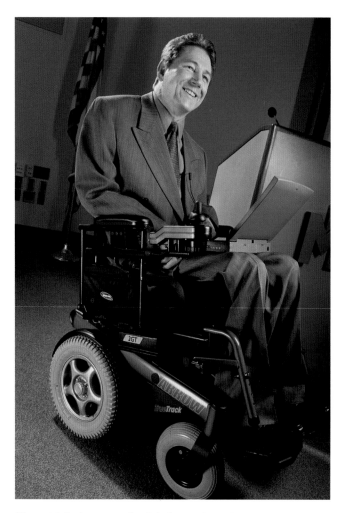

Above: Today's power wheelchairs, such as the Invacare 2GT Arrow Storm Series with TrueTrack, are lighter and more maneuverable than ever. Shown is Jim Lally, former Invacare territory business manager.

Right: Actor Christopher Reeve uses sip-and-puff technology to control his Invacare wheelchair. *(Photo courtesy Christopher Reeve.)*

controlled chair, was the industry leader in the production of power wheelchairs.

The Modern Power Chair

Today, advanced power chairs can be operated by the merest movement of the head, tongue, or limbs—even by simply inhaling and exhaling.[75] In addition, greater technical and clinical progress has led to the development of a wider selection of interface devices, such as the joystick, switch control, and ultrasonic control; intelligent controllers such as speed and acceleration control and controllers with sense faults; plus intelligent accessories like wireless links to computers, robotic arms, and environmental control units.[76] Sophisticated electronic interfaces can enable users to control their home environment as well as the wheelchair.[77]

These devices continue to offer more freedom to even the most severely disabled, such as quadriplegics. Perhaps the most well known wheelchair user in the world today is actor Christopher Reeve, who relies on an Invacare power wheelchair for his mobility. By sipping or blowing air into a straw in varying degrees, Reeve is able to move his wheelchair forward, backward, to the left or right, and fast or slow.[78]

High-tech wheelchairs activated by voice commands entered through a throat-engaging microphone are also available to quadriplegics and are sophisticated enough to understand an excited utterance to "Stop!"[79]

Other amazing advances include a chin-actuated controller system, initially patented in the 1970s, which allows the user to flip a switch with his or her chin to move the wheelchair's control arm. The mouthstick allows those who can't move their arms and hands to manipulate a keyboard, pencil, and book. Another innovation, Richard Cowan's decubitus ulcer–preventing wheelchair— dubbed "The Boss"—introduced a tilt option that

digital controllers for power wheelchairs, which provided improved reliability and increased the chairs' range between battery charges.[74]

The development of the transistor in the 1950s led to electronic speed control of power wheelchairs. However, it wasn't until the 1960s that the demand for power wheelchairs grew sufficiently to create a need for more sophisticated controls and assistive devices. By the mid-1980s, Invacare Corporation, with its novel microprocessor-

reclines the chair to a full ninety degrees, giving pressure relief to the hips and buttocks.[80]

Invacare Corporation made a quantum leap in power wheelchair motor performance and reliability in 1998, when it created and marketed the first wheelchair powered by a gearless-brushless motor.[81] The quiet motor is 45 percent more efficient than other motors.[82]

In the future, said J. B. Richey, senior vice president, electronic and design engineering, computers will drive wheelchair advances. "Power wheelchairs will get 'smarter,'" he predicted. "Eventually, you'll have power wheelchairs that you can control just by telling them where you want them to go, and they will take you....

The Invacare gearless-brushless motor, created by Invacare in 1998, not only has a quieter motor but lasts longer and is more efficient than earlier motors.

Even now they have wheelchairs that will work on eye movements."[83]

The industry is continually evolving and developing new products to offer greater mobility, style, and access to today's wheelchair user. However, the biggest wheelchair advances will likely come when manufacturers are able to surmount development costs and insurance restrictions to make these innovations affordable for consumers.[84]

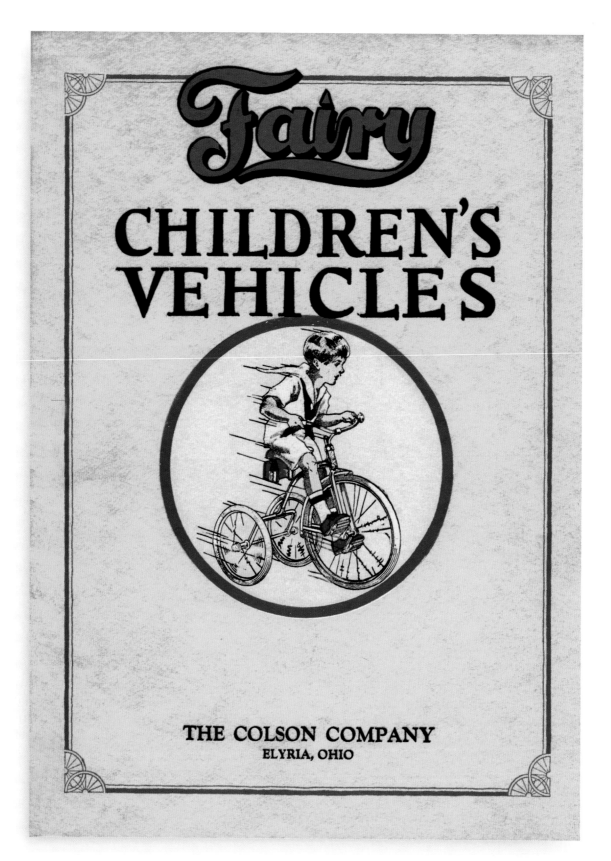

A cover from a 1929 Colson Company Fairy Children's Vehicles catalog. The illustration shows a Fairy Prince Velocipede, or tricycle. *(Photo courtesy Lorain County Historical Society.)*

CHAPTER TWO

THE EVOLUTION OF INVACARE

1885–1976

*Our wheelchair business is founded on the principle that the best is none
too good for [our customers].*

—George Cushing Worthington,
The Worthington Company

THE MODERN INVACARE Corporation might not exist were it not for the Civil War, itself a major impetus in the development of the wheelchair.

That war, in which more than half a million Americans died, left tens of thousands of injured veterans on both sides. Because the medicine of the day was able to stop infection only by removing the diseased limb, amputations were common during the war, and many of these veterans found themselves needing help to get around. This need was later echoed by the thousands of victims of poliomyelitis. The debilitating and paralyzing childhood disease was known as infantile paralysis, and its victims were often confined to hospitals and even sanatoriums.

The desire for the independence and freedom that comes with the ability to move around at will ultimately represented an opportunity for an Ohio inventor whose company was in trouble.

The Fairy Tricycle

His name was Winslow Lamartine Fay, and he founded the Fay Manufacturing Company in 1885 in Elyria, Ohio. From one small plant, the company originally planned to produce the Fay Sulky Scraper and the Fairy Tricycle, which were designed by Fay himself.[1] Both vehicles were carriage style, light weight, and pedal driven. One publication described them as being "built on a low-slung steel frame that was shaped like a bow-handled hayfork."[2]

Although Fay's early models were well received in town, they were soon upstaged by an even more popular kind of self-powered vehicle: the modern bicycle. The first two-wheel bicycles had actually been invented in Scotland almost fifty years before but weren't practical and accessible for everybody. The clumsy and often dangerous early machines featured one huge front wheel and had to be mounted from a special stand or a running start. Riding on cobblestone streets wasn't recommended because falling from such a great height could result in serious injury.

In 1874, however, a new kind of bicycle called a "safety" bicycle began making inroads across Europe and America. Like a modern bike, it featured two medium-size wheels and a chain drive. It was much easier to ride and could be operated by virtually anybody. By 1885—the same year Fay introduced his more cumbersome tricycle—the two-wheeled safety bicycles were well on their way to becoming the most popular self-powered vehicles in the world.[3]

This was hardly good news for Fay, who began looking for new applications for his Fairy Tricycle.

A post-1935-model Colson Baby Prince Velocipede. *(Photo courtesy Chrissy Kadleck.)*

Only a few years after founding his company, Fay overhauled the vehicle's design and aimed at a new market. He figured his convenient machines, if properly designed, could benefit wounded veterans and children.

Soon thereafter Fay introduced an early wheelchair that used hand levers and treadles to steer and pedal. These devices, which were called "machines for cripples," allowed disabled people of various sizes to move around and gave them a greater degree of freedom than was previously possible.[4] (Although the use of the word "cripple," as well as "invalid," is no longer considered appropriate, the evolution to today's preferred terminology—"person with a disability"—would not occur for nearly a century.)

The introduction of Fay's new line was a gamble, but it worked. In 1889, the Fay Manufacturing Company took out an advertisement in the Elyria city directory and pointed out that its products had already spread across the country.

The Fay Manufacturing Co. Manufactures Tricycles for Children, Ladies, Cripples, and Invalids. The manufacturers commenced putting their Tricycle on the market about three years ago. Their trade has been steadily increasing ever since. Their machines have been shipped to nearly if not all the States of the Union and the company [has] recently established agencies in Canada[;] their Invalid Machines are made in great variety and are adapted to almost any condition or affliction. The machines are cheap and at the same time durable and strong.[5]

Before long, Fay took his product line a step further. He began producing specialized "carts for

Employees of the Fay Manufacturing Company outside the company's office at the turn of the century. *(Photo courtesy Lorain County Historical Society.)*

cripples," precursors to the modern wheelchair, which were used in hospitals.[6] Employment at Fay's plant grew to fifty people.[7]

Interestingly, bicycle advances would continue to drive changes in wheelchairs more than a century after their introduction caused Fay to rethink his product line.[8]

Arthur Garford Buys the Company

Like many inventors, Fay became restless with the day-to-day management of his company. By 1891 he was looking for a buyer.[9] Fay soon found Arthur L. Garford, also an inventor and successful businessman based in Elyria. Two years earlier, at the age of thirty-one, Garford had received a patent for his design of a leather bike saddle and founded the Garford Saddle Company. Garford bought the Fay Manufacturing Company with the intention of continuing to manufacture wheelchairs and vehicles for disabled people.[10]

Shortly after buying Fay Manufacturing, Garford hired George Cushing Worthington to

Above: The Worthington Manufacturing Company is visible in the background, identified by a sign that reads "Children's Fairy Machines." Fay Manufacturing became The Worthington Manufacturing Company in the 1890s after Fay, eager to explore new business pursuits, sold his company. *(Photo courtesy Lorain County Historical Society.)*

Below left: Arthur L. Garford, an Elyria businessman and inventor, purchased Fay Manufacturing from Fay in 1891. *(Photo courtesy Lorain County Historical Society.)*

oversee plant operations.[11] Worthington's presence was quickly felt at the company. He shortened the frame of the existing Fairy tricycle and designed a new chassis for a line of bicycle-wheeled rolling chairs. Some of them were even hand propelled, similar to the wheelchairs of today. He also became connected to Garford on a more personal level. In 1897, he married Arthur Garford's youngest sister, Caroline, and was promoted to superintendent of the Fay Manufacturing Company.[12]

Although later corporate publications would record that the modern Invacare Corporation evolved from The Worthington Manufacturing

EVEREST & JENNINGS: AN INDUSTRY IS BORN

IN 1918, HERBERT A. EVEREST, A MINING engineer, was caught in a cave-in that left him with a spinal cord injury. Paralyzed from the waist down, Everest soon discovered that he was limited in unexpected ways.[1] At the time, the only wheelchairs available were wooden vehicles that were either flimsy or cumbersome and awkward. They couldn't be stowed in an automobile and in many cases couldn't even be propelled by the occupant.[2]

Naturally frustrated by the limitations of these devices, Everest turned to a friend, mechanical engineer Harry C. Jennings, to design a better chair. More than a dozen years after the accident, Jennings set out to build a versatile, lightweight chair. Working out of a garage-shop in West Los Angeles and using "cheap Kress tools,"[3] Everest and Jennings began experimenting with lightweight, strong steel tubing—still a relatively new material.[4]

"We tried making a folding wheelchair with airplane tubing, which was just coming to the fore as a structural material," Everest later remembered. "Our first chair had a double x-brace with wooden x-braces. This model lacked flexibility, and Mr. Jennings came up with the idea of the single x-brace. The single x-brace solved the problems of flexibility and lack of durability and eliminated many of the strains in the frame of the chair which had caused failures in previous models."[5]

Before long, the company had produced its first chair at a cost of $108 in retail parts and founded a partnership. This chair was presented to the son of the governor of New Mexico, who attracted considerable attention as he crossed the country in his novel wheelchair. Everest & Jennings the wheelchair manufacturer was established in 1933.[6]

With inquiries coming in, Everest and Jennings continued to work from their respec-

tive garages. At first, Everest spoked and trued the wheels in his garage, while Jennings finished the chair in his garage. The pair then took to the road to sell the completed chairs. This turned out to be a more difficult task than they thought it would be—like "pulling sound teeth," Everest said.[7]

People just weren't used to the idea of putting that much money into a chair, and also they

(Photos courtesy E&J)

were not used to the idea of getting out in public in a wheelchair. Sales were very slow and difficult through the years from 1935 to 1941, but by 1941 we had gotten enough chairs in circulation so that people began to get the idea that even though they were handicapped they could still get out and enjoy living.[8]

When the United States entered World War II, Everest & Jennings was already the world's largest manufacturer of wheelchairs. Its products were used by both President Franklin D. Roosevelt and Sir Winston Churchill (pictured this page). Before long, the chairs became even more international. During a wartime conference in Casablanca, King Ibn Saud of Saudi Arabia admired Roosevelt's attractive metal folding wheelchair. When Roosevelt learned of the King's interest in his chair, he insisted on giving King Ibn Saud one of the many chairs he took on his travels.[9] The king, pleased with the chair's speed and comfort, ordered an entire lot, including an ornate and upholstered lounge wheelchair that was nicknamed the Throne Chair.

The war was good for Everest & Jennings's business because of both its international profile and the sudden and tragic increase in disabled veterans. At the peak of the war, Everest & Jennings was receiving as many as one hundred orders every month. In 1945, the year the war ended, the United States Army ordered one thousand wheelchairs and the American Red Cross ordered another five thousand.[10]

In 1946, after thirteen years as an informal partnership, Everest & Jennings was incorporated.[11] Six years later, the one hundred thousandth wheelchair rolled off the Everest & Jennings assembly line and was presented to Everest as a retirement present.[12] Only a year later, in 1953, the Everest family sold its stake in the company.[13] The Jennings family continued to control the company, although it sold 40 percent of its stock to the public in 1968.[14] That same year, the company expanded internationally and established manufacturing divisions in Canada and Mexico.[15]

By the time of the Vietnam War, Everest & Jennings was synonymous with wheelchair manufacture: In 1973, the company produced its one millionth wheelchair and held about 70 percent of the market.[16] Its products were supplied to the U.S. government and were available in hospitals throughout the United States. It was so big, in fact, that the Department of Justice accused the company of monopolizing its industry, ultimately leading to an agreement that Everest & Jennings would not purchase any of its much smaller rivals.

Although it might have seemed unlikely at the time, the end of the company's dominance had already begun. While the rest of the medical device and supply industry took giant technological strides forward throughout the 1970s, Everest & Jennings devoted most of its time and energy to protecting its products through lawsuits rather than developing new chairs. This stagnation created an environment that invited competition and allowed smaller companies like Invacare to flourish, especially as consumers began to demand more from the growing industry. Invacare has since usurped Everest & Jennings. As of 2000, Invacare's primary competitor was Sunrise Medical Inc., another E&J-era upstart.[17]

Everest & Jennings was purchased by Graham-Field Health Products Inc. in 1996, a move which executives hoped would expand the company's home care product line. Three years later, however, Graham-Field was losing money after a string of acquisitions. In 1999, the company filed for Chapter 11 bankruptcy reorganization. As a result of Graham-Field's money woes, E&J closed its Earth City, Missouri, production plant in June 2000, laying off about fifty workers in the process.[18]

Company in 1885, public records reveal that The Worthington Manufacturing Company itself evolved from the Fay Manufacturing Company. Furthermore, the name wasn't changed until the end of the 1890s. Interestingly, the name change was triggered by Winslow Fay himself. After he had sold his tricycle company, Fay launched a new business to manufacture stockings that were based on a patented design created by his wife. He called it the Fay Stocking Company.[13]

Hoping to avoid confusion, and because of his new brother-in-law's growing influence, Garford changed the name of his tricycle and wheelchair company to The Worthington Manufacturing Company. In 1902, Garford named George Worthington his successor and appointed him the new company president.[14] According to a turn-of-the-century city directory, the company's offices were located at the "foot of Cedar Street."[15]

The business grew rapidly under Worthington. In 1904, the *Elyria Republican* called The Worthington Manufacturing Company "the largest maker of high grade Velocipedes and Tricycles for children, whose Juvenile Bicycles are standard the world over and the acknowledged leaders in the manufacture of Invalid Chairs and Tricycles for cripples."[16] By 1907, the company was large enough that it moved into new headquarters. That same year, it was renamed The Worthington Company.[17]

"Our wheelchair business is founded on the principle that the best is none too good for [our customers]," Worthington said.[18]

When a wheelchair is required, it is either to give a little outing to someone suffering with or convalescing from an acute illness; it is for some aged person or else it is wanted for one who is permanently disabled, who must spend hour after hour in the chair, who lives in it, who has no other way of moving about. In any case the one thing that is vital is the comfort and convenience of the occupant.[19]

Although the company's most popular product would remain wheelchairs, Worthington was always looking for ways to expand. In 1907, he began producing golf balls.[20] One year later, Worthington vice president F. W. Colson engineered the purchase of the aluminum and brass foundry portion of the Machine Parts Company.[21]

Colson, who was responsible for the acquisition, was brought in to run the plant.

Although the Machine Parts Company's largest client was an automotive plant, which was coincidentally owned by Garford, the connection between the two companies was strong.[22]

Before long, Worthington's board of directors moved to the third floor of the Machine Parts Company offices and the two companies struck an agreement. Worthington agreed to divest its manufacturing company. In exchange, Machine Parts would manufacture Worthington products for a fee of no more than 10 percent above cost.[23] This arrangement left The Worthington Company a retail operation rather than a manufacturing one, thus negating the need for manufacturing facilities except "as would be necessary in carrying complete merchandise," according to the company's October board meeting minutes.[24]

The arrangement worked. Fred Colson began to urge the companies closer together. On December 31, 1917, he finally got his wish. The Worthington Company and the Machine Parts Company merged to become The Colson Company.[25] Only a couple of weeks later, on Jan. 15, 1918, The Colson Company was incorporated with Colson as president and majority owner.[26]

Colson continued to produce the company's high-quality wheelchairs and moved to expand in both the medical supplies market and the tricycle business. The Colson Company was soon offering stretchers and service carts. Fred Colson also expanded the Colson line of casters and organized the metal parts production to produce a new line of Fairy bicycles, scooters, and tricycles for children.[27]

In the early 1920s, Colson organized a chain of company-owned branch stores in seventeen

Opposite: An aerial view of Colson's manufacturing plant in Elyria, Ohio. The Worthington Company and the Machine Parts Company were merged in late 1917 to form The Colson Company, which became The Colson Corporation in 1933. Not long after Colson's wheelchair shop was purchased in 1957 and renamed Mobilaid, it became sufficiently fattened by government contracts to require more room to grow. In the late 1950s and early 1960s, the company began construction of a new plant at 443 Oberlin Road. *(Photo courtesy* Elyria Chronicle-Telegram.*)*

A post-1935 Colson Corporation wheelchair catalog showing self-propelled wheelchairs.

major cities throughout the United States.[28] The stores were managed by The Colson Stores Company, which was, in turn, owned and controlled by The Colson Company.[29] By the mid-1920s, Colson took over ownership of these stores and semiretired to manage them.[30]

By that time, the company had grown into an important presence in Elyria. With a workforce of eight hundred, it was the largest employer in the city.[31] According to a 1929 *Chronicle-Telegram*, Colson manufactured 20,000 bicycles, close to 700,000 casters, 5,000 invalid chairs, and 20,000 scooters.[32]

The Great Depression

Unfortunately, that year was to be Colson's best year for some time. On Tuesday, October 29, 1929, after jittering nervously for several weeks, the stock market dropped precipitously, signaling an end to the roaring economy of the 1920s. In one day, the market index lost almost 13 percent of its value (remarkably, it was a drop of only forty-three points). This, coupled with inflation and a crippling drought in the farming states, ushered in the Great Depression. Between 1929 and 1933, the eco-

nomic and psychological damage was intense. Thousands of banks and farms failed. Unemployment skyrocketed to a staggering 25 percent as the government struggled to reignite the economy.

Like virtually every other business, Colson suffered—although it did not go into bankruptcy. In 1933, the worst year of the Great Depression, Colson fell into receivership with some of its suppliers and was reorganized as The Colson Corporation under new management. Neely Powers was named president.[33] Powers would successfully guide the company through the end of the Great Depression and into the World War II era.

The war changed Colson yet again. Up until then, the company had produced mainly tricycles, wheelchairs, and parts for vehicles. After the war began, however, the United States bent its considerable energy and resources to wartime production. Every available factory was converted to defense production, including Colson's. During the war,

Above and inset: In February of 1961, Mobilaid moved into its new quarters, shown under construction. Left to right, W. C. Shea, Charles Hazelton, and William Pivacek, the three long-time Colson employees who purchased the company's wheelchair division and renamed it Mobilaid, survey the construction site.

Colson produced the 2.75-inch "Mighty Mouse" rockets for the U.S. Navy. In all, more than 1.5 million rockets were shipped from the factory, and less than fifty were returned. As a result, Colson was awarded the coveted Army-Navy "E" Award.[34]

When the war ended, production of the rocket ceased and Colson's revenues sagged. This was typical throughout industrial America as companies experienced a short-term reduction in revenues while they retooled for civilian production. In most cases, revenue dramatically increased as America headed into a booming decade of spending and technological progress.

For Colson, however, this was not the case. In June 1953, the Pritzker family of Chicago purchased a weakened Colson Corporation. Instead of rebounding, The Colson Corporation's bicycles and tricycles had been losing market share to foreign competitors. As part of the acquisition, the Pritzker family abandoned the manufacture of bicycles.[35] The company would also be moved from Elyria.[36]

The Birth of Mobilaid

Although Colson was moved from Elyria, important parts would be left behind. In 1957, the wheelchair division of Colson was purchased by three long-time employees: W. C. "Court" Shea, Charles "Chuck" Hazelton, and W. J. Pivacek. Shea and Hazelton said it cost about $250,000 to "establish" the business. They renamed it Mobilaid Inc. and dedicated it to producing primarily wheelchairs.[37] According to Nyal Yost, retired vice president, who was working for the company at the time and bought stock in Mobilaid, Colson would sell the wheelchair models it built in 1957—now made of steel—through the mid-1960s.[38] The company also produced some special-order items, such as custom chairs, belly carts, and gurneys.[39] Ron Thomas, who joined Mobilaid in 1961 and later became director of facilities for Invacare, remembered that the company also made piano dollies for Colson and milk dollies for a local creamery.[40]

Shea, a native Elyrian, had worked at Colson for more than thirty years; Hazelton had worked for Colson for twenty-eight years in the accounting and financial departments; and Pivacek was a nineteen-year veteran and foreman in the wheelchair department.[41]

Mobilaid by itself was a much smaller company than Colson. When it was purchased, the company had fifteen employees and occupied only part of the former Colson factory on Pine Street. Mobilaid had annual sales of about $150,000.[42] At that time, it generally took six man-hours to make a wheelchair.[43]

Within a couple months of the purchase, the group had hired twenty more employees and landed a large contract with the federal government to supply the Veterans Administration with wheelchairs and medical supplies.[44] The company's growth over the next few years was largely due to this

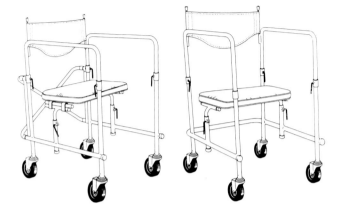

Above: In 1971, Mobilaid and the Rolls Equipment Company—as well as a California-based home health care equipment company called Invalex—were purchased by Boston Capital Corporation. The California Walker-Chair, which combined the features of both a chair and a walker, was one of many new products to augment Mobilaid's growing wheelchair line.

Below: Mobilaid established Rolls as a subsidiary in 1967 to enable the company to sell directly to hospitals and surgical equipment companies. This sketch from a 1971 Rolls Equipment catalog shows one wheelchair offering.

single government contract. "Government contracts we got right away," recalled Yost. "The government had a spec, and we adhered to that and won the contract for that for several years after 1957. So that kind of gave us a good start."[45] In February 1961, the company relocated to a new forty-thousand-square-foot factory on Oberlin Road in Elyria.[46]

In 1967, Mobilaid set up a subsidiary called the Rolls Equipment Company. Instead of dealing with the government or through medical suppliers, Mobilaid would sell directly to hospitals and surgical equipment companies under the Rolls label.[47] This concept was a departure from the accepted practice of selling through middlemen.

Over the next two years, the company continued its focus on wheelchair production. "We were a pretty small company," remembered

Lou Hyster, who started with Mobilaid in 1969 as a lathe operator. "We made a lot of standard wheelchairs and some power chairs that were very poor quality, but nothing high tech. ... It wasn't big business at the time."[48]

By 1970, however, Mobilaid's production had grown more than 350 percent and the plant was producing close to forty thousand wheelchairs every year. Wheelchair assembly had dropped to slightly more than one man hour per chair, during which the metal for the chair was bent to size, chrome plated, and assembled.[49] Because hospitals had to sterilize the chairs, many preferred chrome plating to painting. Heavy but strong cold-steel tubing was still the material of choice, although it

would gradually be replaced by lighter tubing, and finally by plastics in the mid-1980s.[50]

Invacare Is Founded

Mobilaid was by now big enough to attract investor attention. It had prospered through the 1960s and was well positioned at the beginning of the 1970s. This success came despite the fact that Mobilaid basically produced variations of the same chair again and again and was far from the industry leader in wheelchairs. Moreover, this was not an industry that encouraged innovation. Dominated by Everest & Jennings, the old-line manufacturer that had been founded in the 1930s, the wheelchair industry and wheelchair design had hardly advanced since the first modern wheelchairs were introduced.

While this situation wasn't expected to change much in the 1970s, the business of medicine was poised to undergo a rapid evolution. Since the 1950s,

The finished Mobilaid facility on Oberlin Road in 1961. By 1970, the company would be producing nearly forty thousand wheelchairs per year.

the pace of medical innovation had been torrid. New surgeries and technologies, such as catheters and improved diagnostics, were quickly transforming the practice of medicine—and making it much more expensive. At the same time as the disabled community began to find its collective voice, the patient empowerment movement made its first, small inroads into the cloistered world of medicine. Over the next decades, patients would become more involved in their medical treatment and demand more friendly, cost effective, and comfortable treatment options—including home- and self-care. Wheelchairs were but one part of this new trend.

Yet these changes were still emerging at the beginning of the 1970s. The patient empowerment movement was tiny, health care costs were rising unchecked, and the new technologies were often in the hands of the smaller, entrepreneurial companies that had developed them. In the late 1960s and early 1970s, however, consolidation began to sweep through the medical industry as smaller companies joined forces and huge medical device corporations (the largest of which was Johnson & Johnson) jockeyed for position.

Mobilaid represented a small part of this trend. In January 1971, Mobilaid and Rolls Equipment were purchased by Boston Capital Corporation (BCC). At the same time, BCC bought Invalex Company, which had facilities in Long Beach, California, and Lodi, Ohio. That acquisition added walkers, safety side rails, and other home health care products to Mobilaid's wheelchair offerings, laying the groundwork for a full-service home health care company.[51] These companies were later merged to form Invacare Corporation.[52]

BCC

By the time it bought the companies that would become Invacare, Boston Capital Corporation (BCC) had been taking minority positions in companies like Invacare for almost a decade. However, BCC had never exercised managerial control over its acquisitions. Instead, it was content to reap the financial rewards of its investments. In the early 1970s, a new president named Joseph Powell began to change BCC's strategic purpose: Powell wanted to build a company.

To do this, he first turned to Waukesha Industries of Waukesha, Wisconsin, in which BCC owned an 81 percent stake. Waukesha Industries made bearings for heavy equipment, and Powell hired the team of Richard Grimm and Bill Miller to scale up the company. Grimm, the company's new president, remembered the challenge.

We wanted to see if we could run a small business. We felt that if we were any good in a big business we ought to be able to manage a small one. And that's where the fun is—in growing a business. The truth is, managing a mature business can sometimes be damn boring.[53]

Evolution

Although Waukesha was a bearing manufacturing company, Powell's real interest lay in health care. All told, including the acquisitions that formed Invacare, Powell would buy six health care companies.

The first of these, and the one that convinced Powell that medicine was a growth industry, was Ohio-Nuclear, which he purchased a year before creating Invacare. Ohio-Nuclear Inc. was a Cleveland-area company that designed and manufactured radioisotope scanners. These new diagnostic scanners could detect abnormal tissue, making it easier for doctors to find brain tumors, blood clots, and other dangerous conditions.

With the purchase of Ohio-Nuclear, BCC moved into one of the hottest fields in the medical industry. Throughout the 1970s, the field of nuclear medicine advanced rapidly, and Ohio-Nuclear quickly became the focus of Boston Capital's efforts.[54] At the time Grimm was appointed president, Ohio-Nuclear operated from a plant located near a slag pile in Cleveland's historic industrial Flats district. The company had just ten employees.[55]

As part of its focus, BCC moved Waukesha Industries' headquarters to Cleveland, nearer to Ohio-Nuclear.[56] This also put Waukesha close to a subsidiary called Astro Metallurgical Company, based in nearby Wooster, Ohio. Around the same time, Boston Capital Corporation was renamed BCC Industries Inc. and moved its own headquarters from Boston to the Investment Plaza— now Ohio Savings Plaza—in downtown Cleveland.

J. B. Richey, creator of the first full-body CT scanner, the Delta-Scan. A brilliant engineer, Richey would invest first his money and then his time in Invacare.

In 1971, with Grimm as president and CEO, BCC and its subsidiaries—including Invacare—were poised for growth.[57]

"The company enters [1971] fully committed to an aggressive acquisition program focused on finding companies primarily in the business of medical equipment and health care products," Grimm told a reporter.[58]

By late 1973, Ohio-Nuclear had moved to new quarters in suburban Solon to accommodate a growing workforce of five hundred.[59] Then, business took a new turn as CT scanner technology took off.

The CT Scanner

Invented by Alan Cormack, an American physicist, and Godfrey Hounsfield, an English engineer, the CT scanner was introduced in Europe in 1972 by EMI Ltd. of Great Britain and subsequently appeared in the United States. Cormack, the first to develop a tomographic x ray, and Hounsfield actually developed the scanner separately. Cormack's tomographic x ray created an image of a thin section of the head; Hounsfield took a series of tomographic images and joined them in a computer to create a single three-dimensional image.[60]

The computerized axial tomography scanner, generally called a CT or CAT scanner, produced a series of x-ray images that were used to reconstruct a detailed composite of the head. This innovative diagnostic tool could detect tumors and cancers using relatively low levels of radiation, allowing doctors to catch these abnormalities at their earliest and thus most treatable stages.

Because Ohio-Nuclear had the basic expertise to enter the CT field, it sent several staff members to Massachusetts General Hospital, where EMI Ltd. had a unit on display in 1973. Engineer J. B. Richey, head of research and development at Ohio-Nuclear, was part of the delegation. Richey immediately saw the technology's potential. By combining Ohio-Nuclear's previous design exper-

tise in similar imaging system components with x-ray technology and good programming, the company felt it could compete in this new field. "As soon as we saw the unit, we knew this was a business we should be in," Grimm said.[61]

The original EMI scanner could scan only the head, which had to be surrounded by water to prevent x-ray distortion. It also was tediously slow, requiring five minutes for a complete scan, during which time the subject's head had to remain motionless. Richey and the Ohio-Nuclear team thought they could make significant improvements and began working on a prototype in early 1974.[62]

Richey recalled his flash of inspiration upon viewing the Massachusetts General scanner unit:

I came back to Ohio-Nuclear and said, "I think I can make one that will do tomographic CAT scan slices of the whole body." The inventor[s] said that you could never scan the whole body because you had to have a water bag—you couldn't have an air/body interface, and you couldn't put the whole body in a water bag. Well, I figured out a way to do it, and nine months later I had a working unit at the Cleveland Clinic which made medical history. It was the first CAT scanner in the world that would produce diagnostic images of the whole body.[63]

Technicare Corporation and the Delta-Scan

With this promising and growing business, Boston Capital shook off its Boston investment-company roots once and for all in 1973 and acknowledged its new direction by renaming itself again—this time as Technicare Corporation, of which Ohio-Nuclear was a part.[64] At the time, more than 60 percent of the company's sales were in health products. In addition to CT scanners, radioisotope devices, and the Invacare line of patient aids, Technicare was also developing ultrasound equipment. "The market for medical and dental equipment looks extremely good," predicted Grimm. "The demand for increased health care continues to grow in the fields we are currently working in."[65]

By November 1974, Richey's prototype was installed in the radiology lab at the Cleveland Clinic for testing. The Ohio-Nuclear device, which would be called the Delta-Scan, was a full-body scanner and reduced scanning time from five minutes to two minutes—without the use of water bags.

After testing the device, Dr. Ralph Alfidi, director of the department of radiology at the Cleveland Clinic, wrote to Technicare shareholders in glowing terms:

This device provides a new and promising method of diagnosis and detection of abnormalities of the hard-to-image pancreas without the risks and complications of invasive techniques. The unit has also demonstrated that differences between cysts and tumors of the kidneys can be detected.... There is no question that with Delta-Scan, differences in tissue density can be demonstrated in some diseases and that changes in organ size and shape are present in others.[66]

With the success of the Richey prototype and Alfidi's endorsement, company president Grimm envisioned a big future for the device. "We just do not know how large the market will be," he told a reporter. "The x-ray market around the world is known to total about $500 million a year.... The unit has been described as the greatest advance in radiology in the past fifty years."[67]

The CT Takes Over

Technicare began marketing the first scanners in June 1975. Their value as a diagnostic tool became apparent quickly, and the CT scanner was soon sought by most major hospitals, despite being the most expensive piece of medical diagnostic equipment produced at that time.[68] The first Delta-Scan cost about $385,000; others were somewhat more or less expensive.[69] However, because a CT scan often replaced invasive medical procedures that usually required extended hospital stays, some argued that the cost of the equipment was mitigated.[70]

As Technicare rapidly advanced as the leader in computerized scanning and other medical imaging businesses, its interest in its other subsidiaries, including Invacare, waned. This was surprising since Invacare had become the second-largest domestic maker of convalescent products, with a 16 percent market share.[71] In 1974, when Technicare had sales of $43.4 million, the Invacare product line posted sales of $11.8 million, the highest of all the company's divisions. The CT scan business, by comparison, had sales of $10.6 million, but it was poised to take off. Three years later, Technicare's sales had reached $164.4 million, with Ohio-Nuclear contributing $125 million to that total. Invacare added only $17 million.[72]

It was during the mid-1970s that A. Malachi Mixon, III, vice president of sales and marketing for Ohio-Nuclear's CT scanner division, first met Richey. Because the CT scanner technology was booming, Richey remembers teasing Mal Mixon that it would sell itself.

I used to kid him. I'd say, "Mal, you know, you don't have to sell this thing. It's the only one in the world. Just send them a postcard and say, 'Attach check here.'"[73]

With its rapidly rising sales, Technicare became a Wall Street darling in spite of the fact that EMI was the obvious market leader. EMI had sold 230 units by the end of 1975, but Technicare was quickly gaining, having booked orders for 115.

And, although about half a dozen companies, including General Electric, were eyeing the market at the time, it was Technicare's stock that was considered promising by analysts.

The Market Shifts

In 1976, the Department of Health, Education and Welfare required that any hospital using federal funds receive a certificate of need from a regional health-planning agency before purchasing any equipment costing $100,000 or more. This red tape slowed sales of the costly scanners considerably and caused Technicare's profits to tumble to $2.2 million in 1978 from $14 million the previous year. In addition, the business was getting more competitive. Although General Electric took some time to develop a CT scanner as good as Technicare's, the latecomer GE model eventually surpassed Technicare's in sales.[74] By the early 1980s, Technicare had been dethroned as the scanner king.

"Eventually, GE competed," said Richey. "They came out with a lower-cost unit. Technicare earnings started to decrease."[75]

Technicare needed to do something to raise cash, so it began looking for ways to divest portions of its business. In 1977, Waukesha Industries was sold for $12.5 million in cash.[76] Invacare and Astro Metallurgical were put on the auction block the next year, meaning that Technicare planned to put all its fragile eggs in one basket.[77] Jim Dowdell, who joined Invacare in 1971, recalled the company's Technicare years:

> It was my personal opinion that for quite a period of time, because Technicare knew it was going to sell Invacare and was not reinvesting in the business, we were kind of like a stepchild working in the field so the full-blooded child could go off to the prom. Monies were being funneled from Invacare into some of the other businesses that Technicare owned.[78]

However, before the sale of Invacare could be completed, the Technicare board announced that it had accepted an offer of $87 million in stock from Band-Aid giant Johnson & Johnson. Invacare was now a subsidiary of Johnson & Johnson, one of the largest medical companies in the world.

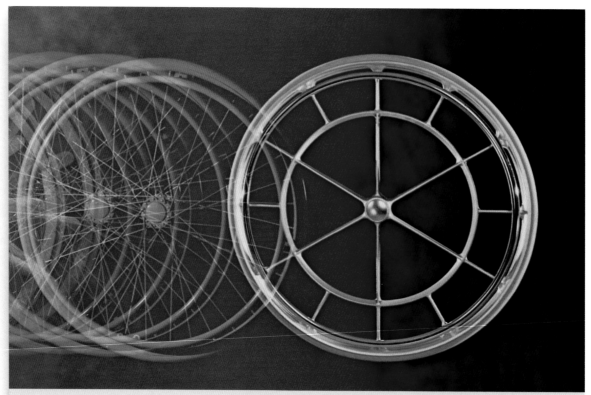

Perfected 1978 AD.

The Endurance Wheel: It'll be 'round for years to come.

Because it was round, the wheel made life a lot easier 5,000 years ago.

Since then, however, there have been problems because many wheels tend to go out-of-round after regular use. This problem is especially detrimental to a wheelchair—which is totally dependent on reliable wheel performance for trouble-free operation.

Now, those problems have been solved by Invacare.

Introducing the Endurance Wheel. We've combined lighter-weight materials in a unique die-cast web design to create the Endurance Wheel. It virtually refuses to go out-of-round.

Spokes have been eliminated, greatly reducing the maintenance usually required on a conventional wheelchair. No spoke tightening. No spoke replacement. No spoke cleaning. No spoke problems.

And even though it's lighter, tests have shown that the Endurance Wheel far exceeds spoked wheel designs in strength—even with heavy loading and hard use.

A completely sealed bearing system adds to the performance of the Endurance Wheel. This system eliminates foreign particles which can impede smooth operation.

The combined result—an Invacare wheelchair that is stronger, more durable, and distinctly easier to maintain—yet adds no extra weight.

The Endurance Wheel. It'll be 'round for years to come. Standard on 400 Series—optional on D200, 200 and 100 Series.

For more information about the Endurance Wheel plus many other remarkable Invacare products, write: Invacare, 1200 Taylor St., Elyria, Ohio 44035.

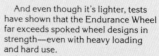

Invacare, then a subsidiary of Johnson & Johnson, "reinvents" the wheel in 1978. Although improved wheels were the only major upgrade made to wheelchairs in years, that was soon to change.

CHAPTER THREE

Invacare's Independence

1977–1979

[Invacare] had all the earmarks of something that could be built into a successful enterprise.

—Dale LaPorte, attorney and former
corporate secretary for Invacare, 2000

LTHOUGH THEY SEEMED LIKE A strange fit, Invacare and especially Ohio-Nuclear were strategic acquisitions for Johnson & Johnson. In the early 1970s, Johnson & Johnson, as well as many other pharmaceutical companies, had decided to enter the emerging medical devices field. This was usually accomplished through acquisition. In addition to its newly acquired CT scanner business, Johnson & Johnson also bought catheter makers and other device companies.

The medical device business, however, was not kind to acquirers. Its technology was still rapidly evolving, and maintaining any degree of market leadership was nearly impossible as new developments rocked the field. Furthermore, the aggressive, start-up companies often didn't fare well in the more constrictive environment of a large multinational, bureaucratic corporation. Many of them were sold in the 1980s.

Invacare was an early casualty. Johnson & Johnson had bought Technicare primarily for its CT scanner business. This was clearly a growth business, and Johnson & Johnson was interested in becoming a long-term player. Invacare, however, never represented much more than a corollary. It was quickly lost in the labyrinthine Johnson & Johnson organizational chart.

According to Nyal Yost, now a retired vice president of Invacare, the company was well aware that Johnson & Johnson had little interest in it.

We knew that [Johnson & Johnson wanted to get rid of Invacare] for three or four years. They had all kinds of people in there, but most anybody who wanted to buy it was what I call a shyster. They wanted to buy it real cheap and probably tear it down and get what they could out of it.[1]

Not surprisingly, Johnson & Johnson announced that it was planning to sell the tiny division in 1979. The asking price was around $8 million. Two groups of potential buyers soon emerged and their offers were considered.

With these two offers still on the table, a third party began planning a bid for Invacare. This group consisted of Mal Mixon, vice president of sales and marketing for CT scanners at Ohio-Nuclear, and J. B. Richey, vice president of engineering for Technicare. The two had become friends while working for Technicare and had long discussed the idea of running a business together. "J. B. and I had talked a little bit about leaving and either buying a company or starting one," Mixon recalled.[2] "After work, we would stop

The Elite Medallion was reserved for only those chairs that met more than three hundred quality control and test inspection standards set for Invacare's Rolls line.

A worker assembles an Invacare wheelchair in 1976. Three years later, Mal Mixon would pull together a team of investors and buy the company.

and maybe have a drink or so and chitchat. It started out as, 'Damn it, we ought to have our own company someday.'"[3]

By the time Invacare was put up for sale, said Richey, Mixon was definitely ready to make his move:

We had discussions, and one day Mal said, "Why don't we buy Invacare?" He was becoming less happy, I guess, at Technicare. I said, "That's a good idea."[4]

During their planning, they met regularly at a Ramada Inn near Technicare headquarters in Solon. Fueled by the free spicy chicken wings served in the hotel lounge, they soon hatched their plan to buy Invacare from Johnson & Johnson.[5] But because he had two buyers ahead of him, Mixon said, "The stars really had to line up for me to get into the position to buy it."[6]

"I was thirty-nine and really wanted to run a company," Mixon recalled. "I wasn't looking for any particular company, but when I heard Invacare was for sale, I took a look and decided it had potential."[7]

Fortunately for Mixon and Richey, the other deals fell through. The first party continued to demand certain conditions that were unacceptable

to Richard Grimm (then CEO of Technicare), and talks were terminated. The second buyer had the money and Invacare was his to close, but he backed out twenty-four hours before a scheduled closing.[8]

The Stars Align

Mixon and Richey were now in a position to set their entrepreneurial dreams in motion, but Mixon quickly encountered the first in a series of small but troublesome stumbling blocks. Convincing Grimm, who was understandably upset at having a second party back out of the sale at the last minute, to entertain a third offer took some doing on Mixon's part.

It was actually Mixon who informed Grimm that the deal was dead. Mixon had even considered joining the second buyer, a Technicare vice president. "I didn't have any money, and so I figured half a loaf of bread was better than no loaf at all," said Mixon of his idea of partnering with the second buyer.[9] Now he had his own shot at the company, but after two unsuccessful attempts, Grimm predicted that Johnson & Johnson would likely take on the selling of Invacare itself, a turn of events he welcomed.

"He said to me, 'Mal, I don't think there's any way I can do this a third time,'" Mixon remembered of his fateful conversation with Grimm.[10]

Yet Mixon persisted, telling Grimm, "Well, I've been here [at Technicare] a long time, and I would appreciate it if you would give me a shot at it." After briefly debating the matter, Grimm agreed to give Mixon sixty days to pull the deal together.[11] "I think he said I had to have $3 million deposited within a week or ten days," Mixon recalled.[12]

Purchasing Invacare, Mixon would later say, proved much more difficult than actually running the company. "I've always said that buying Invacare was harder than running it because I didn't have any money," he said. "I had $10,000, and the company was for sale for $7.8 million."[13]

Thus the only hurdle remaining—and a huge one it was—was funding. Mixon and Richey did not have the necessary financing in place and had precious little time to pull it together. Complicating matters was the fact that local Elyria and Cleveland banks that had arranged financing for the first two parties would not consider a third package for the same purchase.[14] One of the main difficulties Mixon encountered in finding financing was the taint left by the two previously unsuccessful bidders, said Dan T. Moore, III, president of Moore Plastics and one of Mixon's first private investors. "One of the things people asked is, 'Well, if everyone looked at this thing and it's been for sale for so long, how could it be good? What are we missing?'"[15]

In addition, interest rates were an unattractive 15 to 16 percent and on the rise. Mixon had trouble finding mortgage financing for the company's Taylor Street plant in Elyria but was able to procure a loan against the company's assets for $4.3 million from First National Bank of Chicago.[16] He would end up doing a sale lease-back with Cleveland's Smythe brothers, Pete and Jeff, for $2 million, after another real estate firm attempted to change its terms just forty-eight hours before the closing.[17] These difficulties failed to rattle Mixon, who was firm in his resolve to complete the purchase.

"It was always, 'I'm going to get this done. It's just another challenge here.' You get so far into something and you've got everything at stake," he said.[18]

For the remaining $1.5 million in financing—$1 million in common stock and $500,000 in preferred stock—Mixon would take $150,000 worth of common stock, paying $10,000 of his own money, personally borrowing a total of $40,000 from two individuals, and signing a note with the company for the $100,000.[19] He then approached his local Harvard Business School connections for the final amount, which would ultimately come from a group of seventeen investors that began with William M. Jones, president and CEO of Cleveland Machine Controls, and Moore.[20] Moore and Barbara Mixon,

Mixon's wife, had been high school friends. It was through her and the Harvard Business School Club that Mixon and Moore met.[21]

"After reviewing the selling document, I approached two friends I had made through the Harvard Business School Club of Cleveland—Dan Moore and Bill Jones—and asked if they would help me put a group together and attempt to purchase Invacare," Mixon said.[22]

Mixon and Jones had been acquainted through the club since around 1970.[23] "We talked about the long-range possibilities of the company and the demographics," Jones recalled. "I was interested in it from the standpoint of both the company itself and the opportunity for making motorized controls for it, which is what my company did."[24]

Moore, whose company made tires, had similar interests in Invacare. "There were some tires being made in sort of a clumsy fashion. They contained maybe 60 to 70 percent clay," he said. "I knew we could make them better." But his interest also ran deeper: Moore had a cousin in a wheelchair. "For years I'd been doodling ways of making better wheelchairs.... Then [Invacare] came along." He also felt Mixon was equal to the task of running Invacare. "I'm more interested in the size of the fight in the dog than the size of the dog in the fight, and Mal had a lot of fight," said Moore.[25]

Once Jones and Moore bought into Invacare, the final investment pieces began to fall into place. Jones, in turn, brought Francis Joseph "Joe" Callahan—

Above: Friend and Harvard Business School Club member Dan T. Moore, III, was among the first investors Mal Mixon tapped for help in buying Invacare.

Left: In the mid-1970s, wheelchair manufacturing still comprised the lion's share of Invacare's business, but the Cleveland group saw potential for expanding the business.

Joe Callahan joined Mixon's investment team at the suggestion of Bill Jones. A Clevelander like Mixon, Callahan later became a member of Invacare's board of directors.

another Clevelander—on board. Callahan remembered getting the offer:

One night in 1979, Bill Jones called.... The deal Bill presented called for a $100,000 investment from me to join in the purchase of Invacare. At that time, Invacare had annual sales of about $19 million. Bill told me that Everest & Jennings was the leader in the field and had about 80 percent market share. Invacare was the second largest with 10 percent market share, and the other 10 percent was a group of fifteen to twenty small players. I told Bill that I liked the chance of moving number two into having a larger market share.[26]

Callahan threw his $100,000 in the ring. (Both he and Jones would later join Invacare's board of directors.) Like Callahan, Moore, and Jones, most of the remaining Invacare investors hailed from the Cleveland area, including Richey's brother, Dr. DeWayne Richey, Whitney Evans, Larry J. B.

Robinson, William A. Mitchell, Stanley C. Pace (president of TRW Inc.), Robert Files (Robinson and Files were both members of the Harvard Business School Club[27]), Dr. Everett James, John W. Wilhelm, Dr. Ronald Ross, Robert G. Patterson, and Evan Kemp Jr. Most would invest $100,000. Kemp, a disabled attorney who would later become chairman of the U.S. Equal Employment Opportunity Commission[28] and a champion of disabled rights, was a college friend of Richey's. At the time, Kemp—now deceased—was an attorney with the Securities and Exchange Commission (SEC). He was "greatly impressed" by Mixon. "It also helped that he got along well with J. B. Richey, a friend of mine and a brilliant engineer," recalled Kemp in 1991. "Because J. B. and Mal got along well, I thought they had a real shot at making it a success."[29]

Mixon praised the legal advice he received from Dale LaPorte, chairman of the Cleveland law firm Calfee, Halter & Griswold LLP,[30] who would later became Invacare's corporate secretary. The firm served as general counsel to Mixon and his team as they were putting together the pieces of the financing puzzle. The relationship would continue to develop over the years as Invacare grew.

Like the others, LaPorte saw promise in both Invacare and the people Mixon rallied to purchase the company.

It looked like a venture that included a lot of solid people. It had all the earmarks of something that could be built into a successful enterprise. [W]ithout knowing anything about the wheelchair area or medical devices in general, it just seemed to us that the numbers looked right, and ... [Mixon] was pointing out to all of his prospective investors that the demographics were particularly in his favor because ... as the Baby Boomers aged, there would be more and more of a demand.[31]

This same reasoning—and Mixon's sheer determination—helped him weather several sleep-

Although many of Invacare's initial investors felt the company's product line needed improvement—such as an upgrade to its clumsy wheelchair wheels—all saw the potential in Mal Mixon's diamond in the rough.

Dale LaPorte, chairman of the Cleveland law firm Calfee, Halter & Griswold LLP, served as general counsel to Mixon. He has continued to handle the company's acquisitions and public legal requirements.

less nights before everything came together at 5 P.M. on the very last day of Grimm's time frame. Despite the stress of putting the deal together and the huge personal financial stake he had in it, Mixon said he never vacillated in his decision to purchase Invacare. "I was sort of holding this together with baling wire," said Mixon. "I didn't have any money, interest rates were climbing, and I didn't have any room to move anywhere."[32]

With the money in place, Mixon and the group headed by himself and Bill Jones closed the deal for $7.8 million at the end of December 1979. Initially, Mixon would serve as president and COO while Richey stayed on at Technicare, working to develop the scanning technology that would come

to be known as magnetic resonance imaging (MRI).[33] "The company wasn't large enough to support two of us," Mixon said. "So he stayed at [Technicare] but did invest substantially in the company and went on the board."[34] Bill Jones became chairman of the board.

The "Rodney Dangerfield Era"

Although Invacare had the potential to be a thriving enterprise, it wasn't one yet. At the time Mixon and his investment team made their purchase, Invacare's facilities consisted of two plants in Elyria, Ohio, a third in Lodi, Ohio, and around 350 associates. One of the Elyria locations—128,000 square feet on twenty acres—would continue to serve as the company's headquarters.

Although Mixon had plenty of room to grow his new venture, which was already turning a profit,[35] he had inherited a business in need of nurturing.

Assembly of standard wheelchair and patient care products took place at the company's Taylor Street facility in Elyria, Ohio. The plant experienced rejuvenation after the acquisition.

INVACARE'S ORIGINAL
"YES, YOU CAN" – MAL MIXON

MAL MIXON SAW THE SALE slipping away from him. The president of a North Carolina hospital wasn't going to buy a CT scanner from the young Ohio-Nuclear vice president of sales and marketing.

"Mr. Mixon, I appreciate your coming down here," the executive said, beginning his refusal. "You have a great company, but we made a decision. We're going to go with General Electric."

Ever persistent and ever the salesman, Mixon didn't just shake hands and shuffle off.

"I'd like to save you $50,000," he said. "I just happened to notice that GE order on your desk, and I read very well upside down. GE is not selling to everyone at the same price—you're paying $50,000 more than you should. And if you pick up the phone and call the GE district office and tell the manager that Mr. Mixon from Ohio-Nuclear is sitting in the lobby, I think they'll cut the price by $50,000."

They did. But Mixon got the sale anyway.[1]

The story of A. Malachi Mixon, III, gives Horatio Alger a run for his money. He was born in 1940 and raised in Spiro, Oklahoma, a small town twenty miles west of Fort Smith, Arkansas. Spiro had been home to four generations of Mixons, including James Joyce Mixon, a Confederate soldier during the Civil War; Mal Mixon's grandfather, a medical doctor; his father, Aaron M. Mixon Jr., a salesman for a meatpacking company; and his mother, a secretary. The Mixons raised their son and daughter in a one-story house on ten acres of land on the Mixon family property.[2] Since Mixon and his father are of Native American ancestry, Mal Mixon can claim to be one of the few minority chief executives of a large public company.

His parents thrust him into a variety of sports and musical activities, especially trumpet, piano, and voice. "For a while, I even took ballet," he later recalled. Mixon helped the town's high school get into the state semifinals in football and basketball.[3] "Mal was one of the leaders in the school," his former high school coach, Gerald Blankenship, told a reporter.[4]

His parents, particularly his father, pushed him hard. His father stopped picking him up after high school in his sophomore year until he broke into the starting lineup on the varsity basketball team. And it was his father who filled out his application to Harvard University.[5] With the help of scholarships, loans, and jobs, he earned a degree in physical sciences.

While at Harvard, Mixon met his wife, Wellesley College student Barbara Weber. After Harvard he was off to the U.S. Marine Corps. In the mid-1960s, Mixon found himself in Vietnam, where he received several combat decorations while performing air reconnaissance work and directing artillery and air strikes aboard Marine single-engine fixed-wing aircraft and helicopters.[6] He left the Marines after four years, having attained the rank of captain, and headed back to Harvard for an M.B.A.

When it came time to find a job, he looked in his wife's hometown of Cleveland, Ohio. He took a job at Harris Corporation as a management trainee, became a sales representative, and eventually became director of marketing.[7] He worked for two small private companies before joining Ohio-Nuclear, which later took the Technicare Corporation name. There he rose to vice president of sales and marketing.[8] In the late 1970s, Technicare began shopping itself piece by piece. One of those pieces was Invacare, then a small wheelchair maker in

Elyria, west of Cleveland. Mixon took $10,000 of his own savings and borrowed and raised nearly $7.8 million in investments and business loans to buy Invacare.[9] By 2000, his modest financial investment and considerable personal investment had become a $100 million fortune in just twenty-one years.[10]

While Invacare has been the most important business in Mixon's life, he has also built a reputation as a shrewd and successful venture capitalist. Among his ventures is Royal Appliance Manufacturing Company, the maker of Dirt Devil vacuum cleaners. Like Invacare, Royal was ripe for rejuvenation. It was Technicare alumnus John Balch who approached Mixon about the prospect in 1981. As he had done with Invacare, Mixon put together a group of investors to back Balch, this time in exchange for a $20,000 note (10 percent of the company).[11] After the company went public in 1991, Mixon had an investment worth more than $30 million.[12]

In 1992, with friend Francis Joseph Callahan, an original Invacare investor, and Cleveland attorney Ernest P. Mansour, Mixon formed MCM (Mixon, Callahan, and Mansour) Capital Corporation, a venture capital company designed to buy small- and medium-size firms, mostly in northeastern Ohio.

Mixon explained his interest in helping young businesses to a reporter:

Joe [Callahan] and I look at these things as an opportunity to help people who want to help themselves. Many times we invest in people who haven't made their first million. It's a lot of fun to do that....

I like to say that while some people are home mowing the yard or painting a picture or reading a book, I may be ... meeting with an entrepreneur with a new idea. A dinner or a quick meeting on the weekend, and we'll make a decision....

I may make one or two investments a year. It's not that we have a pile of money burning a hole in our pockets. We're opportunistic. We have the money if we find something that we like.[13]

In 1998, MCM raised $50 million for a leveraged buyout and venture fund, topping a fundraising goal of $40 million.[14]

Among Mixon's other private investments: **Advanced Ceramics,** maker of ceramic and other nonmetallic mineral products; **Cencor,** provider of temporary workers to businesses;[15] **NeuroControl Corporation,** maker of electrical implants that restore hand motion to paraplegics; **STERIS Corporation,** creator of a method to quickly sterilize medical equipment.

Mixon has participated in many philanthropic ventures as well. In 1992, he gave $2 million to the Weatherhead School of Management at Case Western Reserve University in Cleveland to boost the school's entrepreneurial programs, including an endowed chair in entrepreneurial studies.[16] And in 1997, he gave $1 million to establish a Mixon Scholarship in each new freshman class at Harvard College for students from Oklahoma and Northeast Ohio. He has also personally contributed $1 million to the Cleveland Clinic for medical research.

His commitment to Invacare has led him into a variety of causes for the disabled. In 1996, the Paralyzed Veterans of America gave him the group's Corporate Patriot Award for his work with the National Veterans Wheelchair Games.[17]

That same year he was named to the inaugural class of the Cleveland Business Hall of Fame, a group that includes John D. Rockefeller, Hector "Chef Boy-ar-dee" Boiardi, and Henry A. Sherwin, cofounder of paint maker The Sherwin-Williams Company.[18]

Mixon was also honored by the Harvard Business School Club of Cleveland in 1984 with the Dively Entrepreneurship Award. In 1995, he was named "Outstanding Philanthropist of the Year" by the Greater Cleveland chapter of the National Society of Fund-Raising Executives.[19] Two years later, he was honored with the National Multiple Sclerosis Society's Hope Award, which he received for his distinguished community service.

Today, Mixon serves on the boards of several public companies and is chairman of the Board of Trustees of the Cleveland Clinic Foundation.

At the time of the purchase, Invacare was producing standard wheelchairs and a few patient products such as walkers, commodes, and canes.[36] The company had no new products under development, no international business, and no strategic plan in place. "[Johnson & Johnson] was trying to operate it at a minimum of any investment to make it as profitable in the short run as they could. So product development was nil," said Mixon.[37] What Invacare did have was a fair share of what Moore called the "down and dirty": wheelchairs that sold for $100 each—but nothing in the prescription wheelchair market.[38]

According to Yost, the company was poorly run from around 1974 until the time that Mixon purchased it.

I kind of headed that [effort] up to clean all the junk out of there—the things that didn't work—and [to] get [rid] of obsolete material.... So when Mal bought it, he had pretty bare bones—good material, but there was no engineering.... There had been no drive to do anything with the company.[39]

Compounding the problem, said Mike Parsons, manager of financial services at the time and later vice president of North American sales, was Invacare's shoestring budget and the fact that no Elyria banks would lend the company money during the early part of Mixon's tenure.

Those were lean years.... No banks would touch us because they didn't know Mal. Even though Invacare was actually one of the oldest companies in Elyria, Ohio, not one bank would loan us a penny, and the Cleveland banks didn't know much about Invacare.[40]

In addition, Mixon found that product quality and delivery times were poor and that Invacare had suffered from neglect under Technicare. Moreover,

Mixon pointed out, "The new CEO, yours truly, had never run a company before."

I remember making my first sales calls in early 1980, and most customers were quick to tell me all the things wrong with Invacare and our products. In fact, I refer to this period as the "Rodney Dangerfield era" because we truly got "no respect" from anyone.

I further recall a first sales meeting I held with Invacare's sales management in which I announced that my plan was to become number one in the wheelchair business. Absolutely no one believed this was possible, and I am confident that group thought the new Invacare CEO was a crazy man who would probably last ninety days at best.[41]

But unlike those who had previously owned what was now Invacare, Mixon and his team—many first-time investors like Mixon—wanted to

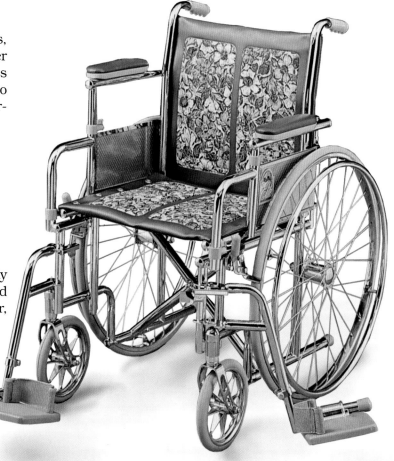

One of Invacare's main product offerings pre-Mixon was wheelchairs like this late-1970s model Rolls Elite wheelchair. That would soon change, however, when Mixon made his first move to expand the company's product line in 1981.

make a real go of building a successful company. Just as he had shown himself to be a persuasive salesman, Mixon would soon prove to be a charismatic leader and an ace planner. Said Moore:

Mal is one of the best planners I've ever seen. I mean, he came from the George Dively School of Planning, and if you overlaid Bill Jones on top of that, another fanatical planner, Invacare was a very well planned company, and it had a fighter as a leader.[42]

As Yost would later remark, Mixon "could sell anything to anybody."[43] This ability would eventually win him many loyal, equally hard-working associates who shared his vision for Invacare. "He's such a driving force," said Debbie Warden, Mixon's assistant for the past twelve years.[44]

Edith Powers, a former executive secretary for Mixon, agreed. "When Mal came it was such a change," she said. "It was wonderful for the company and the people working there. I'm so glad they stayed in Elyria because that's where all the history of wheelchair manufacturing is— in Elyria."[45]

Debbie Warden, who joined Invacare in 1988 as Mal Mixon's assistant, said her boss is a dynamic motivator and driving force.

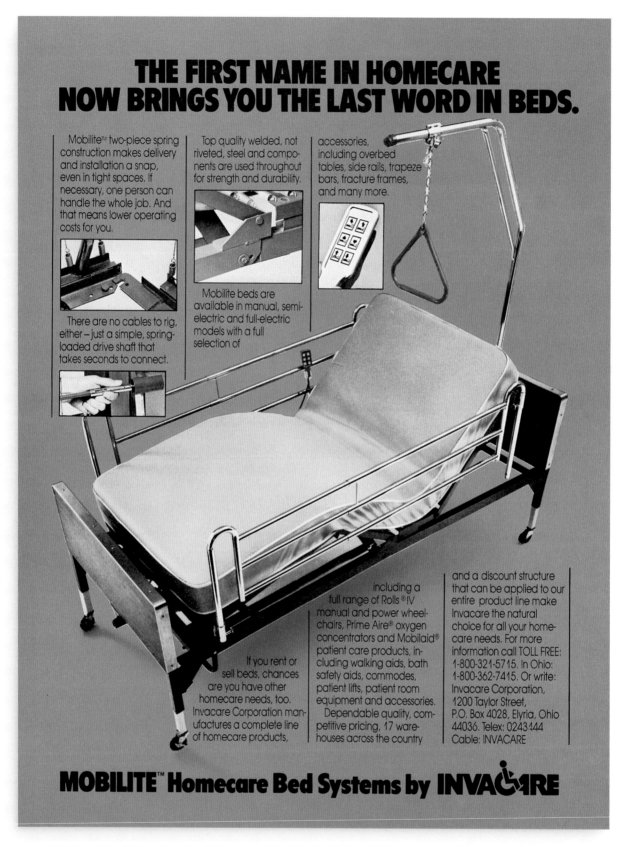

One of Invacare's early acquisitions under Mixon was Mobilite of Sanford, Florida. It would prove to be a profitable acquisition for the company, which wanted to get into the lucrative home care bed market.

CHAPTER FOUR

THE TURNAROUND

1980–1983

When I joined, the entire industry was Everest & Jennings.

—Hymie Pogir, vice president,
product development and Invacare technologies

INVACARE'S NEW OWNER-ship couldn't have come at a better time. Wheelchair giant Everest & Jennings (E&J) had run the industry for decades, and wheelchair design had stagnated. Consumers had few options and were basically forced to accept whatever design Everest & Jennings was selling. In most cases, that meant an institutional-looking wheelchair weighing about fifty pounds and built of steel tubing, with skinny bicycle wheels and a vinyl sling-back seat.

"When I joined, the entire industry *was* Everest & Jennings," said Hymie Pogir, who started at Invacare in 1980 as a sales representative. "They were enormous, and they just ruled the neighborhood."[1] This was literally true in California, where the company had built a huge factory in a town called Camarillo, recalled Pogir, who could see it looming across a mountain range from his home in Ventura County. "I used to look at this and think, 'I better get my damn resume together, because these boys are going to just beat us to death.'"[2]

By 1980, however, Everest & Jennings—once the "only store in town" when it came to wheelchairs—was perhaps more vulnerable than it ever had been.[3] Several of its early and major patents, including the patent for its trademarked folding x-brace, had expired decades before, yet it had spent years and considerable energy bringing patent infringement suits against imitators instead of aggressively pursuing research and development of a new,

more competitive chair.[4] Fear of foreign competition had prompted it to buy overseas wheelchair producers. Moreover, employees weren't willing to relocate to the company's new California manufacturing facility.[5]

In a different business environment, Everest & Jennings would have been quickly swamped with competition. However, the wheelchair business was not a typical business. The largest consumer of wheelchairs in the country was the United States government. Even after Everest & Jennings's patents expired, the government was still actively supporting the company at the expense of innovation in the industry. Until 1976, the government used Everest & Jennings designs to determine its purchasing standards rather than developing any criteria of its own.

In 1976, however, a landmark piece of legislation called the Medical Devices Act was passed, creating the Bureau of Medical Devices under the auspices of the Food and Drug Administration (FDA). This new department was charged with oversight of the rapidly evolving medical devices industry, which included catheters, diagnostic tools like CT

An Invacare logo in the 1980s. Expansion into other areas of the home health care market through acquisitions would prompt the creation of a new one, without a wheelchair, in 1986.

Above: Gil Haury (center, holding plaque, flanked by lab employees), former director of Invacare's test lab, was instrumental in the development of voluntary and comparative standards for wheelchairs.

Inset: Hymie Pogir, vice president of product development, joined Invacare in 1980 as a sales representative.

scanners and MRI devices, and of course wheelchairs and other home care medical equipment. With the passage of the act, a government panel began studying the products on the market and making recommendations about future standards and safety issues.

For wheelchairs, the bureau initially used the Everest & Jennings standards that had been in place for so long. The only area in which it didn't follow Everest & Jennings was the design of electrical components on powered chairs. New standards were set, but these remained almost as constric-

tive as the Everest & Jennings–determined ones. In 1979, Donald Wright, an official with the Veterans Administration, said the federal wheelchair guidelines (really the Everest & Jennings standard) "stifles creativity in the development and severely restricts the use of new materials and methods. It may also fix costs at higher-than-necessary levels."[6]

For a government official to be so openly critical of Everest & Jennings meant trouble. By the late 1970s, Everest & Jennings could no longer expect the government to protect it from competition. In fact, relations between the nation's largest wheelchair maker and the government had deteriorated almost completely. In 1977, the Department of Justice had filed charges against Everest & Jennings for violation of the Sherman Antitrust Act. The Department of Justice alleged that Everest & Jennings, with 90 percent of the domestic wheelchair market, was exercising monopoly-like power over its industry. The Justice Department suit was settled three years later— after it became apparent that Everest & Jennings wouldn't hold on to the lion's share of the market for long.[7]

The Problems at Hand

When Mixon bought Invacare, what was true of Everest & Jennings was true for the whole wheelchair industry. As Mixon quickly discovered, Invacare was also sluggish and tired, its technology outdated, and its manufacturing weak. Nyal Yost, then Elyria plant manager, remembered that under Technicare, the company was "poorly run because Johnson & Johnson wanted to get rid of it. They didn't want it at all, and there wasn't much drive for wheelchairs."[8]

The sole innovation throughout the Technicare years had been the development of a twenty-four-inch magnesium wheel. It was designed by Gil Haury, the future director of Invacare's corporate test lab, and shaved precious pounds off the chairs, making them easier to maneuver. The wheel was honored

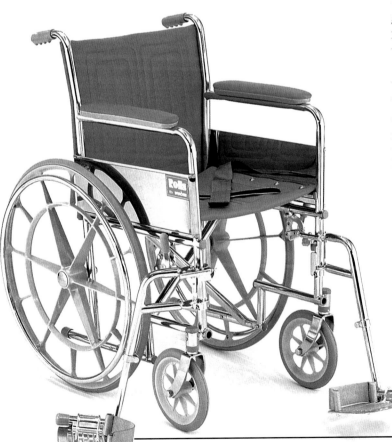

A Rolls manual wheelchair from the early 1980s. In 1981, Invacare would unveil its first powered offering: the Rolls IV.

with an Award of Excellence by the International Magnesium Association. "I received the [award] from the Magnesium Association when that went to production in the late '70s," Haury recalled.[9]

Beyond that, however, Invacare's problems ran deep. According to Mixon, there were several urgent concerns:
- No new products were under development;
- Product quality and delivery were poor;
- Elyria, Ohio, was a high-labor-cost area, surrounded by unions;
- A new offshore competitive threat from Taiwan was beginning to emerge;
- There was no international business of any consequence;
- Interest rates were skyrocketing to 23 percent and Invacare was borrowing at 3 percent over prime; and
- The company had no strategy or business plan.[10]

Furthermore, the sales effort was handled by a "sleepy seventeen-person sales force.... These guys felt sorry for themselves. They really weren't the type of salespeople I wanted to have, and we gradually turned them over," said Mixon.[11] Only a few of the original sales team members survived this cut.

Mixon immediately went to work to address all the problem areas concurrently. He strengthened the distribution network so home care providers could get fast, prepaid delivery and better financing. He began to work on asset management and paying down part of the company's debt by reducing receivables and inventory.[12] In addition, Mixon put Mike Parsons, then assistant treasurer, on task to mend the poor relationship between the company's sales and credit departments. Parsons recalled that "When Mal bought the company, there was about a twelve-foot brick wall between credit and sales. They hated each other. It was the sales prevention department."[13]

Mixon's Marketing Mojo

Mixon also "brought a great [deal of] marketing experience with him from being involved in the Technicare side of imaging equipment," said Gil Haury, director of engineering at

A 1983 Mobilaid product brochure shows Invacare's ever broadening product line.

"He gave us all a chance.... Mal was a super boss to all of us who wanted to really get in there and do something," recalled Yost.[17]

He used the people that were there.... He was capable of sorting out what they were the best at and using them, and he used them well. He made some changes. He brought in others. And then when he was finally able to bring in Richey [in '84], things really went to town.[18]

Building Blocks

While internal product development was moving forward, Mixon turned to another growth strategy: acquisition. Not content to limit the company to selling wheelchairs, Mixon envisioned building an entire health care company around a central theme. Throughout his later career with Invacare, this would become a trademark as he pushed the company both to develop internally and to acquire new technologies and devices that were all related to home health care.

Although Invacare had clearly been focused on its customers in the past, the company now found it was imperative to strike a balance between offering "anything" and being a low-cost supplier, said Gerald B. Blouch, who would later become president and chief operating officer.

It's a challenge to harmonize the disciplines that you need to be a low cost supplier and be able to offer anything anytime to the customer.... If we had a salesman of the year, and he was out with a customer, and he said the customer wanted chartreuse mud flaps on his wheelchair, we gave him chartreuse mud flaps on his wheelchair. That's just the way it was.[19]

Clearly, the key to solving this problem lay in additional acquisitions, which would allow the company to offer a broader range of products at a lower price. However, there wasn't a great deal of acquisition expertise in the organization. What the company did have, said Blouch, was "a lot of smart people with a common objective."

We knew where we needed to get to, and those smart people got us there every time not by pulling

the time.[14] It was Mixon's application of this experience to Invacare's broadening product line—particularly its manual and power wheelchair lines—that would ultimately position Invacare as the market leader. Invacare was an engineer's dream, rife with opportunity and target rich. "Each time we did something, we improved it," Haury said.[15]

In 1980, the company introduced three products—a lightweight wheelchair under the Rollite brand, a tub-transfer chair, and a drop-arm commode. More importantly for the long term, Mixon began to sink money into new product development. He encouraged the company's engineers and designers to create a wheelchair that would far outshine anything on the market. This project would take several years to complete.[16]

out the manual—the acquisition manual—and following the steps, but [by] doing what they thought they needed to do, and at times it could be very exciting.[20]

The First Acquisitions

It didn't take Invacare long to implement a strategy of growth by acquisition. Just weeks after buying the company, Mixon received a call from the top executive at Smith & Davis, a division of an Indiana-based company called Huntco. Smith & Davis, the home care bed leader with approximately 75 or 80 percent of the market, wanted to purchase Invacare. Although Mixon wasn't interested in selling, he agreed to hear Smith & Davis's proposal. The bed and wheelchair markets, they told him, fit together like a glove. If Mixon didn't sell, Smith & Davis would go into the wheelchair business.

So I remember going back to the office and saying, "You know, I've just been threatened, but more importantly, we need to go into the bed business."[21]

In 1981, Invacare purchased a startup bed company in Sanford, Florida, called Easley Medical Products, which had an innovative design for home-use hospital beds that was not yet in production. This design for a split spring bed, which Invacare dubbed Mobilite, folded down the middle and could be delivered by one person. It was a major innovation, and although the design hadn't been perfected, tested, or shipped, Mixon knew potential when he saw it.[22] It was the perfect springboard from which to launch a foray into the home care bed market. The beds could be sold through the existing Invacare dealer network without adding additional marketing costs.[23]

At the same time Invacare moved into the home care bed market, the company also pursued the oxygen concentrator market with the acquisition of Prime Aire Inc. for $75,000 plus royalties and consulting fees. The Hartford, Connecticut, company developed and marketed an oxygen concentrator. These motor-driven compressors filtered regular room air and delivered 95 percent pure oxygen. They replaced more expensive liquid and

Although Invacare's first foray into the oxygen concentrator market was thorny, the respiratory line would become viable once quality control issues were sorted out a couple of years later.

compressed oxygen systems and were used by patients with chronic lung diseases.

Although there was great potential in the concentrators, and they eventually developed into a large business, the first couple of years were rough. Almost immediately, Invacare ran into trouble with the filtering technology of the product and had a recall when the concentrators didn't work as planned. Yost, who worked on this product line, said there were quality control problems with one of the suppliers. The issue took several years to sort out and resulted in a charge against earnings in early 1984.

Above: Mixon and Denis O'Brien, directors of Ortomed Aids Ltd. of Shannon, Ireland. Although Invacare would soon divest itself of this joint venture to manufacture home and health care rehabilitation products, other foreign acquisitions would follow. *(Photo courtesy* Elyria Chronicle-Telegram.*)*

Center: Donald E. Karl was named vice president of operations in 1981.

Below: One of the cost-saving pluses of the Mobilite bed was that it was foldable and could be delivered by one person.

Overseas, Invacare entered into a joint venture agreement in Ireland, where it created Ortomed Aids Ltd. with Denis O'Brien, an Irish business executive. Ortomed, which was founded in May 1981, was created to manufacture home health and rehabilitation products in Ireland for the European market.[24]

Although these early additions were financially taxing for Invacare, which was trying to lower its high-interest debt, they would ultimately prove crucial to its success and would set the tone for the company's acquisition-fueled growth and development. However, because Invacare was still in its adolescence, the company had a number of years of growing pains to endure before reaching maturity.

With his company already growing quickly through acquisition, expansion, and new products, Mixon looked to bring in executive talent that could help run the kind of growth enterprise he hoped to create. He announced four appointments: Donald E. Karl, vice president of operations; E. Patrick Nalley, vice president of sales and marketing; Gary A. Howell, director of personnel; and Daniel Terlaak, director of quality assurance. In comments to Invacare's shareholders, Mixon said he had the needed team in place.

These new executives, together with Fred Barone, chief financial officer, and Gil Haury, director of engineering, have produced a positive impact on operations, and we now have a top management team with the skill and talent to lead Invacare in our continuing rapid growth.[25]

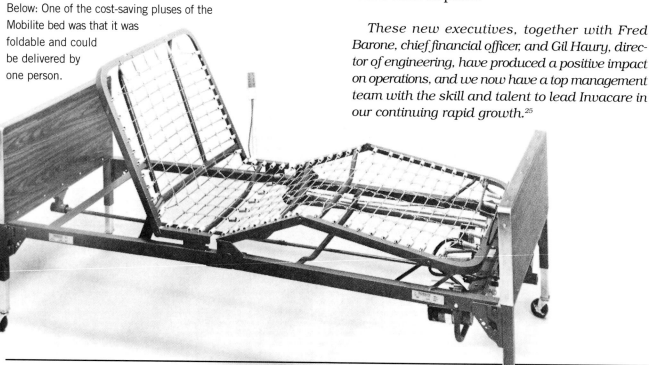

A Trusted Mentor

The relationship between Mixon and Nalley went back some years. The two had worked together at Cleveland-based Harris Corporation, which made printing presses. Nalley was working as vice president of sales when Mixon, fresh out of Harvard Business School, took a position in the company's accounting department. One day as the pair were casually chatting in the company's cafeteria, Nalley inquired how things were going for Mixon at Harris. "Not worth a damn," responded Mixon. "Well," said Nalley, "how would you like to come up and work for me where the action is?" Mixon said yes to an assistant marketing position.[26]

Under Nalley's tutelage, Mixon cut his teeth in marketing. Helpful and eager, he was quickly promoted. However, Nalley felt Mixon needed more experience in sales if he were going to continue his climb up the corpo-

A 1983 Mobilite brochure shows one of the company's electrically controlled beds. Mobilite also offered manual beds and accessories such as overbed tables, side rails, trapeze bars, and fracture frames.

rate ladder. Nalley told him, "If you start telling salesmen and other people how to do their job and you haven't done it, they kind of take a dim viewpoint of that." Off Mixon went into the field, working first as a salesperson, then as a district manager.[27]

Nalley's advice would stand Mixon in good stead in years to come, even after the two parted ways to pursue other endeavors. He continued to mentor Mixon, even throwing job offers his way. In fact, in late 1979, when Mixon was scrambling to pull together financing for Invacare, a Louisiana company to which Nalley had recommended Mixon was holding a job for him. "If he got [Invacare], he wouldn't want the job, but if he didn't get [Invacare], he could have it," remembered Nalley.[28]

As it turned out, after Mixon bought Invacare, he persuaded Nalley to visit him at a small trade show in New Orleans. Nalley, who at one time had been selling $1 million and $2 million printing presses, wasn't impressed with the company's $200—$300 wheelchairs. "I said, 'My God, man, we'd have to sell a lot of those things in order to make any money. Besides, that sounds depressing, so I don't think I'd care for it much,'" Nalley remembered.[29]

However, making money, Mixon would later say during a Newcomen speech in 1996, was not necessarily high on his list of priorities for Invacare. Rather, it would be a product of successfully serving customers. "Customers are the only purpose of a business—fulfilling a need," he said. "Profits are a result, not the purpose of a business."[30]

Never one to give up easily, Mixon persuaded Nalley to travel with Millard Watts, one of his regional sales reps, and give the company another shot.

So he and I traveled around, and I saw people who were handicapped, and it kind of got in your blood that you were doing some good and helping them out.[31]

Mixon brought Nalley on board in 1980 as "international manager" in order to avoid ruffling feathers,

Pat Nalley and Mal Mixon (above, left and right) developed Invacare's Total One Stop Shopping concept with Mike Parsons (inset).

eventually promoting him to vice president of sales and marketing. He would remain a part of the Invacare sales team until his retirement in 1992. Nalley continued to serve as a trusted mentor to Mixon, helping to shape and guide the company in its infancy.[32] During Invacare's "Rodney Dangerfield" days, it was Nalley who urged Mixon to demand respect from some of the company's biggest clients.

One of these clients was Abbey. In the early 1980s, said Nalley, the company wasn't playing fair ball, even going as far as to pass Invacare leads on to E&J.[33] This prompted a visit to the company's California headquarters from Nalley, who used a football analogy to illustrate the fact that Invacare would not be pushed around. He made his point forcefully.

What we want to do is play ball with you guys and work with you, but if you're not cooperating

with us, I'm going to tell our guys to fake you and do whatever the hell is necessary—to lower their shoulders and run over you bastards.[34]

Invacare even fired a Boston-based Abbey distributor who refused to see Mixon—a bold move considering that the company was Invacare's largest dealer in the early 1980s. Mixon agreed to reinstate the dealer only when he came to Elyria to tell Mixon personally that he would "fairly and properly and legitimately represent my products and give us a substantial opening order consistent with that.... So we had a nice visit, and evidently there were just enough people that wanted our line that they wanted to make amends." The dealer would eventually leave Abbey, open his own business, and become one of Invacare's best customers, Mixon said.[35]

However, although Invacare was quick to challenge nonsupportive distributors, the company also made it a point to reward those who were doing well, said Nalley.[36] In fact, the company's continuing support of dealers would prove to be one of its strengths.

One Stop Shopping and Invalease

Invacare took another step toward future success when Mixon, Nalley, and Parsons developed the company's trademark "One Stop Shopping" concept. Parsons recalled how the idea was born.

We had this idea of offering one stop shopping to our customers, where you could make one phone call and get everything you needed. You know, wheelchairs, beds, patient aids, walkers, and you name it. The only problem is, we only had one product back in those days, and that was the wheelchair.[37]

As a result, said Parsons, the company often had to put the proverbial product cart before the horse. "We knew what we wanted to do, and sometimes you kind of just have to catch up with yourself as you're going out and getting the business," he said. "That's what we did in the early years before we could really get all the products together to complement a true one stop shopping."[38]

One Stop Shopping was developed around the same time as Invacare's Invalease program

The ingenious One Stop Shopping concept, introduced in the early 1980s, would prove to be one of Invacare's strengths as further acquisitions broadened the company's home health care lines.

was created, which itself was a response to customers' needs.[39]

Engineering Pays Off

In 1982, the wheelchair industry jointly established the American National Standards Institute (ANSI) and the Rehabilitation Engineering and Assistive Technology Society of North America (RESNA). These agencies were created to set vol-

untary testing and comparative standards for wheelchairs.[40] In an effort to better serve disabled consumers and to help set the standards, Invacare became an active member of ANSI and also of the International Standards Organization (ISO). "We developed a lot of the tests that were ... put into these specifications," said Haury, who later became a committee member of ISO and an active member of ANSI.[41]

There had never been a greater need for industry standards, especially considering the technological innovations that would come that year. After working for two years, Invacare's engineers began introducing new products and focuses. First, Invacare moved into the "prescription wheelchair" business. Unlike the standard production chairs, prescription chairs were custom products made to suit the individual needs of disabled patients.[42] Next, Invacare introduced its much-praised dual sealed precision ball bearings for wheelchairs.[43] "Our dealers loved this because they steam clean [wheelchairs] and re-rent them," said Richey.[44]

Prior to that, in 1981, Invacare had unveiled a power wheelchair called the Rolls IV. Looking back, many industry observers would credit this first major product with much of Invacare's later success. It represented a tremendous leap forward in technology for the entire wheelchair industry and, more than any other factor, hastened the demise of the beleaguered Everest & Jennings.

As Invacare introduced products like the Rolls IV, "It gave people the ability to do more," said Ron Thomas, director of facilities. "So, they expected more and they wanted more."[45] With a talented and growing staff, Invacare was ready to deliver. The company's introduction of a power chair also meant that home care providers were more inclined to pay attention, said Richey.

Right away, the home care providers thought it was wonderful because they had been told all along by Everest & Jennings, "This is the best, this is all you're going to get." Well, when they saw a better mouse trap, they liked it.[46]

Such innovation came with a price tag, however, and, like all new technology, had its share of bugs. The battery-powered Rolls IV, priced at $3,500, was the product of a $500,000 development program—

a staggering sum for an industry whose latest innovation had come decades before. The new chair could travel twenty-seven miles before it needed a recharge and had a maximum speed of 4.8 miles per hour.

Mixon tried out a test model of the new chair himself on a loading dock at the Elyria plant. At the touch of a button on the left armrest, he took the new wheelchair down a forty-five-degree ramp, demonstrating the automatic braking system. "Just the slightest movement in the direction you want to go will move the chair," Mixon said, adding that under power the chair could move "forward or backward with a slight touch and even in a circular motion."[47]

Although the chair would ultimately position Invacare as a leader, the company spent some time working out issues with its control mechanism, recalled Otmar Sackerlotzky, retired vice president of quality control. Due to what Sackerlotzky termed a "process control problem," one wheel would sometimes receive more power than the other, causing the wheelchair to move in circles. Another problem was that the motors on these early power models were too small and really required a feedback loop between two stronger motors for control.[48]

By 1983, however, Invacare had chosen to purchase its controllers from Dynamic Controls in New Zealand, a company it would eventually purchase. Invacare's use of Dynamic's controllers—improved upon by Invacare engineers—coupled with the use of an inductive joystick manufactured in England, helped to make the company's power chair safer and more reliable.[49]

When the Rolls IV was introduced, Invacare's sales had already begun an upward trend. In 1980, sales stood at $25 million. One year later, as

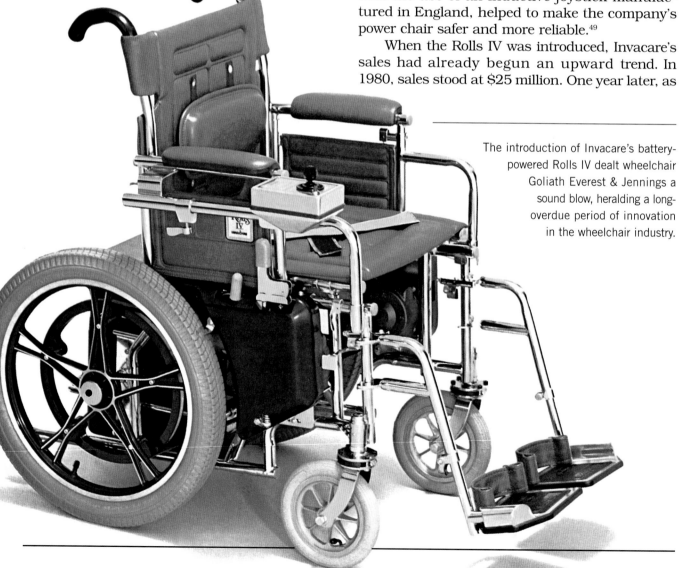

The introduction of Invacare's battery-powered Rolls IV dealt wheelchair Goliath Everest & Jennings a sound blow, heralding a long-overdue period of innovation in the wheelchair industry.

Rolls IV

The Wheelchair Worth Prescribing.

INTERNATIONAL YEAR OF DISABLED PERSONS, 1981
FULL PARTICIPATION AND EQUALITY

a result of the acquisitions, the Rolls IV, and a new sales mentality, revenues had risen to $38 million.[50] In this time, the marketing staff had increased from two to fifteen people and three-quarters of the company's salespeople had been replaced. As a result, sales per person rose from $750,000 to $1.2 million.[51]

In May 1982, Mixon announced a round of promotions and new additions to his senior management. Karl was promoted to senior vice president of operations, Nalley to senior vice president of sales and marketing, Howell to vice president of personnel, and Yost to vice president of manufacturing.[52]

Above: A 1981 brochure produced during the International Year of Disabled Persons featuring the Rolls IV, "The Wheelchair Worth Prescribing." As an up-and-coming health care leader, Invacare was a strong and early proponent of working toward full participation and equality for the disabled.

Left: Otmar Sackerlotzky, former vice president of quality control, worked to help get the bugs out of Invacare's first power wheelchair offering, the Rolls IV.

As Invacare grew, Everest & Jennings's revenue remained flat. Mixon pointed out to shareholders: "When our sales were at $19 million, [Everest & Jennings's] were at $150 million. When our sales were at $25 million, they were at $150 million. Today [in December 1981], when our sales are at $38 million, they are still at $150 million."

Fighting for Position

Everest & Jennings, however, was still by far the largest wheelchair maker in the world and had no intention of letting an upstart company like Invacare threaten it. Although the antitrust suit brought by the Justice Department had been settled in 1980, Everest & Jennings nonetheless remained fiercely protective of its market share. As Mixon remembered,

Right after we bought Invacare, almost to the day we announced we were going to come out with a motorized wheelchair, Everest & Jennings announced severe price cutting on standard wheelchairs. At that time, this made up about 80 percent of our business. I think they were offering a 17 percent discount plus free freight, which was another 5 percent. In total, it was 22 percent.[53]

To Invacare, this didn't seem like fair play, and in April 1982 it filed a suit against Everest & Jennings for predatory pricing practices in violation of the Sherman Antitrust Act and Ohio law. The $4.5 million suit claimed that the Everest & Jennings price cuts were designed "for the purpose of maintaining its monopoly in the industry and to injure or eliminate competition."[54] The lawsuit caused a lengthy legal battle between the two companies. Invacare was also prompted to file a patent infringement suit when its patent attorney discovered that E&J had violated one of Invacare's wheelchair patents for a swing-away and hook-on leg-and-footrest.[55] The suits, which also accused E&J of interfering with Invacare's business relationships, were eventually settled for $1 million.

Elyria Extends a Helping Hand

The lawsuits, and even the price war with Everest & Jennings, were signs that Invacare was doing something right. The company was growing quickly, with new products and increased revenue, and soon needed additional space. Mixon looked to Elyria and surrounding Lorain County for expansion. A part of the Cleveland metropolitan area, Lorain County had a rich industrial heritage and was home to several automotive assembly plants and a major steel mill operated by the U.S. Steel

Company. The Ridge Tool Company was headquartered there, and General Motors' Fisher Guide parts plant was a key employer.

In its 1950s and 1960s heyday, Lorain County was home to several steel plants and was ground zero for innovations like the Troxel bicycle seat, the first glass-lined water heaters, and the Garford car. "In this [county], which had been an industrial mecca, pre- and post-World War II, there were over four hundred patented products which were invented and manufactured," said Libbie Lockard, former manager of trade shows and special events, who started with Invacare in 1982.[56] By the time Mixon purchased Invacare, however, the economic climate had cooled considerably. Labor was heavily unionized and unemployment was on the rise; the local economy was not faring well.

Between 1978 and 1982, unemployment in Lorain County climbed from 5.2 percent to an alarming 18.9 percent, with the county losing twelve thousand jobs. Near the end of the decade, Frank DiTillio, economic development manager of the Greater Lorain Chamber of Commerce, observed that "In the past five years about one hundred companies have closed or moved out of the county either because of labor relations problems, tax benefits offered in other areas, [or] needs that could be met in another location or because the grass is greener somewhere else."[57]

Public officials knew that they had to help area employers in any way they could in order to maintain the area's vitality, and so began an ambitious campaign to improve the county's roads, bridges, and sewers and to assist businesses with tax abatements and federal and state financial assistance.

Invacare, which was ready to expand and wanted to stay in Elyria, sought help and found it. In September 1982, the company was awarded $2.33 million in government-subsidized loans to help finance a $3.5 million, 120,000-square-foot addition to its Taylor Street plant. The addition would allow Invacare to increase employment by about 280 and double its production to 250,000 wheelchairs a year.[58] Groundbreaking was scheduled for the spring of 1983.

The planned expansion didn't work out, however. Before Invacare even started construction, company officers announced that Invacare would lease a 137,000-square-foot plant on Cleveland Street, also in Elyria. The plant had recently been idled by the Bendix Heavy Vehicle Systems Group. In addition to increasing the size of the company's manufacturing operations, the new location would house corporate and division headquarters.[59]

Poised

Only a few years after orchestrating the buyout of Invacare, Mixon was predicting sales of $100 million by 1985. This would put his company, which had quickly claimed the number two spot in the wheelchair industry, within striking distance of snatching market leadership and ousting Everest & Jennings from the top spot.

This event—when it occurred—would be the result of careful planning and company structuring. Early in 1983, Invacare was reorganized to allow for more growth. The Mobilite bed unit, located in

Thomas J. Buckley took charge of the Patient Systems Division, which included the Mobilite bed unit, after Invacare reorganized in early 1983.

Sanford, Florida, and Lam Craft Industries, a small manufacturer of nursing home furnishings acquired in 1982, were grouped into the Patient Systems Division, to be headed by Thomas J. Buckley, vice president and general manager.[60] And the company created a Respiratory Products Division, which handled the Prime Aire oxygen concentrator business. In addition, M. Louis Tabickman joined Invacare that year as vice president of engineering.

With distinct units—each joined by the common thread of home care and institutional products—and expanding facilities, Invacare prepared for the next major step in its evolution: a public offering.

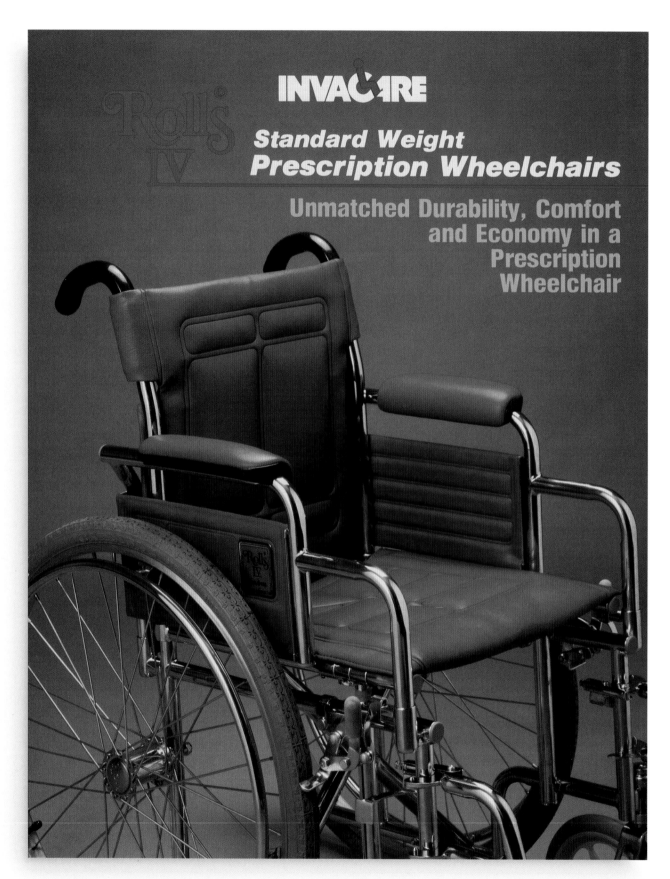

Invacare moved into the prescription wheelchair business in the early 1980s with its Rolls IV standard-weight prescription wheelchair.

CHAPTER FIVE

PUBLIC SCRUTINY

1984–1985

When we emerge again as a profitable company, I'm going to enjoy talking to investors about the good things.

—A. Malachi, Mixon III, 1985

MAL MIXON'S AMBITIOUS PREDICtions seemed to be coming true. In the first few years of his tenure, Invacare's sales rose at an annual rate of 38 percent. But growth like this often comes at a price. By 1984, Invacare had accumulated $32.7 million in debt, and the company was looking for a way out.[1]

"To support our growth, our borrowings increased very rapidly," Mixon told a reporter. "We decided that a public offering was the best vehicle for us to raise the necessary funds to continue our growth."[2]

In late 1984, Invacare announced its initial public offering (IPO) of 1.9 million shares of common stock.[3] Invacare had high hopes for its public offering and expected to raise as much as $38.3 million at between fourteen dollars and sixteen dollars per share. Much to Mixon's disappointment, however, the shares sold for only eleven dollars each.

There were several reasons for this drop. The market for new issues was getting soft, making the timing of Invacare's offering unfortunate. Hindsight, Mixon found, was perfect. "If we'd gone public a year earlier, we'd have found a very bullish market with people paying high prices for new issues," he said.[4] The lower selling price meant that Invacare would continue to carry a significant portion of its debt and that earnings wouldn't be as strong as hoped, leaving less funding for the company's aggressive acquisitions strategy.[5] Unfortunately, the stock

price would actually drop much lower over the next year, sliding down to what analysts dubbed a "bargain" price in mid-August 1985, at four dollars per share.

Had he been able to find private funding, Mixon later reflected, the company might not have gone public at all. At the time of the offering, however, Invacare was not particularly attractive to investors. "A venture capitalist looks for a very high return because of the risk involved," said Mixon. "As it was, we only sold about 9 percent of the company to the public, so the original owners still held a majority of the stock."[6] As part of the public offering, several early investors sold portions of their holdings. Mixon himself sold 57,000 shares, reducing his ownership interest from 14.2 percent to 9.2 percent.[7]

Although the offering raised only half of the desired funds, it substantially reduced the company's expensive short-term debt load from $28.5 million to $13.3 million.

A New Commitment

Although the financial outlook—particularly in light of the stock offering—wasn't what Invacare's

---

This 1985 brochure shows what is probably a Colson-era wheelchair and an Invacare model.

The company expanded its wheelchair operations by moving prescription wheelchair assembly to a facility adjacent to the existing plant on Taylor Street (shown here). *(Photo courtesy Elyria Chronicle-Telegram.)*

executive team had hoped, leaders still believed that Invacare was well positioned for the future. The demographics of the United States were changing in Invacare's favor. The population of home-health care product consumers—those age sixty-five and older—was growing rapidly. Moreover, the life expectancy in the United States continued to rise as medical advances made it possible to live a quality life for longer. At the same time, the cost of medical care was rising relentlessly, causing Medicare and other insurance providers to press for shorter hospital stays. Patients began to spend more of their recovery time at home than in hospitals or nursing facilities, which created a need for home care equipment. Along with many industry analysts, Invacare believed this demand would increase the network of home care providers necessary to distribute home health products and push the market into drugstores and other new outlets.[8]

To meet this demand, Invacare mapped out a plan to expand its field sales force and build a network of warehouses to speed delivery time. By the middle of 1984, the company had increased the number of its warehouses to twenty-three.[9] A larger distribution network, Invacare executives reasoned, would make the company's products more attractive because it would allow home care providers to reduce their inventories and costs. Invacare would sweeten the pot by instituting volume discounts to home care providers across the entire product line. Ultimately, these moves helped Invacare not only in the short run (that year it won two "Supplier of the Year" awards from key customers) but also over the long run as the health care industry continued to grow.

More crucial still was the company's new-found commitment to "achieving design and performance superiority throughout Invacare's product line."[10] To attain this goal, Invacare expanded its Elyria wheelchair-making operations, moving prescription wheelchair manufacturing to a facility adjacent to the existing plant on Taylor Street. Respiratory product manufacturing was moved from West Hartford, Connecticut, to a larger, more efficient, 18,000-square-foot home in nearby Newington. A new, 67,000-square-foot facility was leased in Sanford, Florida, to replace Mobilite's 24,000-square-foot facility for manufacturing its line of manual and powered home care beds.[11]

By this time, Invacare had already earned a reputation for innovative and high-quality products. In 1983, the company announced that almost

Inset: Invacare found a new home for the company's Mobilite facility. Here, the new Sanford, Florida, plant is dedicated during an October 1984 open house. Nyal Yost (third from right, first row) helped with ribbon-cutting festivities.

Bottom: The new, larger Mobilite facility was located on Silver Lake Drive in Sanford, Florida.

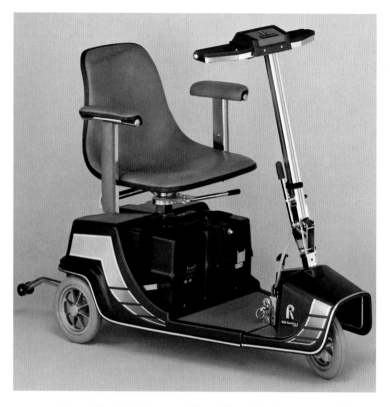

Above: The Rolls Runabout Three-Wheel Scooter, introduced in the early '80s, was one of several new revenue-generating products.

Right: The Action Power 9000, a successor of Invacare's early power chairs, would be developed in part by engineer Gunter Meier, whose company, Gunter Meier GmbH, Invacare purchased in 1984.

40 percent of its revenue came from products introduced since 1980. These included the Power Rolls Arrow line of prescription power wheelchairs; the Rolls Runabout, a three-wheeled electric scooter; the Rolls 500 series of superlight sport-type prescription wheelchairs; and the Rolls 700 series of stainless steel prescription chairs.[12] These products boosted company sales by more than $20 million in 1984 alone.

As Mike Parsons, assistant treasurer at the time, recalled, the mid-'80s was when Invacare really began "hitting the streets" with its newer electronic power-chair technology.

Therapists inside the rehab facilities really started to understand that we had the best possible solu-

tion for most of the consumers that went into power chairs with our electronic ability. We just kept expanding on it, either engineering the products to go along with that to complement those core products or making key acquisitions along the way.[13]

Expansion on the European Front

Despite the lower-than-expected IPO fundraising, Invacare still had enough money to begin expansion and soon moved into the international market. In the summer of 1984, Invacare negotiated with Diasonics Inc. to acquire its subsidiary, Carters (J&A), a large wheelchair maker based in Bridgend, South Wales. The purchase included Rajowalt/Carters in the United States. Rajowalt, located in Atwood, Indiana, made splints and other equipment for repairing bone fractures.[14] Together, the businesses posted revenue of $12.3 million with income of $70,747 in 1983.[15] Invacare paid $5.4 million in cash and notes.[16]

Until this purchase, Invacare had only a small European presence through Ortomed Aids, Ireland,

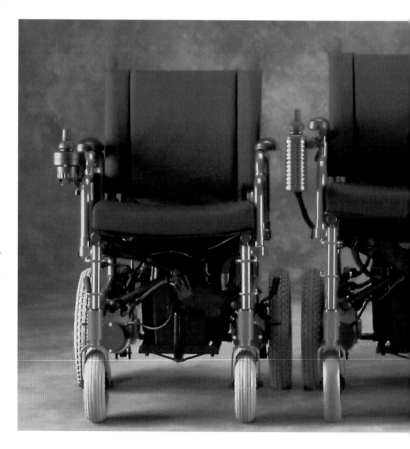

which it had formed as a joint venture in 1981. (It was divested in 1984 due to unprofitability.) With Carters, however, Invacare hoped to firmly establish itself and gain profitability in the European market. Carters had been selling medical equipment in Europe since 1850. It made manual wheelchairs and other patient aids, and it had recently introduced a power wheelchair with a curb-climbing attachment.

Invacare had plans to expand Carters' product line and told Welsh officials it would swell the ranks of the company's workforce from two hundred to five hundred over the next four or five years. Among the products Invacare planned to add to the Wales operation were oxygen concentrators, which continued to replace more expensive bottled, compressed oxygen.[17] It also planned to transplant its own successful sales strategies and reduce operating costs, a modus operandi that Invacare would soon implement throughout its U.S. operations.

Later that year, Invacare again added to its European presence with the purchase of an 85

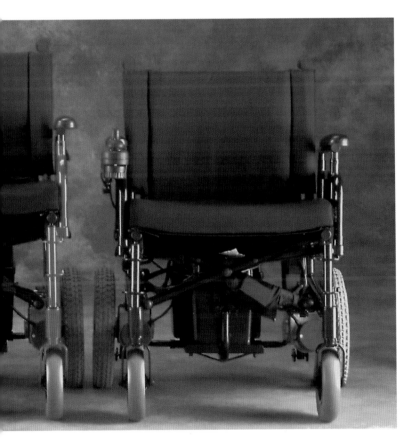

percent interest in a small West German wheelchair firm, Gunter Meier GmbH, for $250,000.[18] With 55 percent of its European sales in the United Kingdom and almost none in West Germany—the largest European market for chairs and other aids—Invacare saw an opportunity for significant growth.

The purchase of Gunter Meier, which had a plant in Eschweg, West Germany, would later prove pivotal when engineer and owner Gunter Meier, under the direction of J. B. Richey, rigged a clever way to bolt a motor directly onto one of Invacare's popular prescription manual wheelchairs, the 9000, to create the Action Power 9000.[19] The resulting low-cost motorized wheelchair and its incarnations would be resoundingly successful, particularly because they were introduced at a time when insurance companies began to reimburse less for power chairs. "We were there to meet [the change in reimbursement] with our new low-cost chair," Richey recalled.[20]

Over the next two years, Invacare would innovate the use of digital controls on wheelchairs, allowing users to revert to factory settings at the push of a button.[21] Later, this technology would be further advanced to allow computerized diagnostics of wheelchairs—and even reprogramming—by modem.[22]

Trouble Looms

Despite the strong start, 1984 wasn't destined to be a good year. By December 31, the company had lost $6.1 million.[23] According to Mixon, the loss was attributable to several factors.

First, the company was forced once again to meet price cuts from Everest & Jennings.[24] Just as sales had begun to rise, E&J pulled the rug out from under Invacare. "It was as if someone had phoned us and said there's an earthquake, and the wave is on its way," remembered Hymie Pogir, national sales manager at the time.[25]

These price cuts were particularly worrisome because "We knew we didn't have very much money, and we didn't know how long we could last or how bad it was going to be," said Pat Nalley, senior vice president, sales and marketing.[26] Nonetheless, the company was determined to survive—and surpass—E&J. The question was how to do it, said Parsons.

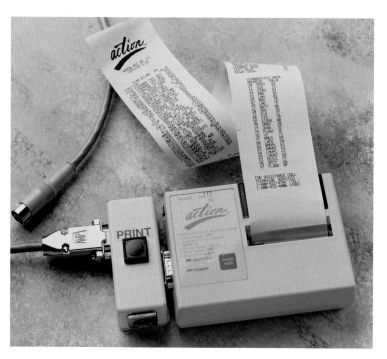

In the mid-'80s, Invacare revolutionized the use of digital controls for wheelchairs and later added computerized diagnostics, such as this system for the Action line, introduced in the '90s.

We were bound and determined to fight it. Mal said, "We're not going to let them get to us. We're going to match them. We're going to find a way to get our costs down, and we're going to hit them right in the street." They tried that for about four quarters running, until they finally realized that Invacare wasn't going to go away.[27]

"It was pretty rugged fighting in the early stages, but we were capable of holding our end of it and we did," remembered Nalley. "They were fat and lazy because they'd had it made all this time. We had to be scrappers because we didn't have it made."[28]

It was particularly important to win because wheelchairs still comprised about 80 percent of Invacare's business, recalled Mixon, who redoubled the company's efforts to beat E&J at its own game. "We worked really hard to get our costs down," he recalled.[29]

There were other factors affecting the company's bottom line, however, such as inventory shrinkage caused by inefficiency in opening the Cleveland Street plant.[30] On the financial and operations side of the business, Invacare definitely had room for improvement. "When I came [to Invacare], the opportunity was so large because everything you touched, you could improve," said Otmar Sackerlotzky, retired vice president of quality control, recalling the push to "solve the problem" of Invacare's business controls and manufacturing inefficiencies.[31]

To address these issues, Invacare chose a new problem-solving methodology: Statistical Process Controls (SPC). Not long after that, the company would implement Total Quality Management (TQM). "Mal is very much a driver to improve," said Sackerlotzky. "So that made it easy for the company to constantly improve."[32] Both SPC and TQM were geared to keep Invacare "running lean" and to ensure that Invacare kept its priorities in order. Still, at the top of the list were customers, said Sackerlotzky.

That was the most important thing, that we have satisfied customers, which we still live by.... The customers get to us and they are satisfied, and they get the product they need. This basic philosophy, I think, really drove us.[33]

Perhaps more troubling than the price cuts and business controls issues, however, were problems with the company's "PA-O_2" line of oxygen concentrators, which faced recall. Nyal Yost, then vice president of operations, said the problem stemmed from the inconsistent quality of a chemical—zeolite, actually a hydrous silicate that acts as an ion exchanger[34]—that helped draw oxygen out of the air. There were also problems with the compressor. Considering the company's poor showing after its IPO, the timing was bad, said Parsons.

All of a sudden, our results didn't look too good. Wall Street didn't take it too well, but we knew that we had one hell of a company. It's pretty hard to keep something like that from getting you down, but we knew we were doing things right. We knew that we were on a road to success and that all we had to do was work harder and get that behind us and prove to Wall Street and the investment community that this was a solid company.[35]

As conditions deteriorated throughout 1984, Invacare attacked the problem by being up front

Honesty about oxygen concentrator problems helped to pave the way for a promising relationship with customers, said Lou Tabickman (left), president of Invacare's European operations.

with its customers, a move Lou Tabickman, today Invacare's president of European operations, credits with "giving us the foothold that launched us to where we are today."[36]

Resolving the zeolite problem took a couple of years, recalled Yost. "Once we got that under control, the concentrators worked much better," he said.[37] But doing so cost the company $4 million in replacement fees and warranty claims in 1984.[38]

Just as Invacare was resolving its zeolite issues, the respiratory industry as a whole faced problems with concentrator valves, which were prone to clogging, especially from moisture. Richey solved the problem by finding a company that made ceramic valves for steering systems on ships. Using the same technology, Invacare got proprietary rights for medical use of the valves. "It's so good, we have a lifetime guarantee on it, and we've never had one fail. Never is a strong word," said Richey.[39]

To rebuild the battered oxygen concentrator line, Invacare closed its respirator manufacturing facility in Hartford, Connecticut, in June 1985 and moved production to unused space in Elyria to reduce fixed costs.[40] A new oxygen concentrator, the Mobilaire III, which Mixon described as "99 percent reliable," would be introduced in mid-1986 to replace the troubled line.[41]

Lastly, the company, always vulnerable to changes in federal government policy, got a jolt in February 1985 when new guidelines for Medicaid and Medicare reimbursement required patients to purchase, rather than rent, home care equipment costing less than $120.[42]

This particularly hurt medical equipment manufacturers like Invacare when home care providers began selling used, previously rented products, curtailing purchases from manufacturers. Typically, home care providers stretched income over a rental term. With the new guidelines, they had to adjust to a system that expected them to make money through a one-time sale at a government-established price.[43]

According to Jay P. AuWerter, Invacare's chief financial officer at the time, although a dealer may have had one hundred chairs on rental contracts with twenty to twenty-five in stock for sales or backup at one time, he or she would now have to cut inventory in half. Compounding the problem was the fact that home care providers had started purchasing lower-cost products because quality was less of a concern for sales equipment than for rentals.[44] Consumers, now paying more out of their own pockets, wanted reasonably priced equipment.

An Efficiency Overhaul

While many of these factors were outside Invacare's control and hurt results for 1984, Invacare was determined to focus on the things it could control, including the poor record keeping. As the *Insiders' Chronicle* reported, "What stood out above all these 'adjustments' and losses was the absence in Invacare of the financial and operating controls that might have obviated some of them and at least softened the edges of the rest." Analysts felt that the company, privately held for the five previous years, had placed such controls secondary to longer-term strategic positioning.[45]

Mixon moved quickly to acknowledge that problems existed and began looking for solutions. "We've always been a sales-driven company," Mixon later told a business reporter. "And as chief executive officer, I've focused on growing the company. We didn't spend a lot of time on efficiency."[46]

That soon changed. Invacare immediately increased capital spending by 50 percent,[47] using some of the money for automation equipment and reconfiguring production lines to increase efficiency.[48] It also redesigned several key products, introducing less-costly parts and more-efficient production techniques. New walkers and standing commodes, for example, were designed with lower steel content and smaller-gauge tubing, lowering production costs by 10 percent.[49] Cost-cutting measures such as these helped bring the products below the Medicare/Medicaid threshold of $120, thereby boosting sales.

Nevertheless, the year was a trying one. "It was like God had it in for us that year," Mixon said. "I had to really reach down into my own motivation.... It was embarrassing going around town when my stock fell from eleven dollars to four dollars."[50] As the leader of a public company—one with falling earnings—he was forced to take time out from problem solving to discuss issues he had previously examined only with his colleagues. There were many pressures in running a publicly held company, he said.

The public exposure and disclosure take you away from the freedom of running a private business.... It takes quite a bit of time to prepare news releases, to answer questions from investors, and to meet with investors.

First, there's a time factor for the chief executive who might better spend that time running the business. However, that's a necessity if you're going to be fair to your investors.

Second, I think the whole disclosure area is frustrating because it telegraphs to our competitors a whole lot of things about our strengths and weaknesses.

Third, there are a lot of additional costs involved in going public. You have to make annual 10-K reports, quarterly 10-Qs, and reports to the SEC [Securities and Exchange Commission] on everything from profit-sharing plans to stock options. We have lawyers do that, and they run up a pretty big bill.[51]

On the other side of the coin, however, Mixon acknowledged that going public also had advantages, such as enabling him to recruit top executives with offers of stock options and acquisitions. And he still firmly believed in Invacare's success. "When we emerge again as a profitable company, I'm going to enjoy talking to investors about the good things.... So, all in all, I think the pluses outweigh the minuses," he said of going public.[52]

No Laughing Matter

Still, some employees found it difficult to buy into Mixon's forward-thinking optimism in the face of recent losses. "He went on record telling everybody that we were going to be a *Fortune* 500 com-

pany someday," recalled Jan Lovelace, a director of human resources. "He just had this belief that he was going to be able to make this business go. Everybody laughed."[53]

For his part, Mixon was well aware that believing in his goals required much faith, at least in the early years, and that some thought him "crazy" for thinking he could achieve them.

I'm sure they did, and I kept saying it, and at some point, when they saw what we were beginning to do to E&J, they started believing it, and then you could almost sense the energy in the company change. People started working later. They were driven, you know. We're really going to do it.[54]

"Mal had a way early on of injecting his energy and vision into the business," said Tom Buckley, later senior vice president of marketing, who joined Invacare in 1981. Mixon's optimism and good humor helped buoy the company's spirit even during the lean, "no respect" years. Needless to say, when Mixon announced some fifteen years later that the company would achieve $1 billion in sales, of "those of us that have been with Mal ... and had heard his prior speech, not a soul laughed," said Lovelace.[55]

Richey Comes to Invacare

Recruiting and promoting talented executives were key parts of Mixon's strategy. In keeping with this, Otmar Sackerlotzky, a Technicare alumnus, was named vice president of quality assurance, and George Uveges was added as corporate controller.

J. B. Richey II, a gifted engineer and one of Invacare's original investors, finally came to work for Invacare as senior vice president of product development. Richey had headed Technicare's new ventures division and was responsible for many of the company's innovative CT and nuclear magnetic resonance scanners.[56] He was "not an ivory-tower brain, but a hands-on, practical person," according to Mixon. With Richey in place, Mixon felt confident that there was "nothing technical Invacare couldn't undertake."[57]

One of Richey's first assignments was to get the oxygen concentrator line under control.

Bouncing Back

Even during the worst of the slump, Mixon was outwardly positive, telling a reporter that the company was turning the corner and would "return to profitability sometime in the fall of 1985."[58] To aid in the company's recovery, the directives Mixon had outlined in late 1984 were solidified into a three-year plan to strengthen its manufacturing and management practices.[59]

It worked. By the last quarter of 1985, the company had begun a turnaround, showing a profit for the first time since the third quarter of 1984.[60] "Our significant improvement is based on several factors, including aggressive management efforts to reduce costs; additional sales volume from new products and product upgrades; and reorganization of management along product lines," Mixon said.[61]

By early 1986, he could report to shareholders that cost cutting was working and new products were finally beginning to produce revenue, which rose from $91.31 million in 1984 to $95.79 million in 1985. In fact, 1985's revenue increase actually came in the last three months of the year, when sales jumped from $21.99 million to $27.83 million.[62] The company also paid down $9.7 million in debt, avoiding the need for another stock offering.[63]

The recovery helped the stock price rise to nearly $5.50 a share by the end of 1985, up $1.50 from its low point. Securities analysts, who had previously shied away from recommending Invacare's stock, began to take note of the company's visible turnaround. By fall 1986, Invacare was back in favor.[64] Douglas A. Fox, an analyst with McDonald & Company Securities, felt that cost cutting had trimmed the company's working-capital needs, which suggested "that Invacare has solved many of its problems and was on its way to becoming a low-cost producer."[65]

With financial and operational concerns abating, Invacare was now free to turn its attention to new innovations such as building better products.

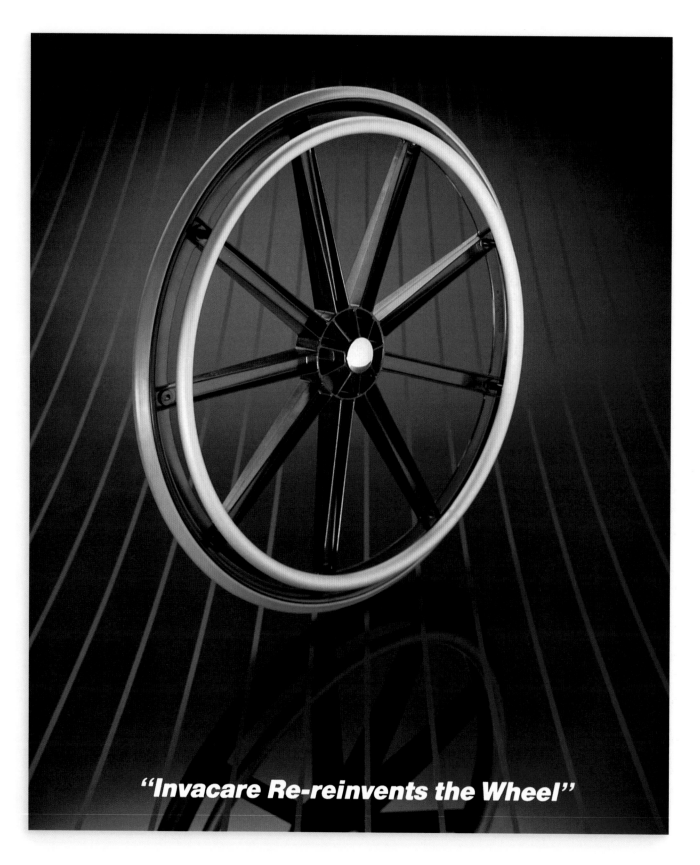

"Invacare Re-reinvents the Wheel"

This 1986 product brochure shows Invacare's revolutionary 2222 Composite Mag Wheel. Made of plastic in collaboration with General Electric, the wheel was lighter and more durable than metal wheels.

CHAPTER SIX

BUILDING A BETTER MACHINE

1986–1988

We really got the little stumble on Wall Street behind us and started gaining market share from our competitors because we started to deliver the full basket of our One Stop Shopping products and programs.

—Mike Parsons, vice president of North American sales

By THE MIDDLE OF THE DEcade, Invacare was able to turn its attention to product development and manufacturing efficiency, investing nearly $5 million in 1986.[1] The expensive operational overhaul was well worth the effort; over the next several years, Invacare would turn out a spate of new products and modifications.

The company's biggest challenge, however, was to cut manufacturing costs at all levels, including suppliers, said Ron Thomas, director of facility engineering.[2] To do this, Invacare began importing more raw materials and brought the manufacture of many electronic components in-house.[3] It also redesigned its product lines, striving for changes that would yield both cost and quality benefits. One striking example was the introduction of the composite wheel in 1986. This wheel, the product of more than two years' collaboration with General Electric's plastics group, was made of a molded plastic and was less expensive to produce than a metal one. Nonetheless, it was just as strong and better able to resist front impact and side-to-side pressure. Its finish didn't chip like a magnesium casting,[4] and as an added bonus, it weighed less and was virtually maintenance free.

Manufacture of the wheel was contracted to Majestic Molding of Elyria, and the specially designed tire was made by Invacare investor and board member Dan T. Moore III's company in Cleveland.

The composite wheel, which was introduced into the standard wheelchair line, was only one of many new products rolled out in the mid- to late-'80s. The company also introduced its Rolls ATS wheelchair, which replaced steel and chrome with lighter titanium and an epoxy-coated aluminum frame. The Rolls ATS wheelchair weighed just thirty pounds, just over half the fifty pounds of most comparable chairs.[5] A similar chair, the Rolls STS, had a chrome steel frame and weighed only slightly more at thirty-three pounds. Both reflected a growing consumer demand for stylish, sporty chairs—and for choices.

In Thomas's eyes, Invacare's success was tied to its ability to listen—and then deliver—to its customers.

We've always been pretty receptive to the customers' needs, and that has been one of the things

---

Invacare had made a number of subtle but important improvements to its wheels since its Technicare days. Among these advances was the 1982 introduction of the lightweight D.T.M. Polymer Tire, shown here. The initials "D.T.M." stand for board member Dan T. Moore. Moore's company would produce the wheel for Invacare.

that's helped us to grow. In fact, our salesmen are out there meeting with people all the time. They have an idea of what the people need, and they bring it back to manufacturing and to the engineers.[6]

For the first time, the chairs were offered in a wide array of colors, such as pewter, red, black, and blue, and were adaptable for sports.[7] Though wheelchair sports were not a new phenomenon, having been first introduced in England post-World War II as a form of therapy, modern-day athletes were demanding more functional, attractive chairs for their activities.[8]

A Battle Won

Invacare's wheelchair division got another boost in March 1986, when the Canadian Federal Court ruled in its favor after a protracted patent battle with long-time industry leader Everest & Jennings. Invacare filed suit against the company in Canada and the United States, alleging that E&J's Canadian subsidiary had infringed on an Invacare patent. The courts subsequently found in favor of Invacare and ordered E&J to quit making chairs with the contested front foot-support mechanism.[9]

E&J tried to settle the suit three times, for $500,000, $700,000, and $900,000, respectively, but Invacare would not agree to terms until the company paid $1 million, recalled Mixon.[10] To this day, said Libbie Lockard, former manager of trade shows and special events, Mixon still has hanging in his office a copy of the single check written as part of this settlement.[11]

Product Improvements

Invacare continued to introduce notable products and make improvements to existing ones. New products included a line of economical patient aids, such as walkers and bathroom and bedroom aids, and several new, lighter-weight wheelchairs designed for purchase rather than rental. During a 1986 demonstration, Mixon featured two new power wheelchairs for children. The chairs sported smaller chassis and lighter frames. "These features result in a better turning ratio and increased maneuverability—very important considerations for a child," he emphasized.[12]

Mixon was also enthusiastic about a new line of continuous passive motion (CPM) rehabilitation aids being marketed under the name TOTAL CPM. These devices helped patients to recover more quickly from orthopedic surgery—particularly knee surgery—by using continuous motion exercises to strengthen the injured joint.[13]

To increase marketing of these new rehabilitation products, Invacare created a special six-person sales team. Beyond selling to medical equipment dealers, the new team members would run clinics and in-service seminars for rehabilitation workers, as well as participate in community and sports activities. They would also market Invacare's CPM products directly to orthopedic surgeons and clinics.[14]

Restructuring

Invacare also had other important organizational changes in store, including a structural overhaul that would result in the creation of five new

Louis F. J. Slangen joined Invacare's marketing team in late 1987.

divisions. At Invacare's annual meeting in May 1986, Mixon outlined the changes: The company would add divisions for durable medical products, rehabilitation, and respiratory products; European operations; and customer service. Jay P. AuWerter took on the role of general manager of durable medical products (DMP). J. B. Richey would retain his role as senior vice president for product development but would also take on the role of general manager of rehabilitation and respiratory products (R&R). Pat Nalley, who had recently been sent overseas, continued as general manager of European operations; and Louis Tabickman, who had been vice president and general manager of patient aids, beds, and respiratory products, would take charge of customer service.[15]

The creation of these new divisions would also bring about the need for stronger, more individualized marketing for each separate unit and, eventually, a more central marketing structure. Louis F. J. "Lou" Slangen joined Invacare in late 1987 from Philips. He would initially handle marketing duties for the company's new R&R division. As Invacare's marketing strategy gradually shifted over the next few years, however, he would soon be tapped to handle marketing for the entire company and, finally, all sales and marketing.

Despite all the focus on internal improvements, Mixon hadn't forgotten about his plans for growth by external acquisition. He told a reporter in 1986 that he "would be disappointed if [the company] didn't make one small acquisition a year" in the $4 million to $6 million sales range, and that he had his eye out for candidates.[16]

True to his word, in April Mixon and his team settled on an agreement to acquire Huntco Health Care, which owned Smith & Davis Manufacturing, the same company that had first prompted Invacare's move into the bed market. In addition to beds, Smith & Davis made oxygen systems, wheelchairs, and other patient aids and would augment Invacare's home health care offerings.

With this purchase, Mixon saw an entrée to the institutional health care market. "Smith & Davis equipment has an exceptionally strong presence in the nursing home field, and with the acquisition, we will become an important force in providing more health care equipment to extended care facilities," he said. "We will also gain a foothold in the hospital side of the institutional bed market through the acquisition."

Mixon believed the acquisition would help Invacare at the low end of the market, which was suffering from a glut of cheap Taiwanese chairs.[17] "All of a sudden, the market was flooded with wheelchairs that were selling for $105 to $110, and we were selling that same wheelchair for an average of $275.... It was a huge difference," recalled Mike Parsons, Invacare's future vice president of sales.[18] There was also a huge difference in quality. Choosing between an Invacare chair and one of these chairs was choosing between "a true carbon steel, platable-grade chair with three mils of chrome plating, proven to be the most durable finish for the rental market," and a gummy grade of stainless steel that would rust within three months of use, said Lockard.[19]

In addition, said Ron Thomas, director of facilities, if people purchased the chairs and had problems with them, they couldn't get replacement parts. "They couldn't get them repaired because there wasn't anyone in the United States who could do it," he said.[20]

To purchase Huntco, Invacare offered stock valued at $6.8 million, $300,000 in cash, and an agreement to assume $22 million in debt for the business. B. D. Hunter, whose family owned Huntco, was offered a spot on the Invacare board.[21] Press reports estimated that the company had about $45 million in annual sales and employed 425 people at four U.S. manufacturing sites at the time of the proposed sale.[22]

Above: The Invacare logo and tag line got an overhaul to reflect the company's growing product diversity and emphasis on innovation.

Right: Ron Thomas, Invacare's director of facilities. Thomas started with the company when it was Mobilaid in 1961.

New Products, a New Look

Invacare continued its restructuring and cost-cutting efforts well into 1987. The company closed its wheelchair manufacturing plant on Oberlin Road in Elyria and its patient aid plant in Lodi, Ohio, transferring the functions to plants on Taylor Road and Cleveland Street in Elyria in January 1987.[23] Employees at the two closed plants were offered positions at the relocated Elyria plants.[24]

At its annual meeting in May, Invacare gave shareholders a peek at a new line of exercise equipment designed for older and disabled consumers and people recovering from, or working to prevent, heart attacks. The fitness line included exercise cycles, treadmills, and rowing machines. Although the products would be sold through Invacare's distribution network, their fabrication would be subcontracted.[25]

Because the company had diversified beyond wheelchairs, its logo was due for an overhaul.[26] The new logo still emphasized the company's name in block letters but eliminated a stylized individual in a wheelchair and the word "Corporation." To reflect the company's broader range of health care and rehabilitation products and its emphasis on innovation, a new tag line was also in order: "Invacare—Innovation in Health Care."

Stymied

In August 1987, Invacare encountered a stumbling block with the impending Huntco transaction. The Federal Trade Commission (FTC) believed the merger would substantially reduce competition in the manufacture and sale of home care beds. Invacare and Huntco, it determined, were the two largest bed makers in the country.[27]

The FTC rejection came as a surprise to both Invacare and industry watchers. "It is a relatively small market and a small acquisition," said analyst David Goldsmith, a close Invacare follower with San Francisco–based Robertson, Colman & Stephens. "It would have led one to believe that the FTC would not be that concerned about this one." Although Goldsmith didn't think the loss would have a major impact on Invacare, the company did take an after-tax charge of $300,000 to account for costs of the attempted transaction.[28]

While Invacare could have fought the FTC, it didn't want to take on the cost of an extended legal battle. The company believed the market was open for competitors, despite the fact that Invacare and Huntco made similar beds. "What we hear from our counsel is that the FTC was under pressure from Congress to try more cases," A. Chace Anderson, vice president, told the *Plain Dealer.* "We believe we happened to be caught in a period of time that the FTC needed to find cases."[29] FTC official James C. Egan, however, denied the charge and said that all four of the five commissioners who were present voted against the acquisition.[30]

Mixon and his team were disappointed with the termination of the Huntco deal, but they weren't yet ready to call it quits on their acquisition strategy. The company still had its eye on other opportunities, "but nothing the size of Huntco," said Anderson.[31]

Huntco would eventually sell to Everest & Jennings, which would end up selling the company to St. Louis investors, who renamed it Heathtech and sold it to Invacare in 1996. It is now called the Invacare Continuous Care Group (ICCG). "Had the government not interceded, the owner's Invacare stock would have been worth $100 million when we ended up buying the company," mused Gerry Blouch, president and chief operating officer. "Instead, they took the E&J stock, which ended up being worth nothing."[32]

With the prospect of Huntco gone, management turned its attention back to business, introducing several new manual wheelchair lines during 1987, among these its well-received 2000 series. Invacare had indeed diversified, but wheelchairs still comprised one of its largest divisions and biggest revenue generators.

At the top of the standard manual chair line, the 2000-series chairs weighed only thirty-seven pounds with footrests and included standard options such as composite mag rear wheels and swing-back removable arms. Another new series, the 5000 Ride Lite, was introduced as the company's top-of-the-line manual prescription chair. It weighed only thirty-three pounds.[33]

Special Delivery

To expand on its strategy of increasing warehouse locations to decrease delivery time, Invacare began to offer customers an enticing new perk—

free shipping on products sent from the nearest warehouse, a strategy competitors were unwilling to copy.[34] "Our distribution is a distinct competitive advantage," said Mixon, who had built up inventories to back up this offer,[35] though doing so contributed to an overall increase in borrowing, from $32 million to $50 million.[36] "The free freight program loses its edge if the product isn't in stock at the warehouse," Mixon told shareholders.

With the inventory buildup, the company could offer 90 percent of its standard products with same-day pickup or next-day delivery.[37] Mixon later attributed the company's 29 percent increase in sales during the first six months of 1988 to this strategy.[38]

Operationally, the company consolidated its United Kingdom manufacturing, moving operations at Westbury, England, into its plant at Bridgend, Wales, reducing workforce needs by 15 percent.[39]

Two years of operational fine-tuning were finally beginning to pay off: In 1987, Invacare's sales rose 17.2 percent over 1986, beating Mixon's prediction in March that internal sales growth would be in the 10 percent to 15 percent range.[40] For the year, sales totaled $130.8 million, against $111.5 million for 1986. Net earnings for the year, however, were $2.4 million, down from $3.4 million a year earlier. Mixon

Above: The exterior of Invamex, Invacare's Mexican manufacturing facility in Reynosa. The $5 million manufacturing facility was built to help Invacare compete with Taiwanese wheelchair makers.

Inset: Mal Mixon presents Nyal Yost with an award for his design of Invamex. Once it was fully operational, the plant enabled Invacare to deal with plating license issues and fight back against the cheap Taiwanese chairs flooding the market in the mid-1980s.

attributed the decline to charges for the Huntco transaction and costs of the Bridgend consolidation, as well as a higher tax rate.[41]

Invamex

In 1988, to increase its manufacturing capability and compete with the low-cost Taiwanese chairs, Invacare took its business south of the border and began building a new, $5 million manufacturing facility in Reynosa, Mexico.[42] Dubbed Invamex by Mixon, the plant was the largest single capital-spending project in the company's history.

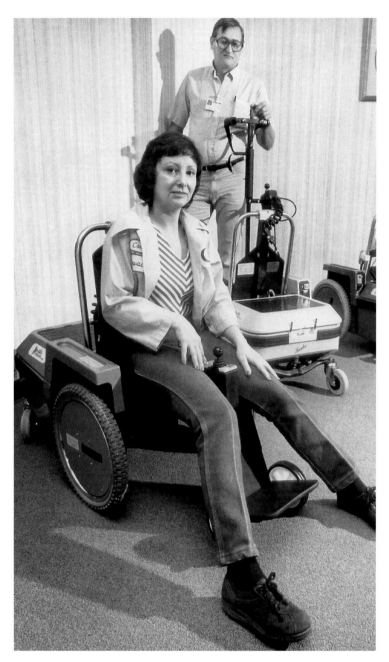

Invacare employee Carol Pierce, in charge of quality assurance in 1987. Pierce, shown with production supervisor Dallas Deal (standing), is sitting on a seventy-pound Turbo power wheelchair. During the late 1980s, cutting costs and improving quality were high on the company's priority list. *(Photo courtesy* Elyria Chronicle-Telegram.*)*

Invamex would fabricate, assemble, and plate wheelchairs and could produce plated bed rails.[43]

With labor rates under one dollar an hour, Invamex was seen as a means of fending off the low-priced imports from Taiwan and elsewhere. Rather than compete with Taiwanese wheelchair makers on their own turf, Invacare opted for the best logistical solution—a plant in Mexico "rather than somewhere over there where you have boats going back and forth," said Otmar Sackerlotzky, retired vice president of quality control.[44]

Mixon was quick to emphasize, however, that the new plant would not affect domestic employment. "It's important to note—here in our home town—that no Elyria jobs will be lost as a result of Invamex," he said. "In fact, the competitive edge provided by the facility actually improves Invacare's stability as an employer."[45]

The company simply couldn't handle the volume of chairs it was producing domestically, said Tabickman. "So nobody lost their job, and, in fact, jobs grew from that point," he said.[46] By October 1988, the Mexican plant began shipping its low-cost wheelchairs.[47] Mixon believed the low end of the market would continue to be competitive but that the company's cost reduction programs would offset the declines.[48]

We still view Taiwanese wheelchair imports as a competitive threat, although their market penetration has declined, with unit sales off 39 percent in 1987 versus 1986. To be sure, some of the decrease was due to the appreciation in Taiwanese currency compared to the U.S. dollar; however, our customers tell us that Invacare's superior quality, distribution expertise and competitive pricing have been principal reasons imports have declined.[49]

Looking back at the company's reaction to the so-called Taiwanese invasion," Parsons recalled the strategy.

We knew that we had to get our operations in line and reduce our costs, but at the same time ... we stuck with the quality issue that we were selling. We stuck with the programs that we were selling. We proved to our customer that if you buy a quality product, you can pay more for that product because in the long run, it's going to be less costly than if you go out and buy something from offshore that you can't get parts [for], you can't get repaired, and, of course, our customers started to find that out very quickly after about twelve months.[50]

The decision to keep its operations closer to home proved to be a good one; E&J had taken the production of its lower-cost chairs offshore to Indonesia. E&J's earlier move from St. Louis to California had given Invacare "a break," said Sackerlotzky. "They never could get the logistics right."[51] The strategy ultimately cost E&J the low-end market.

A Banner Year

As it turned out, 1988 was a banner year for Invacare. Sales climbed to $160.8 million, while earnings hit a record $5.1 million. The company attributed the records to improved results by all divisions, including international.[52] By 1988, Invacare was doing $35 million in business overseas, from only a few hundred thousand dollars a decade earlier and $15 million in 1984.[53] "We really got the little stumble on Wall Street behind us and started gaining market share from our competitors because we started to deliver the full basket of our One Stop Shopping products and programs," said Parsons.[54]

The year also saw the introduction of the Ride Lite 9000 series of lightweight, manual, prescription wheelchairs, which Mixon described as the most successful new product in the company's history.[55] Invacare made several improvements to the power wheelchair, including the development of a microprocessor control system—first used on the Arrow power wheelchair—that allowed the user to modify the chair's performance and ride characteristics and included a self-diagnostic system for repair technicians.[56] The Arrow chair also offered an "Extra Power and Range" (XPR) system that doubled the range of the chair on a single charge from twelve miles to twenty-four miles.[57]

In December 1988, the company revamped its hourly piece-work incentive, which Mixon believed pitted employees against each other, discouraged employee innovation, and was difficult to administer. It was replaced with a merit-based, hourly pay program that would begin in January 1989.[58] The company also increased its employee profit-sharing program contribution. Employees now had a vested interest in helping to grow Invacare. In the years to follow, the company would add a 401(k) to its employee benefits.[59]

Invacare's profit-sharing contribution, equal to 10 percent of the company's pre-tax profits at the time, was a 50 percent increase over the previous year. "The company is finally beginning to show some profit improvement, and we want the employees to share in that improvement," Mixon said.[60]

As Invacare continued to expand its product lines through acquisitions and internal growth, both dealers and consumers benefited. Home care providers were able to simplify their supply issues through Invacare's One Stop Shopping program, and consumers, such as this child, got a broader range of products to meet their needs.

CHAPTER SEVEN

MEETING THE MARKET

1989–1991

In business, you never win: At best, you are temporarily ahead.

—A. Malachi Mixon, III

INVACARE'S GROWING success was drawing the attention of more than just associates, who welcomed the new profit-sharing program. Its strong results also caught the eye of Wall Street, though Invacare's stock was trading at just $9.75 a share at the time. Analysts, it seems, were finally beginning to take note of the company's investment potential. By 1991, Invacare's stock would more than double to $25.[1]

Two analysts—Jeffrey Stein, of Cleveland's McDonald & Company Securities, and Vivian Wohl, of Robertson, Colman & Stephens—gave Invacare's stock a "buy" recommendation based on the company's growth and performance, as well as the overall industry recovery from Medicare reimbursement changes. As Stein saw it, Invacare had "established itself as the lowest-cost producer with the broadest line of products and the best distribution system in the industry." With these considerations in mind, Wohl predicted that institutional investors, mutual funds, and pension plans would soon be adding Invacare stock to their portfolios.[2]

Despite 1988's promising figures and recommendations such as these, Invacare was fighting hard to make money. On one hand, the efficiency changes were finally beginning to yield tangible results. On the other, additional modifications to the Medicare reimbursement guidelines—called the Six-Point Plan—had slowed sales as home care providers adjusted. Compounding the problem was the fact that Everest & Jennings, still the wheelchair-industry leader by a small margin, had begun another aggressive price-cutting strategy.[3]

Instead of pushing Invacare out of the market, this competition only spurred the company to fight back. "We had our sights set on E&J, and we loved to have somebody to hate," said Mike Parsons, assistant treasurer at the time.[4]

This meant going after more customers and improving contact with home care providers and therapists. To do this, Invacare created the "Rehab Van," a thirty-foot-long vehicle stocked with wheelchairs, oxygen concentrators, and other products. The company scheduled new product seminars at Veterans Administration hospitals and rehabilitation centers in more than twenty cities. The van "allows consumers to have hands-on experience with the equipment," explained Randy Potter, manager of training, at the van's open-house rollout. "This is really important to people who are buying rehab equipment for the first time."[5]

In 1989, Invacare began working aggressively to improve its contact with health care professionals. With the "Rehab Van," Invacare brought its products directly to health care facilities.

Up and Running in Mexico

By 1989, earnings were improving in spite of operational glitches. For one thing, it was taking longer than forecast to get the Invamex plant in Reynosa, Mexico, up and running at optimal efficiency. This delay forced Invacare to continue making some wheelchair components at less-efficient plants. In addition, a new, computerized warehouse-management system (WMS) was proving difficult to bring online, a problem Mixon hoped to resolve by year's end.[6] "The system had basically blocked things, so we couldn't get our shipments out," recalled Judy Kovacs, vice president of product and customer support services.[7]

Mexico became more of a concern in July, when a labor dispute shut down Invamex and, consequently, several other U.S. companies" assembly operations. The costly three-week strike left two thousand area workers idle and resulted in a $500,000-per-day loss for the affected plants until around half of the workers crossed picket lines, locked themselves in their plants, and resumed work.[8] "The important thing is that we're at our jobs," Invamex worker Gustin Villanueva told an Associated Press correspondent. "We don't want these plants to close."[9] Invacare officials, for their part, made it clear that the company would pull out of Mexico before signing an unreasonable contract.[10] However, Invacare executives note that no additional labor problems have arisen since the resolution of the 1989 strike.

Management Changes

To trim management overhead and to keep operations firmly in hand, Mixon announced in September that Invacare would again restructure its leadership. J. B. Richey, who had been senior vice president and general manager of rehabilitation and respiratory (R&R) products, would become senior vice president and general manager of North American operations. R&R products included prescription wheelchairs and respiratory equipment, so this move expanded Richey's responsibilities to include standard wheelchairs and other durable medical products. Even after the reorganization, however, Richey—the engineer who had spearheaded so many Invacare innovations—continued to lead the company's product development.

Invacare also continued to watch for opportunities in Europe. A. Chace Anderson, who joined Invacare in 1986 as director of corporate development, relocated from Elyria to England to better focus his attention on international markets. Moving Anderson to Europe was Mixon's recognition that international operations would play a greater role in the years ahead.[11] In addition, "Lou" Slangen would soon trade his divisional marketing duties for company-wide responsibility for marketing. "We needed some programs and procedures in place," Slangen recalled. "The problem that we ran into a lot of times was that the ideas came faster than the organization could follow them.... When you move, you've got to make the whole thing move with you."[12]

Mixon announced this reorganization even as it was still taking shape. The last anticipated change —the addition of a chief financial officer—was long overdue and would require a careful search. Though the company had its manufacturing and marketing operations running smoothly, outside observers still saw the need for better financial controls. Byam K. Stevens, an analyst with H. G. Wellington & Company of New York, noted in March 1990 that "a seasoned chief financial officer is one of management's current top priorities."[13]

It would take until May 1990 for Mixon to round out his reorganized senior staff with the appointment of Gerald B. Blouch as chief financial officer. Mixon wooed Blouch from Inacomp Computer Centers Inc. of Troy, Michigan, where he had been executive vice president and CFO.[14] In his new position at Invacare, Blouch would oversee the company's finances, corporate development, and shareholder relations.[15]

Judy Kovacs, vice president of product and customer support services, said a new computerized warehouse-management system eventually helped Invacare ship efficiently in 1989.

Above: Gerald B. Blouch joined Invacare in May 1990 as the company's first chief financial officer. He would quickly become an important member of the company's executive staff and now serves as president and chief operating officer.

Right: In 1991, Mixon launched a six-year battle fighting restrictive Medicare reimbursement, among other issues, said David Williams, Invacare's director of government relations.

Getting Involved

Over the years, Invacare had weathered the effects of governmental changes to medical-expense reimbursements. In 1989, however, Mixon decided it was time to increase the company's activity in government affairs, especially in light of the impending Americans with Disabilities Act (ADA). This historic civil rights legislation was meant to expand the 1973 Rehabilitation Act, which mandated that no organization receiving federal funds could discriminate "solely by reason of handicap." The ADA expanded this basic protection to any public service, to all commercial areas (like stores, banks, and theaters), and to public and private transportation. The ADA, which was eventually passed, promised to overhaul the nation's attitudes toward accessibility for disabled people.

Mixon believed the effects of this pivotal piece of legislation would reverberate throughout the industry: as people with disabilities gained greater entrance into the world of the nondisabled, they would need more of the products Invacare made. He also understood that health care cost containment would be an issue for years to come.[16]

Among those issues Mixon would champion in Washington were the capping of home medical equipment rental costs and allowing Medicare recipients to upgrade their equipment by pooling their own money with the government's reimbursement.[17] "Medicare said they would pay what was allowed under these guidelines, but that if a patient wanted more, they would have to pay the full price out of pocket," said David Williams, Invacare's director of government relations for the past nine years.[18]

Furthermore, under Medicare's restrictive guidelines at the time, it would only reimburse for equipment it deemed "medically necessary to perform the activities of daily living within the four walls of the home," said Williams.[19] This flew in the face of Invacare's enabling philosophy, causing the company to launch a six-year campaign for what would become the Consumer Choice Initiative. There were other battles as well: Invacare fought against reductions in fee schedules and the imposition of what it considered to be intrusive rules, and for fair treatment under the new reimbursement system.

In the late 1980s, the government's reimbursement system got a much-needed overhaul as it switched from making payments based upon wholesale manufacturer pricing to using a Six Point Plan.

"The transition was huge—it was almost a tsunami for our industry—because you went from basing pricing on a catalog to using these complex fee schedules that were extrapolated based on historical data and so forth," said Williams.[20]

Mixon would also participate in several organizations to lobby for the home care industry, including the Health Industry Manufacturers Association (HIMA), the Health Industry Distributors Association (HIDA), and the National Association of Medical Equipment Suppliers (NAMES).

Invacare in France

Further focusing international activities in 1990, the company created Invacare SARL, a French distribution company that formalized Invacare's European presence. With manufacturing in Germany and the United Kingdom and a distribution company in France, Invacare now had a strong presence in Europe's three largest markets. With its distributor network in the other European countries, Mixon told shareholders, "We are well prepared for the eventuality of a single European market."[21]

At the annual meeting in May 1990, Mixon laid out the company's strategy for the years ahead:

Despite the changes taking place in our industry, we continue to focus on our five core strategies. Invacare offers the industry's broadest product line and continues to expand it, provides the highest level of customer service, continues to be the product and marketing innovator, maintains the industry's most productive sales force, and is the industry's low-cost producer. These five strategies are key to our success today and will help us get where we want to be tomorrow.[22]

This plan got a surprising boost from Everest & Jennings, which had started a round of price cuts in 1989. In 1990, a new majority owner disagreed with the price cut strategy, among other things, and shuffled the company's top executives. To counteract E&J's $33 million loss in 1989, the new management then raised prices 5 percent, cut its workforce, and trimmed its sales staff.[23]

Stock market analysts saw this as a huge opportunity for Invacare. Analysts like Byam Stevens thought that cutbacks would hurt E&J's ability to service its distributors, who might then turn to Invacare. "If Invacare doesn't gain major market share out of this, I'd be real surprised," he told a *Plain Dealer* reporter.[24]

Mixon's strategy of offering a broad product line was also paying off. "Instead of going to thirty different manufacturers, the home care providers are coming to Invacare," observed analyst Vivian Wohl. Wohl also believed home care providers appreciated the company's extensive warehouse network and pledge of speedy delivery, which

Opposite: The introduction of its Action Technology line of wheelchairs, including this Ranger X, helped Invacare depose competitor Everest & Jennings once and for all.

Left: The Action MVP was one of the contemporary composite and aluminum ultralightweight chairs Invacare introduced through its Action Technology division. In addition to stylish looks and features such as this particular chair's ability to fold, Action wheelchairs were designed to highlight the individuals using the chairs rather than the chairs themselves.

WHEELCHAIR RACING

THE BEGINNING OF WHEELCHAIR sports can be traced to two researchers, Tim Nugent at the University of Illinois and Dr. Ludwig Guttman of the Spinal Injury Center in Stoke Mandeville, England.[1] In the years following World War II, these two pioneers noticed a large number of young men returning from war with disabilities and with a desire to continue active lives.[2]

The two men helped develop the first wheelchair sport competitions as a way to build strength, provide enjoyment, and build self-esteem among wheelchair users.[3]

The National Wheelchair Athletic Association was created in 1956 to organize competitions and events as the idea of sporting events for wheelchair athletes gained popularity in the United States. (The group later changed its name to Wheelchair Sports, USA.[4])

Able-bodied people were at first leery of wheelchair athletes and worried about the disabled men and women hurting themselves or falling out of their chairs. Others figured there would be a shortage of spectators. Nonetheless, early wheelchair sports included track and field events, bowling, archery, and basketball.

Perhaps the best-known wheelchair sport, however, is road racing. In 1975, wheelchair racer Bob Hall, at thirty-four years old, made history when he competed unofficially in the 1975 Boston Marathon (although records show he was preceded by five years by Eugene Roberts, who finished the race in seven hours).

His first time on the course, Hall finished in two hours, fifty-eight minutes.[5] By today's times of an hour and a half or less, Hall's showing seems like a crawl, but he was using a standard rehab wheelchair weighing about fifty pounds.[6]

By 1977, Hall had recruited six other wheelchair racers, including a woman, to race in the Boston Marathon, which marked the beginning of the National Wheelchair Marathon Championships.[7] That same year, Hall took a blowtorch to his dinosaur of a wheelchair to produce a leaner machine for racing.[8]

His tinkering spread like brushfire through the wheelchair sporting circuit. Everyone wanted a lighter chair that they could propel faster on the roadways. Other wheelchair athletes—a group known for altering chairs for a competitive edge—started their own garage businesses across the country because the larger companies had not yet recognized the market.[9]

In 1978, Hall started Hall's Wheels in Somerville, Massachusetts, to design and manufacture racing wheelchairs.[10] Some of his older, bolder racing chair designs were honored for their innovative style and functionality. In fact, a Bob Hall racing chair is on permanent display at New York City's Museum of Modern Art.[11]

As more people joined the sport—including future champions like George Murray and Jim

Wheelchair sports such as racing developed from rehabilitation exercise programs designed for disabled World War II veterans looking to continue their active lives. Here Team Invacare members strategize before a race.

Knaub—sport wheelchair design became more standardized. Racing regulations shifted to allow twelve- and fourteen-inch wheels in the front instead of casters, which paved the way for major improvements.[12] Before long, the chairs' basic design was radically changed. The axles on the altered chairs were moved forward and upward, pushing the center of gravity backward and toward the ground. This allowed the wheeler's arms to reach farther along the pushrims and thus to achieve faster speeds.[13]

In 1983, George Murray, winner of the 1978 Boston Marathon, became the first wheelchair athlete to be featured on a *Wheaties*® box.[14] Around the same time, Invacare entered the field with the Invacare Cup, a nationwide series of seven races that helped promote the sport, including the Kaiser Roll, a ten-kilometer race in Phoenix; a half marathon in Long Beach, California; and a marathon in Miami, Florida.[15]

In June of 1985, Murray gave the sport another boost during a race in Pennsylvania when he broke the four-minute-mile barrier. He and his friend Chris Peterson went on to establish Top End, a company that focused on building custom racing wheelchairs as well as other sports chairs.[16] Peterson would later design the first three-wheeled chair for tennis, which would become the industry standard.[17] Invacare would purchase the company in 1993, merging Top End with its Action wheelchair line.

That same year (1985), Hall rolled out a controversial racing chair with only three wheels. He was able to slide the chair onto the course under an international rule that allowed a chair with three wheels or more.[18]

Jim Knaub, another wheelchair racing champion, became an outspoken defender of the athleticism involved in racing. The former specialist in development of high-performance wheelchairs for Invacare once remarked that

Above: Women, such as top-ranked Team Invacare member Louise Sauvage, are becoming more and more visible in racing.

Below: Five-time Boston Marathon winner Jim Knaub is one of the most accomplished racers on the circuit. Knaub worked for Invacare as a performance products and programs specialist.

when wheelchair racers first started competing in the mid-1970s, runners would gush and say how incredible they were. But once the wheelers' times improved and they started competing for first place, the runners said it was unfair because wheelchair racers had a mechanical advantage.[19]

In the late 1980s and early 1990s, wheelchair sports mushroomed. Besides road racing and tennis, athletes began competing in a myriad of sports including skiing, kayaking, mountain climbing, sailing, and even bungee jumping.[20] The sporting world was quick to embrace athletes of all ages and genders. Although men easily outnumber women in racing competitions today, female competitors such as Team Invacare member Louise Sauvage are making their mark.

allowed the home care providers to save money by keeping inventories low.[25]

Mixon also redoubled the company's efforts to simplify the production process. For example, oxygen concentrators were redesigned so that the three- and five-liter Mobilaire units shared the same injection-molded cabinet. Also, a new line of nine bath safety products was designed to share several modular components.[26]

Taking Action

In November 1990, Invacare created Action Technology to market lightweight, sporty-looking wheelchairs to active users. "Most of the players that we were dealing with during that time period were fairly small companies dedicated to doing only one thing," said Parsons of other lightweight chair manufacturers at the time.[27]

Mixon believed the Action line of wheelchairs could make inroads into what he estimated was a $50 million sport-wheelchair market, comprised of people who competed in tennis, basketball, or road races.[28] "The physically challenged—just like the rest of America's population—are leading more active lifestyles than ever before," said Mixon when the new division was announced. "Yet until now, mobility has been hampered by a lack of style and performance in the wheelchairs our industry has offered."[29]

At the top of the Action line were the Action AC chairs, which had one-piece composite frames made from materials such as carbon fiber, Kevlar,

ceramics, and glass and were lighter than traditional steel or aluminum. The line also included six Superlite aluminum chairs, as well as accessories and clothing with the Action logo.[30]

Overtaking Everest & Jennings

As 1991 began, Invacare was in the process of overtaking Everest & Jennings as the leading wheelchair maker in the United States and the world. More and more, Invacare was becoming the company to watch. "The health care industry is known for its breakthrough products and lavish research spending, but Invacare favored a more basic approach," the *Wall Street Journal* reported in late December 1990. "It broadened its offerings of home health care products, found out what its customers' needs were and made sure they were met. Its success

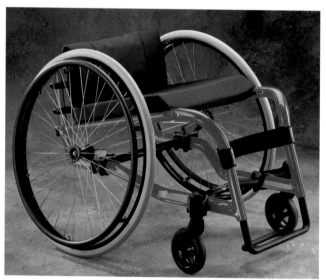

Above: Weighing less than twenty-one pounds, the Action FX was made of advanced carbon fiber composites and could be tailored to a variety of sports needs.

Left: The rigid aluminum Action Super Pro-T wheelchair has a low center of gravity; roller blades instead of front wheels produce a sharp turning radius.

Opposite: Invacare started marketing its sporty Action wheelchairs in late 1990. Mixon believed that the disabled, like many Americans, were leading more active lives and needed special wheelchairs that would enable them to pursue their interests despite their disabilities.

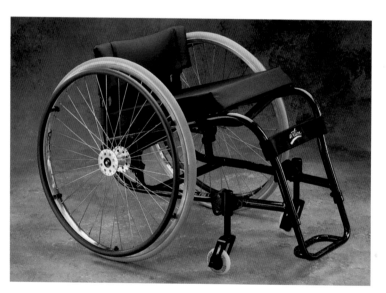

illustrates how painstaking attention to simple marketing and distribution can revitalize a company sputtering along on stale, almost forgotten products."[31]

Capping off its profile, the *Wall Street Journal* made Invacare's decade-long recovery official. "What's more," the article said, "Invacare's wheelchairs now outsell Everest & Jennings, and the former leader is mired in red ink after launching a price war in an unsuccessful attempt to win back market share."[32]

Invacare wasn't about to rest on its laurels, however. "Mal has a great line.... I use it quite a bit," said Lou Slangen, senior vice president, sales and marketing. "Mal always says, 'In business, you never win: At best, you are temporarily ahead.'"[33]

To retain its position of leadership, and in particular to boost European sales, Invacare began the ISO 9000 certification process worldwide. ISO 9000 certification would give the company license to sell European products produced worldwide when the European Union began to impact trade within Europe in a few years. The ISO 9000 rules set standards for improving product quality in areas such as employee training, manufacturing process controls, product design, and statistical process control.[34]

Though many U.S. companies moved slowly on international certification, Mixon considered it a high corporate priority. "Hopefully, once you get the certification, you will be able to ship anywhere in

Europe," he told a reporter. "My English plant will need it if it wants to ship into another European country."[35]

Improving Customer Service

In addition to implementing ISO 9000, the company began a broader, companion Total Quality Management (TQM) system in the United States. This program was designed to improve the performance of every aspect of the company, which also created its own Quality Council to track quality and customer satisfaction.[36] Years later, in 1999, Invacare would adopt another problem-solving methodology called Six-Sigma.[37] In the meantime, however, employment of TQM yielded results across the board.

Invacare had been receiving complaints from home care providers who had difficulty getting through to Invacare's customer service department. While reviewing a computer analysis of customer service response, the company's top executives sought confirmation. "We were in an executive committee meeting looking at the phone statistics," Richey recalled a few years later, "and I said, 'Let's just call us.'" They were treated to several minutes of tinny recordings. "It was terrible," Richey said.[38] The company quickly hired twenty people and reorganized the customer service department so that customers waited no more than fifteen seconds before getting a human voice.[39]

Though this early quality management effort came from the executive suite at Invacare, TQM required that management relinquish some control over its business processes to employees closer to each situation. Traditionally, Richey explained, engineers would create a new product and a prototype and then "plunk it down in manufacturing" to let them figure out how to make it, which often led to production problems. But, with TQM, said Richey, "We put together a team of marketing, quality, manufacturing, purchasing, engineering, and financial people at the concept stage."[40] This method

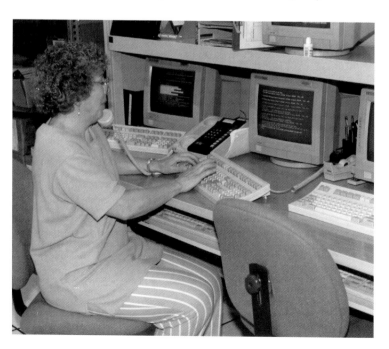

After a test of the company's customer service response time put Invacare executives "on hold" in 1991, the staff was quickly augmented so that customers had to wait no longer than fifteen seconds to speak with a live representative.

enabled the company to expose and resolve problems at an earlier stage—before production—thereby reducing cycle time.

Implementing both processes initially created added work. "At the same time we were telling people TQM, we were putting ISO 9000 procedures into place, and regular work had to be done," Richey said. "Workers asked, 'What are we going to do first?' The answer was, 'You have to do everything, but with enough resources.'"[41]

"It's a pretty tough place to work insomuch as we demand a lot from our people," admitted Michael Devlin, former director of health care professional marketing. "Invacare has a lot of bright people who work very, very hard, as evidenced, I think, by the company's success. So that's very much the culture, but the beauty of it, and what attracted me to Invacare, is the freedom that everyone is afforded in doing their job."[42]

Though initiating TQM was difficult, Invacare reaped its benefits. In his report to shareholders in the 1992 annual report, Mixon said that "Substantial improvements were made during the year in customer service, especially telephone responsiveness, transaction accuracy and reduced lead times."[43] These improvements were accomplished through regionalization of customer service by adjusting time schedules so that reps handling Western region home care providers would be on Pacific time.[44]

Moreover, TQM freed employees to take an even more active role in the company's success. Said Gil Haury, retired director of Invacare's corporate test lab:

We have the freedom to make suggestions, and there's no problem talking to anybody all the way up the ladder. If you've got a suggestion or a problem, or if we find a problem in the lab or something

To market the new Action line in 1991, Invacare invested in a series of ads aimed at home care providers, therapists, and consumers. These ads, which featured athletes, such as former Invacare endorsee Mike Schlappi, showed that wheelchair users could continue their active lifestyles with an Action wheelchair from Invacare.

*in the product, ... it's taken care of immediately.
We get 100 percent backing.*[45]

Above and beyond cost cutting, however, was Invacare's "raison d'être": the customer. "What was driving product development was that Mal had a real passion to provide unique, better products to people with disabilities. That really drove the company," said Tom Buckley, who was later named Invacare's senior vice president of marketing.[46]

Alongside these organizational changes, the company also moved to put its financial house in order. In April, the company changed its shareholder rights plan, a so-called "poison pill" designed to prevent a hostile takeover.[47] A month later, Invacare offered one million of its shares to the public, raising $32 million, which it planned to use to retire debt and reduce annual debt payments by $2.3 million.[48] That fall, the board of directors declared a 100 percent share dividend and a two-for-one stock split to make the stock more widely available for trading and more attractive to investors.[49]

Wall Street began to applaud the company's efforts. In its July 15 issue, *U.S. News and World Report* included Invacare in its list of top fifty growth stocks that had generated consistent and superior earnings over the long term. Invacare ranked thirty-third, putting it in the top 2 percent of the twenty-five hundred companies considered.

Marketing Action

To raise awareness of its new Action wheelchair line, Invacare began its largest-ever marketing push in May 1991. The effort was centered on a series of six print ads tied together by the theme, "Action speaks louder than words." The ads appeared in magazines for home care equipment providers, health care professionals, and consumers, including *Sports 'N Spokes*, a magazine for active wheelchair users. The campaign included a video that was sent to home care providers and health care professionals, and Invacare even contemplated a sixty-second television commercial based on the video.[50]

At the company's annual meeting on May 24, Mixon announced that he had hired a Washington, D.C., lobbyist; organized a political action committee, InvaPAC; and begun to personally lobby for both "mainstreaming" the disabled and protecting

the Medicare and Medicaid reimbursement that home care providers—and indirectly Invacare—relied on. "Mixon really took the lead in terms of legislation by serving as the interface between Washington and the industry," said Buckley.[51]

The federal government's Omnibus Budget Reconciliation Act of 1990 imposed new limits on some reimbursement levels, and the industry was worried about the financial fallout.[52] With approximately 50 percent of a dealer's annual revenue coming from reimbursements, according to Mixon, these sales were critical to both the industry and Invacare.[53]

In addition, Congress, concerned about the safety of medical devices after reports of failures of more complex medical equipment, such as defective heart valves, was looking to strengthen regulatory protection.[54] "I wasn't really aware how much [Congress] controlled my business," Mixon said at year's end. "Now, getting Congress to understand and support home health care is my number one priority."[55]

A New Headquarters

Invacare caused a minor uproar in its own backyard when it announced in August 1991 that it was scouting locations for a new world headquarters and other new operations. The lease on its Cleveland Street headquarters and plant in Elyria would expire in September 1993.[56]

The mayors of Elyria and neighboring North Ridgeville, home to Action Technology's plant and an Invacare warehouse, wanted the new facilities for their communities and said they would offer tax abatement to the company. But plans bogged down when neither community, according to one press account, was willing to accept only one piece of the pie.[57]

Frustrated by the inaction, Invacare tried a new approach. Though Elyria and North Ridgeville were preferred, the company announced it would consider sites within a thirty-minute drive of its Elyria facilities. This brought several Cleveland and Akron suburbs with attractive industrial and office sites into consideration.

The mention of a move outside the neighborhood got the attention of both communities. By the end of September, the company struck a complicated three-way agreement with both Elyria and

North Ridgeville to build a new headquarters and plant not far from existing facilities. In the end, though, the company decided to work harder to use existing space more efficiently and deferred the construction expense.[58]

Expanding in Canada

In a busy year for internal growth, the company didn't completely ignore growth by acquisition and made two small Canadian purchases. In October, Invacare augmented its wheelchair division with the purchase of Canadian Wheelchair Manufacturing, a wheelchair maker with Can$6 million in sales annually, for an undisclosed sum. Canadian Wheelchair had fifty employees and manufactured chairs under the Voyager and Magic brand names at a plant in Mississauga, Ontario.[59]

In November, Invacare added Canadian Posture & Seating Centre (CPSC), which made seating products. The Kitchener, Ontario, company had annual sales estimated at Can$1.3 million. Its products would be sold under the Avanti seating products brand name, which the company unveiled at the same time it announced the CPSC purchase.

This would be the company's first significant move into the lucrative seating and positioning business, estimated at $60 million annually.[60] To lead the development of the Avanti line, Invacare hired Allen R. Siekman, formerly head of clinical services for the seating department at the Rehabilitation Engineering Center at Stanford University Children's Hospital.[61]

Product Innovation

The early 1990s heralded several product innovations in the home health care division. In 1991, Invacare introduced its bed synchronizer, which virtually eliminated most bed quality issues. Consist-

---

It was Invacare's little innovations, such as the use clamps on its commode seats, that made the quality difference in the company's products, said Dale Nash, director of distributor accounts and a long-time employee.

ing of a "motor and a slip nut housing in the pull tube," synchronizers eliminated problems such as broken motor housings and bent frames, which were caused when a bed's motor would get out of sync with its position and jam.[62]

Another brainstorm was the use of clamps, rather than hardware, for the installation of commode seats. Hardware was problematic because it often got lost or rusted, said Dale Nash, director of distributor accounts. In addition, the connection points were fairly weak, sometimes causing the seat to move —a dangerous combination when the user was already unstable. Not only were the new seats more secure, they were easier to install. "It turned out to be a huge innovation," said Nash.[63]

The company also redesigned its institutional lifts—which previously looked like "something commercial"—for added stability and patient comfort.[64]

Simple but effective product changes such as these proved financially rewarding for Invacare and were typical of the company's innovative, creative spirit. Often these ideas were germinated from conversations with home care providers, health care professionals, and consumers.

Earnings Rise, Growth Slows

For the full year 1991, earnings rose to $14.1 million, up from $7.6 million a year earlier, with $263.2 million in sales, up 14.5 percent from 1990's $229.8 million.[65] Although sales for the last quarter of 1991 had grown over the previous year's figures, the company's growth was actually slowing as the year ended. Invacare leaders attributed this to a strong U.S. dollar, which hurt exports, and to changes in Medicare reimbursement brought about by the Omnibus Budget Reconciliation Act of 1990, which negatively affected home care providers' purchases as they reduced their inventories.[66]

The purchase of Poirier S.A., France's largest wheelchair maker, in 1992 marked one of the company's most pivotal European acquisitions. Shown are (left to right) Gerry Blouch, Mal Mixon, and Poirier president Benoit Juranville.

CHAPTER EIGHT

ROOM TO GROW

1992–1994

*We've always been driven by One Stop Shopping to make it easier and
less costly for the home care provider to do business.*

—Louis F. J. Slangen, senior vice president,
sales and marketing

DESPITE SLOWING GROWTH IN
the last quarter, 1991 was still
a watershed year for Invacare.
Operational improvements had turned
the company into a well-oiled machine
that was more than capable of handling its burgeoning role as industry leader. Invacare's stock,
having risen to twenty-five dollars a share, had gained
the attention of both analysts and investors, and
international growth was booming with several
key acquisitions. In addition, the company was
growing by leaps and bounds as it continued to
expand its ever broadening product lines.

"I came to Invacare, and the first thing that
struck me was the fast-paced environment," recalled
Thomas Wiegand, former director of corporate pricing and sales administrative services, who joined
the company in 1989 in the finance department.

*Everything moved at the speed of light, and
change was nothing to be afraid of. Everyone at the
company was just moving like a train on the tracks
as fast as it could go, and it didn't stop to let you get
on. You needed to get on while it was moving, but
it was great—it was absolutely great. I found out
very quickly [that] it wasn't a place for someone
who didn't like that type of environment, a very
quick and changing environment.[1]*

Despite the fast-paced environment, however,
the company noted that sales growth had actu-

ally slowed as the year was ending.[2]
Reimbursement issues were a constant
headache on the financial side of the
business. Home care providers, having
provided patients with equipment, would
often be bogged down for months in a quagmire of
paperwork and documentation. Consequently,
home care providers were "usually pretty cash
starved because they don't have capital to necessarily float the government and/or the large insurance companies when they delay in payment, and
yet they still need to provide the equipment to the
patient, who is in need of the equipment and the
service," said Bill Corcoran, vice president and treasurer, Invacare Credit Corporation.[3]

Invacare's innovative solution was to offer
creative financing plans through Invacare Credit
Corporation, the company's captive financing subsidiary. Approximately 15 percent to 18 percent of
the company's business was facilitated through
Invacare Credit Corporation, said Corcoran. This
additional service allowed Invacare to further dif-
ferentiate itself from its competition.

*If you're a manufacturer and you want to compete
with Invacare, I think you have to look at the fact
that we've got the broadest product line in the*

Poirier helped Invacare reach "critical mass" in Europe.

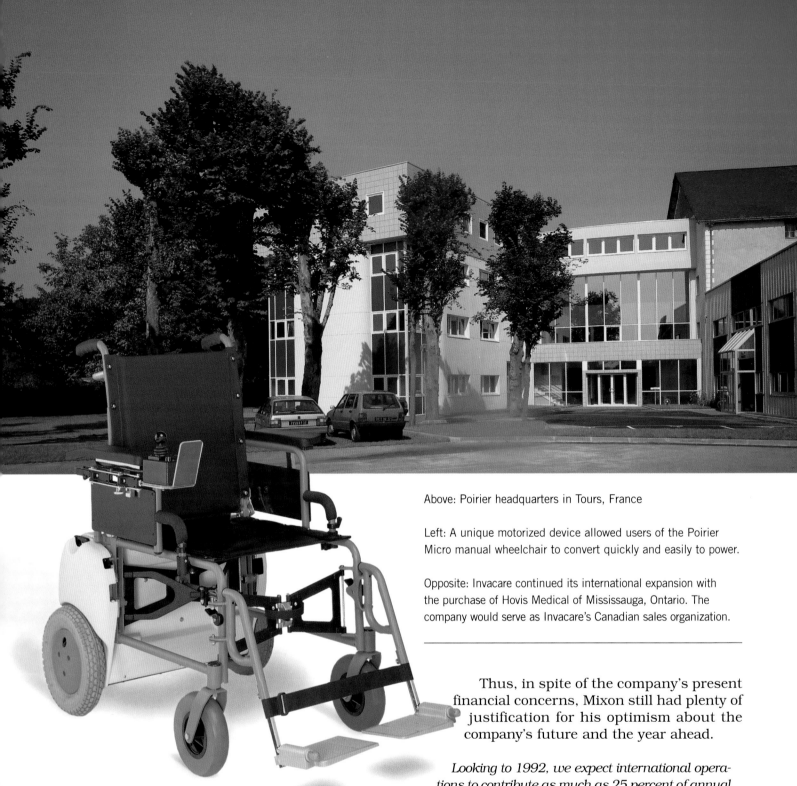

Above: Poirier headquarters in Tours, France

Left: A unique motorized device allowed users of the Poirier Micro manual wheelchair to convert quickly and easily to power.

Opposite: Invacare continued its international expansion with the purchase of Hovis Medical of Mississauga, Ontario. The company would serve as Invacare's Canadian sales organization.

Thus, in spite of the company's present financial concerns, Mixon still had plenty of justification for his optimism about the company's future and the year ahead.

Looking to 1992, we expect international operations to contribute as much as 25 percent of annual sales as opportunities abroad continue to develop nicely. Our products are recession resistant, and the underlying fundamentals driving growth in home medical equipment are very strong. The well-documented aging of the population, technological advancements in home medical technology, enactment of the Americans with Disabilities Act to mainstream persons with disabilities, and growing awareness of the emotional and financial ben-

industry. We've got the major market presence in the field with our sales organization [plus] major customer service support, and when we go in to a customer or a provider, we can offer all of those products and services, and at the same time bundle them in a way that makes it financially palatable for a company to purchase from us. That's the winning formula we use.[4]

efits of home care are all expected to continue build-ing greater demand for our products.[5]

A New European Headquarters

Hoping to strengthen the product base that would meet this growth, Invacare continued its foray into the international market. In fact, 1992 marked one of Invacare's most significant European acqui-sitions—that of Poirier S.A., France's largest wheel-chair maker and Europe's premier lightweight wheelchair maker. Purchased for $57.3 million, Poirier would double Invacare's European sales.[6] "Poirier gave us a presence in Europe," said Thomas R. Miklich, who joined Invacare in May 1993 as chief financial officer.[7]

"When we bought Poirier, which was larger than the combined European companies we had, we became a player to be reckoned with," recalled Otmar Sackerlotzky, retired vice president of qual-ity control. "Before, they looked at us [and said,] 'Yes, Invacare is from America. They buy everything up ... but they don't know how to run Europe.' But with Poirier, we are at critical mass."[8]

Founded in 1928, Poirier was a privately held, Tours-based company headed by Benoit Juranville, who would stay on as European company presi-dent. Poirier now formed the core of Invacare's new International unit, and was scheduled to open a new world-class manufacturing facility near Tours in August—just one month after Invacare announced its purchase. One of Poirier's most popular offerings was its unique Micro manual wheelchair, which was equipped with a motorized device that allowed the user to convert quickly to a power chair.[9]

While Invacare was an aggressive acquirer, Poirier had surveyed the trends in the industry and decided to look for a company with which to partner. Several years later, Benoit Juranville, Poirier's president, recalled the circumstances.

As I saw the industry consolidation occurring, I had two objectives. First, the company needed to expand dramatically in order to remain a force in the marketplace. Second, all family assets were tied up in the company and I needed to protect that investment. A capital infusion was the solution, and I began looking at potential partners. There had to be a good cultural fit, they needed to meet minimum financial standards, the deal had to be completed quickly, and I needed assurances that my employees would be taken care of.

Invacare exceeded my criteria in all areas and created an atmosphere of trust throughout the negotiation period. Their words were supported by their actions, and management worked diligently to structure a transaction that was good for all par-ties. I was also impressed by Invacare's flexibility and entrepreneurial spirit; they were a large cor-poration, but they did not act like one.[10]

After years of being an acquirer, Invacare had learned that retaining the creativity, autonomy, and entrepreneurial spirit of a company it had purchased was essential to successful growth—for all parties concerned. "Sometimes you're buying uniqueness, and you need to preserve that. Having autonomy is part of preserving that.... It's not the simple process of an anaconda swallowing its prey," said Blouch.[11]

Canadian Acquisitions

Just as Invacare was expanding in Europe, so was it broadening its holdings to the north. Hovis Medical, the company's independent Canadian sales representative, was acquired in April 1992. Based in Mississauga, Ontario, Hovis had sixty employees in Ontario, British Columbia, and Quebec.[12]

Hovis was folded into the new Invacare Canada division, along with Canadian Wheelchair

Manufacturing and Canadian Posture & Seating Centre (CPSC), acquired in October 1991. Production space was doubled at CPSC, bringing upholstery fabrication in-house and adding an electrostatic powder-coat paint line.[13] "CPSC was really an acquisition that allowed us to expand in the Canadian market—it was a combination of Canadian Posture & Seating and Hovis Medical, which was our big distributor," said Tom Miklich.[14]

As the company continued to acquire operations and brands, it merged them under the Invacare name. In Canada, for example, the CPSC plant moved from Kitchener, Ontario, to the Canadian Wheelchair plant in nearby Mississauga. In addition, a single sales force was forged from the three separate Canadian organizations.[15]

Invacare's globalization would take another giant step forward when the company introduced its first international product in 1993. Called the Action Patriot in the United States, the Action Elite in Canada, and the Action 2000 in Europe, this superlight, manual, prescription wheelchair would be manufactured in both the United States and France.[16]

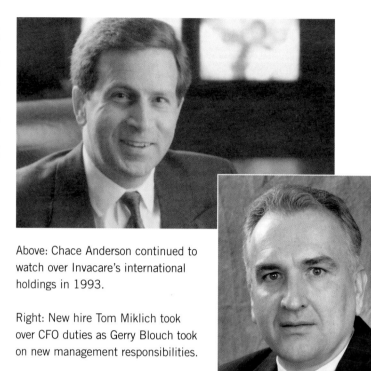

Above: Chace Anderson continued to watch over Invacare's international holdings in 1993.

Right: New hire Tom Miklich took over CFO duties as Gerry Blouch took on new management responsibilities.

Below: Invacare's first international product offering was a superlight, manual, prescription wheelchair introduced in 1993 under the Action Patriot name in the United States, the Action Elite name in Canada, and the Action 2000 name in Europe.

Expansion Pays Off

The bolstered international operations generated $80.8 million in net sales in 1992—26.4 percent of overall sales. Five years earlier, international sales had been just 13.3 percent, or $17.4 million, of overall sales.[17]

Continued growth—both internal and external—brought about the need for additional changes in Invacare's organizational structure. The company was divided into six units, each led by a general manager: Home Care, led by Gerry Blouch; Rehab, by Lou Slangen; Aftermarket Parts, by Vice President Richard Sayers; Technologies, by J. B. Richey; Canada, by Louis Tabickman; and International, by Chace Anderson.[18] Along with its own manager, each unit also had divisions for manufacturing, engineering, quality, marketing, and finance.

In April 1993, Thomas R. Miklich, a new hire, replaced Gerry Blouch as chief financial officer as Blouch took over new duties as president of the Home Care division.[19]

Sales of respiratory products increased approximately 7 percent per year from 1987 to 1992, growing in conjunction with increasing consumer demand for portable home respiratory products.

Future Prospects

The slowing sales growth that marked the end of 1991 was clearly over by the fall of 1992, when Invacare boasted record third quarter sales and earnings. "Business conditions have improved steadily through the year," Mixon said. "The acquisition of Poirier S.A., France's largest manufacturer and distributor of home medical equipment, has solidified Invacare's position as the largest home medical equipment manufacturer in the world, and enhances the company's long-term growth prospects."[20]

The recovery didn't surprise Mixon, who continued to like the company's long-term opportunities and still believed that the recently passed Americans with Disabilities Act would boost business. "Many people think of this law only in terms of providing access to public facilities, but the goal of the legislation is to integrate people with disabilities into the workforce," he said. Invacare's products could help the disabled to mainstream, Mixon reasoned.[21]

In 1992, the rehab business—particularly power and manual prescription wheelchairs—was growing especially fast. Over the past six years, it had grown at a compounded rate of 29 percent. Despite this, management was still cautious in its outlook, projecting growth between 10 percent and 12 percent per year at the company's annual meeting in 1992.[22]

Other areas of the home health care business were growing for Invacare as well; in fact, home respiratory equipment sales had grown at a compounded rate of 7 percent a year since 1987.[23] The company solidified its success in the home respiratory market, a part of its Home Care division, with the introduction of the Passport nebulizer, which delivers liquid medication as an aerosol to be inhaled. This product, Mixon told shareholders at the company's 1993 annual meeting, became the number two product on the market just twelve months after its introduction.[24] Invacare's expanded respiratory product line also included flow meters, aspirators, and portable oxygen.[25]

Invacare's position in the respiratory market was further bolstered in 1992 when it acquired Perry Oxygen Systems of Port St. Lucie, Florida. Perry gave the company a foothold in the liquid oxygen products market and patent rights to an oxygen delivery system that conserved oxygen, reducing cost and stretching the time between refills. Invacare planned to move the Perry operation to its existing Sanford, Florida, facility and market a line of products under the Mobilaire brand name.

John J. Turanin, former director of respiratory product marketing, said the new product line would give Invacare the broadest line of home respiratory products in the industry. "Offering liquid oxygen along with our concentrators and compressed gas systems gives us every oxygen modality for home respiratory home care providers," he said.[26]

Invacare's domestic aftermarket parts unit was new in 1992 and combined both the Invacare parts operation and its Canyon Products subsidiary. Canyon Products manufactured and sold parts for equipment of other manufacturers. In 1993, the division would fill more than one hundred thousand parts orders with the goal of ensuring that parts for any product made in the last twenty-five years either were in stock or could be fabricated within five days.[27]

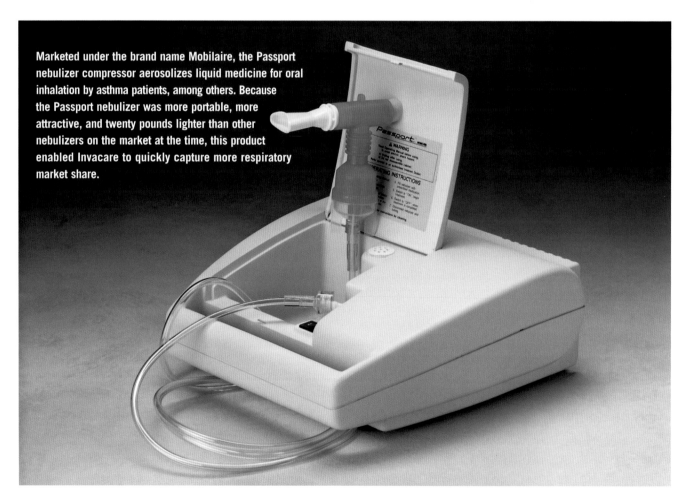

Marketed under the brand name Mobilaire, the Passport nebulizer compressor aerosolizes liquid medicine for oral inhalation by asthma patients, among others. Because the Passport nebulizer was more portable, more attractive, and twenty pounds lighter than other nebulizers on the market at the time, this product enabled Invacare to quickly capture more respiratory market share.

Invacare began to be a more active community partner in the early 1990s. To support its outreach activities, the company created the Invacare Foundation. In 1992, sponsorships, activities, and awards included (counterclockwise from left) the Ms. Wheelchair America competition—pictured is Dawn Blodgett, Ms. Wheelchair America 1993; Cleveland Ballet Dancing Wheels; and the Invacare Award for Excellence in Home Respiratory Care.

An Active Partner

To lend its support to organizations for the disabled and other charities, the company formed the Invacare Foundation in late 1992. The funds for the Foundation came from a one-time invested gain Invacare had realized from a start-up investment in another Cleveland-area company, STERIS. The Foundation's activities, coupled with Invacare's many marketing-sponsored events, would increase the company's visibility within the community through its involvement with organizations and events like the National Veterans Wheelchair Games, the National Junior Wheelchair Championships, Easter Seals, the Ms. Wheelchair America competition, and Cleveland Ballet Dancing Wheels, a dance company featuring dancers with and without disabilities.[28] The Foundation also created an endowment fund with the American Respiratory Care Foundation for the Invacare Award for Excellence in Home Respiratory Care, to be awarded to an outstanding respiratory-care worker.[29]

As it had in 1991, Invacare and its leaders continued to receive recognition from the industry: the Northeast Ohio Entrepreneur of the Year program honored Mixon with its 1992 Master Entrepreneur Award;[30] *Forbes* magazine put Invacare on its list of "200 Best Small Companies in America";[31] *INC.* magazine noted the company's

Ben Lucas · Chantal Petiticlerc · Cheri Becerra · Krige Schabort

INVACARE'S TOP-NOTCH TEAM

INVACARE SPONSORS AN ELITE GROUP OF some eighty athletes and endorsees, all of whom serve as ambassadors for both Invacare and wheelchair athletes and users worldwide. This top-notch team, which includes the world's leading wheelchair racing, tennis, handcycling, quad rugby, and basketball athletes, also helps Invacare continually refine its sports wheelchairs for better performance. This winning combination of talented athletes and Invacare's technology proves successful wherever Team Invacare members compete and perform in events such as the Paralympic Games and the Boston Marathon, among others.

The Paralympic Games

At the 1996 Paralympic Games, Team Invacare captured eighty-nine medals, most of which were won on the track.

The Paralympics, which take place in the weeks following the Olympic Games in the same country at the same facilities, allow the best athletes from around the world to compete. In 1996, more than one thousand disabled athletes competed in the Paralympic events in Atlanta, Georgia. The Olympics also included two exhibition wheelchair events—the women's eight-hundred-meter and the men's fifteen-hundred-meter races.[1]

Team Invacare members also fared well at the 2000 Paralympic Games in Sydney, Australia. Thirty-nine team members brought home seventy-four medals—including thirty gold, twenty-six silver, and eighteen bronze, and dominated the tennis, track, and racing events in their Invacare Top End wheelchairs.

The Boston Marathon

Besides the Paralympics, wheelchair athletes consider the Boston Marathon a showcase event. From 1997 to 1999, **Louise Sauvage** and **Franz Nietlispach** were the top winners in the women's and men's open divisions at the Boston Marathon; in 2000, they captured the second and first place spots. Nietlispach and Sauvage also won second place and first place, respectively, in the 2000 Sempach Marathon in Switzerland.[2] Sauvage and Nietlispach also earned top honors at the 2000 Paralympics, with Sauvage bringing home gold medals in the 1,500- and 5,000-meter, and a silver in the 800-meter, and Nietlispach winning a gold medal in the marathon and a silver in the 10,000-meter.

Other prominent Team Invacare racing competitors include:

Krige Schabort—Winner of the 1999 Twin City Marathon, the 1999 Detroit Marathon, and the 1999 Honolulu Marathon, fourth-place winner in the 2000 Peachtree 10k, second-place winner in the 2000 North American WC Champion 10k, and a silver medal winner in the 26.2-mile marathon in the 2000 Paralympics;

Cheri Becerra—Silver medal winner in the 100-meter and 200-meter races at the 1996 Paralympics, winner of the Boulder 10k in 1999 and 2000, second-place winner in the 2000 Wilkes-Barre National 10k, a gold medal winner in the 100- and 400-meter and a silver medal winner in the 200-meter in the 2000 Paralympics;

Scot Hollonbeck—Third-place winner of the 1999 Boston Marathon, winner of the 1999

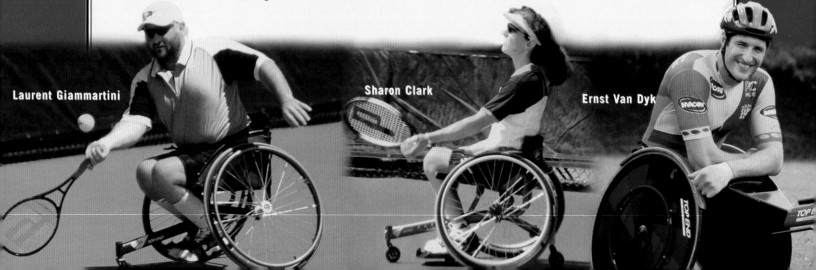

Laurent Giammartini · Sharon Clark · Ernst Van Dyk

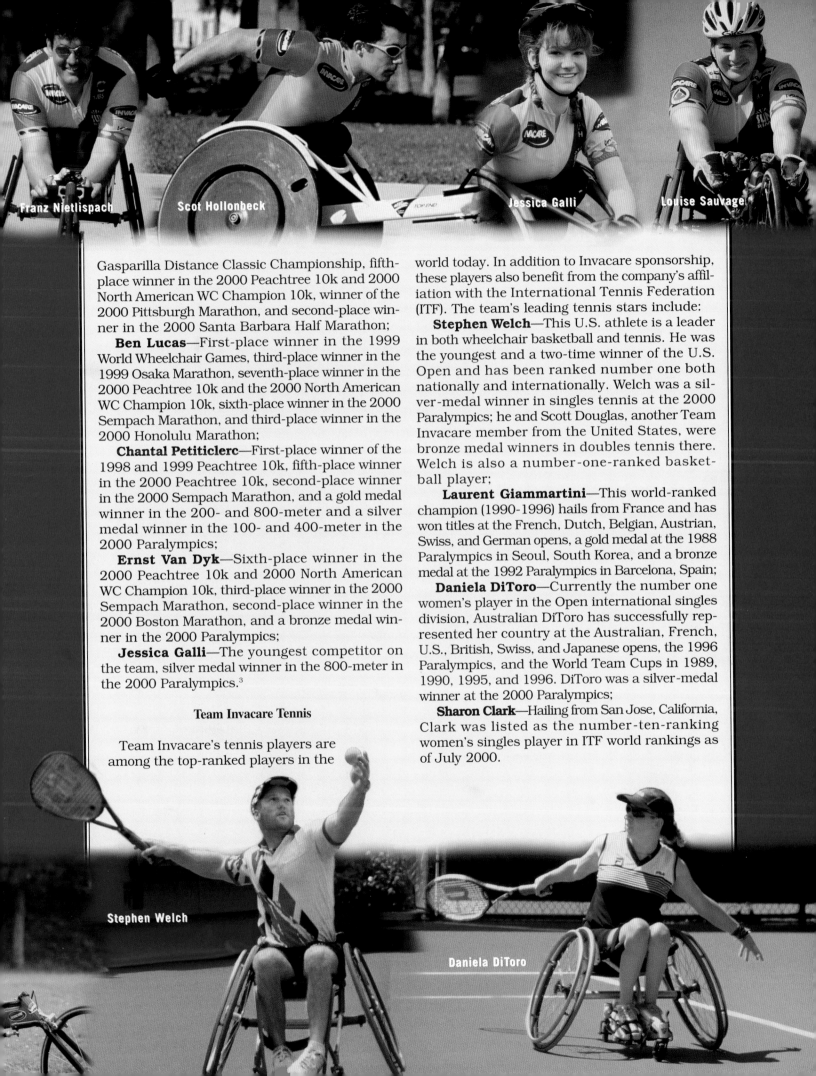

Franz Nietlispach

Scot Hollonbeck

Jessica Galli

Louise Sauvage

Gasparilla Distance Classic Championship, fifth-place winner in the 2000 Peachtree 10k and 2000 North American WC Champion 10k, winner of the 2000 Pittsburgh Marathon, and second-place winner in the 2000 Santa Barbara Half Marathon;

Ben Lucas—First-place winner in the 1999 World Wheelchair Games, third-place winner in the 1999 Osaka Marathon, seventh-place winner in the 2000 Peachtree 10k and the 2000 North American WC Champion 10k, sixth-place winner in the 2000 Sempach Marathon, and third-place winner in the 2000 Honolulu Marathon;

Chantal Petiticlerc—First-place winner of the 1998 and 1999 Peachtree 10k, fifth-place winner in the 2000 Peachtree 10k, second-place winner in the 2000 Sempach Marathon, and a gold medal winner in the 200- and 800-meter and a silver medal winner in the 100- and 400-meter in the 2000 Paralympics;

Ernst Van Dyk—Sixth-place winner in the 2000 Peachtree 10k and 2000 North American WC Champion 10k, third-place winner in the 2000 Sempach Marathon, second-place winner in the 2000 Boston Marathon, and a bronze medal winner in the 2000 Paralympics;

Jessica Galli—The youngest competitor on the team, silver medal winner in the 800-meter in the 2000 Paralympics.[3]

Team Invacare Tennis

Team Invacare's tennis players are among the top-ranked players in the world today. In addition to Invacare sponsorship, these players also benefit from the company's affiliation with the International Tennis Federation (ITF). The team's leading tennis stars include:

Stephen Welch—This U.S. athlete is a leader in both wheelchair basketball and tennis. He was the youngest and a two-time winner of the U.S. Open and has been ranked number one both nationally and internationally. Welch was a silver-medal winner in singles tennis at the 2000 Paralympics; he and Scott Douglas, another Team Invacare member from the United States, were bronze medal winners in doubles tennis there. Welch is also a number-one-ranked basketball player;

Laurent Giammartini—This world-ranked champion (1990-1996) hails from France and has won titles at the French, Dutch, Belgian, Austrian, Swiss, and German opens, a gold medal at the 1988 Paralympics in Seoul, South Korea, and a bronze medal at the 1992 Paralympics in Barcelona, Spain;

Daniela DiToro—Currently the number one women's player in the Open international singles division, Australian DiToro has successfully represented her country at the Australian, French, U.S., British, Swiss, and Japanese opens, the 1996 Paralympics, and the World Team Cups in 1989, 1990, 1995, and 1996. DiToro was a silver-medal winner at the 2000 Paralympics;

Sharon Clark—Hailing from San Jose, California, Clark was listed as the number-ten-ranking women's singles player in ITF world rankings as of July 2000.

Stephen Welch

Daniela DiToro

entrepreneurial leadership; and *Medical Industry Executive* called the company one of the top U.S. medical equipment makers.

In 1993, the company would again be named one of *Forbes* magazine's "200 Best Small Companies,"[32] and *Business Week* included Invacare on its list of "250 Companies on the Move."[33]

Invacare's early lobbying efforts also earned plaudits: In 1992, the company received recognition from the National Association of Medical Equipment Suppliers, which honored Invacare with its first "President's Award for 'grassroots' lobbying and advocacy efforts on behalf of the industry."[34]

Mixon was becoming more and more visible in Washington and even visited the White House the day after President and Mrs. Clinton unveiled their health care reform proposal. "They told me firsthand of their commitment to keeping a strong home health care component in the minimum benefit package," he reported back in 1993.[35]

Top End by Action

Invacare made more acquisitions in 1993, purchasing Top End, Dynamic Controls, and Geomarine Systems (GSI). With growing consumer interest in sports and recreational wheelchairs, Invacare wanted to expand its presence in that niche.

The company bought Top End Wheelchair Sports of Pinellas Park, Florida, in March of 1993 for less than $5 million,[36] merging the seven-year-old company with its Action line to create Top End by Action.[37] "We pursued the acquisition of Top End because of the firm's reputation for innovation and quality in sports wheelchairs," Mixon said.[38] The company would continue building Top End chairs in Florida under the supervision of Chris and Mary Carol Peterson, two of the company's founders.

The Petersons started Top End with George Murray, the veteran wheelchair racer who started wheelchair racing in 1963 in a hospital wheel-

chair in a parking lot. Like many active wheelchair users, Murray began tinkering with chairs both to improve his racing performance and because those on the market weren't meeting his needs. Peterson was a medical equipment sales representative. He met Murray in the early 1980s, and together they formed Top End in 1986.[39]

Invacare's other two 1993 acquisitions would also prove to be important for the company's growth. Dynamic Controls was a New Zealand company that manufactured electronic controls for more than fifty wheelchair makers worldwide. The purchase doubled Invacare's output of control systems, allowing the company to eventually consolidate all its electronics manufacturing in New Zealand.[40]

"That was really a vertical integration because they had electronics technology," said Tom Miklich. "We use a lot of electronics on our wheelchairs, and they were the market leader outside of us. We had made our own, and they were a lower-cost manufacturer. So, it allowed us to kind of get in and have the full gamut of electronics."[41]

Since 1986, New York–based GSI had been manufacturing bed and mattress systems that used low air loss (LAL) therapy to prevent decubitus ulcers, or bed sores, and to treat other skin ailments, such as burns. "We have followed the development of this therapy closely for several years, and feel its clinical viability in the home care setting is now widely accepted in the medical community. With Invacare's financial resources and unmatched distribution capabilities, we are optimistic about the growth potential for this product line," said Mixon at the time of the purchase.[42]

Sales of GSI's microAir Turn-Q—a pressure-adjusting mattress system—had, in fact, been

After purchasing Top End in 1993, Invacare merged the company with its own Action line to create Top End by Action. Because the Top End name was already well respected among athletes with disabilities, the pairing gave Invacare a new edge in the sports wheelchair market.

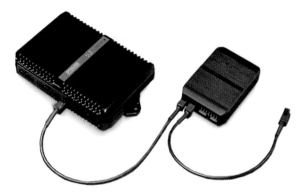

robust.[43] Because of this, Invacare was able to pay for the purchase in just one year, said Otmar Sackerlotzky, retired vice president of quality control.[44]

A Continuing Commitment to Home Care Providers

Though it was committed to expanding product lines, Invacare resisted imitating some competitors who took sales from loyal home care providers by selling directly to consumers or through health maintenance organizations (HMOs). While the company saw the obvious potential for additional sales, it believed that home care providers supplied necessary training and after-sale service.

Instead, Invacare bolstered its commitment to dealer programs that provided financing and free shipping for home care providers, and, beginning in late 1991, the company began to strongly emphasize its "One Stop Shopping Plus" marketing program, which provided incentives to home care

Above: An electronic wheelchair controller manufactured by Dynamic Controls of New Zealand. The company was added to the Invacare fold during the summer of 1993. Because Dynamic sold its wares to more than fifty wheelchair makers worldwide, the purchase in effect gave Invacare control over its competitors' controllers.

Below: GSI's successful microAir Turn-Q mattress system helps to prevent bedsores by continuously readjusting the patient's positioning. Invacare bought the company in 1993 and quickly recouped the cost of the purchase.

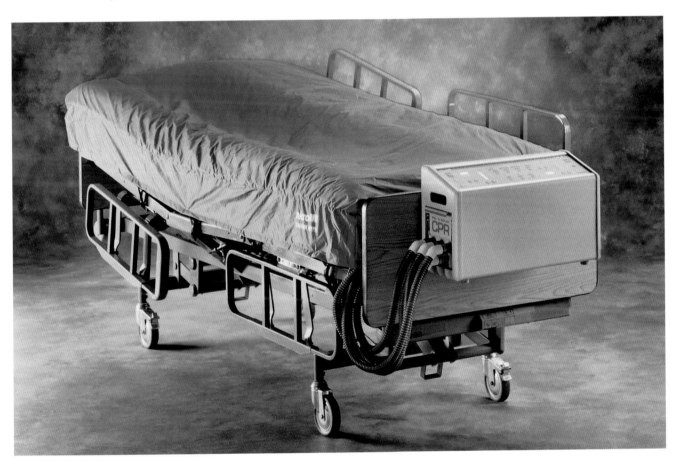

With warehouses, distribution centers, and sales offices located strategically across the country and in Toronto, Invacare providers could get needed stock at a moment's notice.

providers who made Invacare products their preferred brand.[45] "We've always been driven by One Stop Shopping to make it easier and less costly for the home care provider to do business,'" said Slangen, then head of Rehab and today senior vice president of sales and marketing. "For twenty years, we built Invacare through a push marketing strategy [that made it] easy for the dealer to order the merchandise from Invacare and have the broadest array of products and programs available to the dealer so that he doesn't have to go anywhere else."[46]

In 1993, the company added the slogan "Your partner, not your competitor" to emphasize its commitment to its home care providers.[47] This became the rallying cry as the company launched programs to help home care providers with advertising and showroom design.[48]

At the end of 1993, the federal Health Care Financing Administration (HCFA), which administers Medicare payments, reduced the number of Durable Medical Equipment Regional Carriers (DMERCs). Mixon estimated that this act caused a backlog of two million payment claims from home care providers, leading them to experience cashflow problems as they waited for reimbursement.[49]

Invacare could help in this situation—at least with its own products—with its innovative Invalease dealer inventory financing program. During the transition, Invacare created several such programs to carry home care providers through the drought, which lasted into the third quarter of 1994.[50]

Forging Ahead

Having won success through its acquisition and administrative strategies, Invacare was forging ahead with clear objectives, outlined by Mixon in the company's 1993 annual report:

- Sustain a sales growth rate of 50 percent above the industry's growth rate;
- Surpass the $500 million mark in sales;
- Earn *Fortune* 500 status;
- Achieve and sustain a 20 percent return on equity;
- Realize continuous improvement in after-tax profit margins; and
- Continue technological leadership in all product lines.[51]

However, *Fortune* changed its rules of eligibility shortly thereafter to include retailers, making *Fortune* 500 status an unrealistic objective for the near term.

Although Invacare's Canadian and European subsidiaries did boost earnings in 1992 and 1993, both regions were hit by recession and unemployment in 1994. Worldwide, but especially in Europe, the company was fighting to cut costs to compensate for reduced government reimbursements for durable medical equipment.[52]

In 1993, sales were up 20 percent to $365.5 million, and earnings took a healthy jump, climbing 25 percent to $22.1 million. As in past years, the company's fitness was a function of the increasing value the health care industry was putting on home care and the aging population, as well as Invacare's strong strategic acquisitions and empowered management team.

As 1993 was ending, the company made several important announcements. Just days before the year's end, Gerry Blouch, president of the home care division, added European operations to his portfolio of responsibilities. As vice president in charge of international operations based in France, Chace Anderson would report to Blouch.[53]

While foreign concerns were clearly essential to Invacare's growth strategy, the company also understood the necessity of tending its roots back home in the United States—not an easy task in light of recent expansions. "With our core business still in the United States, part of our challenge continues to be [to] think globally ... [and] support our global strategy but at the same time keep the lights on here in the U.S.," said Bill Corcoran.[54]

Industry Politics in the United States

Part of keeping "the lights on in the United States" involved lobbying politicians in support of the industry. In March 1994, U.S. House majority leader Richard Gephardt, a Missouri Democrat, paid a visit to Invacare's Elyria facilities and spoke at a fundraiser sponsored by InvaPAC, the company's political action committee.

Mixon was visiting Washington, D.C., on a monthly basis in those days, shaking hands and lobbying to keep Medicare and Medicaid reimbursement levels from dropping further and to push the Food and Drug Administration to lift its hold on approvals of power wheelchairs. "I'm advocating a very selfish position," he told a reporter. "But I also know I'm not selling tobacco or guns. I'm selling [home] health care at a third the cost of institutionalized care."[55] Mixon also confided to a reporter that he believed government action limiting reimbursement for the home medical equipment Invacare sold, rather than any competitor, was the company's greatest threat.[56]

Always loyal to its home care providers, Invacare continued to support them through special financing programs, One Stop Shopping Plus, and other incentives—especially when federal changes to health care policy hit home care providers hard at the end of 1993. To emphasize this commitment, Invacare added the slogan "Your partner, not your competitor."

THE TOP END STORY

THE STORY OF TOP END BEGAN IN 1986 when friends Chris Peterson and George Murray joined forces to create racing wheelchairs.[1]

The time was ripe for a fledgling company to redesign the clunky wheelchairs: athletes across the country wanted to improve their speed and trim the weight off their chairs during racing competitions.

As an accomplished wheelchair racer himself, Murray was in touch with the pulse of the racing community. He was the first racer to break the four-minute mile in a wheelchair and the first wheelchair athlete to be featured on a *Wheaties*® box. He beat out one thousand other nominees in 1983 to be the face on the cereal box known for highlighting only the best of the best in sports.[2]

Peterson became involved in wheelchair sports when he worked at a New York–based home health care company that provided wheelchairs. As the company's technical expert in the lighter sports models, Peterson became an avid spectator at wheelchair sporting events all over the world in 1983.[3]

Two years later he relocated to Florida and began designing his own sports chairs at a small company called Hand Crafted Metals, where Murray also worked.[4] The two left the following year

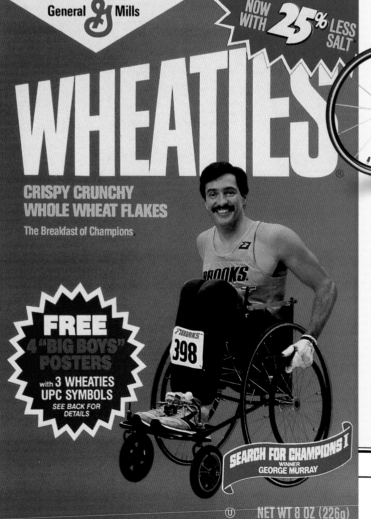

to start their own company, calling it Top End.

"I was involved in wheelchair racing during the 1980s, the exciting times when I made a new design almost every week for George Murray…. In 1986, George won the Invacare Cup Race Series, the first significant racing series for the sport," reminisced Peterson. "Originally, we just made four-wheelers, custom built of chrome-moly steel, and the front wheels were only available in sixteen-inch.[5]

There were steering levers and compensators and hill climbers. Then came the athletes who wanted a three-wheeler. This was in 1987. I remember building the first T-frame then, which

is now the industry standard. The chair has evolved with subtle, significant improvements. Racing chairs are safer, faster, better constructed, and more aerodynamic.[6]

From its beginnings Top End led the industry in innovation and design for custom-made wheelchairs for both everyday use and sports. The Terminator basketball and everyday chair was a marked addition to the product line in 1988. In 1990, Peterson became the first in the industry to design and manufacture a hand cycle. In 1992, he designed the first three-wheeled chair for tennis, which continues to be the industry standard.[7]

Peterson began brainstorming for a new design for the tennis chair after attending the

Paralympics in Barcelona, Spain. Several athletes told Peterson that they wanted a chair specifically designed for tennis.[8]

"I went home after the games thinking of a custom tennis chair. I thought of the racing chair with three wheels. Then I thought, why not three wheels for tennis?" Peterson explained. "Tennis is a noncontact sport. The court is smooth and the players sit low. So I built a three-wheel chair called the T3. Mike Bond, a Team Invacare tennis player, went to the U.S. Open with the T3 and got a lot of funny looks. But, wheelchair tennis was changed forever."[9]

Top End became the sports wheelchair division of Invacare Corporation in 1993. The acquisition allowed Invacare to fill a void in its product line and offer sports and recreational chairs.[10] Peterson remained manager of product development at Top End, and Murray, who took a break from the business for a while, returned to work part-time in customer service.

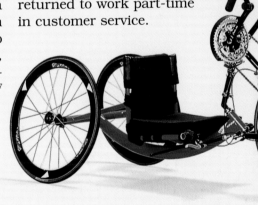

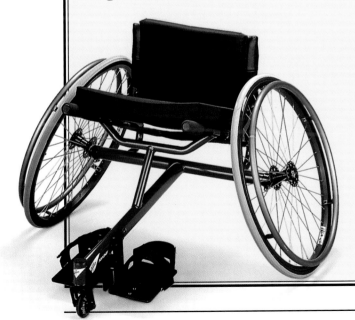

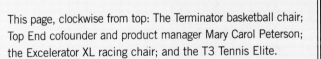

This page, clockwise from top: The Terminator basketball chair; Top End cofounder and product manager Mary Carol Peterson; the Excelerator XL racing chair; and the T3 Tennis Elite.

Opposite, clockwise from top: Top End cofounder Chris Peterson; a Top End racing wheelchair; Top End cofounder George Murray, the first wheelchair athlete to be featured on a *Wheaties*® box. (*Wheaties* is a registered trademark of General Mills, Inc. Photo used by permission.)

Survival in this environment, said Gerry Blouch, hinged on Invacare's ability to continually innovate every aspect of its business, from product design and engineering to manufacturing and operations. "The government has been cutting reimbursement prices for our products almost at a nonstop pace over the last decade, and our competitors haven't discovered any way to compete other than cutting prices," he said.[57]

After shuttling between Elyria and Washington for three years, Mixon was finally beginning to make a name for himself. "They recognize he has built an excellent company that produces first-class equipment," said Frederick H. Graefe, a lawyer with the Baker & Hostetler law firm and the company's Washington lobbyist.[58]

Said Mixon: "It was either get run over or get involved. We won't be run over."[59]

Know Thy Consumer

Just as Mixon wanted Washington to hear industry concerns, so did wheelchair users want the industry to focus on their needs. Invacare was listening. Less than a year after Invacare's March

1993 acquisition of Top End, Invacare's high-performance wheelchair unit, now named Top End by Action, brought out three new chairs. This new line included the Eliminator X, the T3, and the T2. The Eliminator X, the company claimed, was more aerodynamic than any chair on the market and was a championship-level racer.[60] The T3 and T2 were created for tennis and basketball players.

Both the company's new line and its lengthening list of wheelchair athlete endorsements demonstrated that Invacare was listening to consumers. At the recommendation of racer Phillipe Cupre, for example, the Eliminator X was designed with a triangular front fork that gives the chair a lower center of gravity and enhanced turning and control.[61] The T3, which was designed for basketball, tennis, and softball, was made of aircraft aluminum and weighed only about eighteen pounds. It had an open front that allowed a user to bend down to scoop up a ground ball. When Rick Cooper, manager of consumer marketing, showed off the chair at a ball field, the response was positive. "I could easily scoop up the ball," said Cooper, who was a former pitcher for the Oakland As and a wheelchair user himself after being injured in a car acci-

The aerodynamic Top End Eliminator X racing chair helped racing competitors achieve top speeds like never before.

Above: Invacare Consumer Marketing Manager Rick Cooper—who was also a ranked tennis player—was honored along with Invacare endorsee Scott Law (not shown) by the United States Tennis Association for their work at wheelchair sports clinics cosponsored by Invacare and Easter Seals. Here Cooper and clinic participants work on their swings.

Right: Invacare looked to wheelchair users—particularly its own associates—for guidance in fine-tuning products. Because of the volume of chairs manufactured at Invacare, able-bodied associates such as Steve Penfound, associate project engineer for power wheelchairs, also became wheelchair experts in their own right.

dent. "The other players saw that, and I got some good comments."[62]

Although Invacare's research indicated that only an estimated seventy thousand of the 1.4 million Americans in wheelchairs needed specialized chairs, the demands of this particular group of users, particularly athletes, were driving innovation for the whole industry. For example, those attributes that made Invacare's racing chairs sought after—their light weight and easy maneuverability—were features that standard users were beginning to look for as well.[63]

Made out of aluminum instead of steel, these chairs weighed about fifteen pounds and were aerodynamic, allowing the athlete to safely increase speed.[64] The push rims were small so the chair

could be propelled by the upward motion of the arms as well as the normal downward push. Most racers sat with their legs tucked under their bodies for optimum speed.

"Every one of these chairs is built around the person who is sitting in it," said Michael Devlin, former director of health care professional marketing, who joined Invacare the same year Top End was purchased. "There's no such thing as a warehouse full of these chairs sitting somewhere, waiting to be purchased.... Every one of them is made to measure."[65]

For a company with $366 million in sales, Invacare's sports chair division—Top End by Action—was relatively small, with sales of about $2 million and 20 percent of the sports chair market.[66] Meeting the needs of sports wheelchair users, however, was vital to the company's success in this niche.

Some of Invacare's associates were, in fact, wheelchair users and made recommendations for modifications. And Invacare's other associates, by virtue of manufacturing some two hundred thousand wheelchairs a year, became experts of a kind. The problem, said Ron Thomas, was that if "you've never had somebody in a wheelchair or been involved

in one yourself," it was difficult to relate to the needs of wheelchair users.[67]

Thomas had an aunt who required a wheelchair because of severe arthritis, and he remembered the chair's inadequacies. "You'd say, 'Boy, if you just had this, it would make it much easier,'" he recalled. "So that's one of the reasons that I stayed in this business for years."[68]

I've had opportunities to go other places, but I stay here because I like the product, and I see the product as a way to help people. That's the reason why I've really been involved in it.[69]

To really understand what consumers were looking for in a wheelchair, Invacare formed focus groups to critique existing equipment and suggest improvements. After all, said Thomas, a better product was a coup for everyone involved. "It helped our business because people got more mobile," he said.[70]

Suggestions that met safety and reliability standards were then field-tested to see if users actually wanted the new features.[71] Wheelchair users continued to push Invacare and other makers to develop lighter, stronger chairs with features such as high-pressure tires and quick-release axles that would eventually become more common.

The company further demonstrated its commitment to building better sports wheelchairs in 1994, when Jim Knaub, a champion wheelchair marathoner, rejoined the company as a product support specialist. Knaub, who had been a rehab manager for Invacare from 1982 to 1987, returned after having won the wheelchair division of the famed Boston Marathon three years in a row. His new duties included training sales people and visiting rehabilitation centers to find out what features users wanted.[72]

Other wheelchair athletes signed with the company, including Stephen Welch, Laurent Giammartini, and Chantal Vandierendonck—all top wheelchair tennis players.[73] By 1994, more than

150 athletes and celebrities were endorsing Invacare's products.[74] And by 2000 the company was the clear leader in the sporting arena, a success that was fueled by Invacare's Top End acquisition.

"The changes have been fast and dramatic, and really led by Invacare from a technological standpoint," said Susan Elder, director of marketing communications, who is responsible for the company's consumer marketing program today.[75]

By 2000, Invacare would be the largest supporter of wheelchair sports in the world, sponsoring two of the biggest international events: the Invacare World Cup, the premier wheelchair tennis event, and the Paralyzed Veterans Games. "We're the primary sponsor of both those events, and outside of the Paralympics, those are the two largest wheelchair sports events in the world," Elder said.[76]

The Invacare World Cup is a team tennis tournament that takes place in various locations around the world with three hundred to five hundred wheelchair athletes representing forty to fifty countries. The Paralyzed Veterans Games is a huge multisport wheelchair event that takes place annually.

New Products

The coming year, 1994, would bring about changes to the company's other wheelchair lines and much more. Invacare had revealed much of its 1994 product line—more than forty new products—at the National Home Health Care Exhibition (NHHCE) held in Atlanta in November 1993.[77] Highlights of these offerings included a new line of liquid oxygen products with self-calibrating, microprocessor-controlled LED content indicators and a redesigned and reengineered Tracer line of standard, manual wheelchairs.[78] These wheelchairs required less maintenance and offered greater longevity than earlier models.[79]

In addition to its Tracer line, the company launched an enhanced line of Action power prescription wheelchairs, the Tiger series of pediatric wheelchairs, the A-T and the A-4 prescription chairs, and the Mark IV power controllers.[80] In April 1994, after the FDA finally lifted its months-long hold on clearing new power wheelchairs for sale, Invacare also rolled out its award-winning Storm Series line of wheelchairs. As a result of the FDA's concerns, Invacare and other manufacturers began increased

Opposite: Many Invacare associates, such as Rick Cooper (pictured), said they stayed with the company because they felt its products truly made a difference in helping people with disabilities lead more active and fulfilling lives.

New offerings at the National Home Health Care Exhibition, held in Atlanta in November 1993, included a new line of Action power chairs (below) and a reengineered line of Tracer manual wheelchairs (left). The sale of power chairs had been put on hold for the whole industry while the FDA sorted out concerns over the chairs' controllers and also implemented testing and safety standards. Invacare stepped to the forefront and helped to institute nonmandatory standards that would become an industry guideline.

testing of power wheelchairs and other equipment to ensure user safety.[81]

Boasting one of the industry's first shock-dampened suspension wheelchairs, the Storm Series line offered superior comfort, often helping users with posture and spasticity problems by reducing vibration.[82] Best of all, the new chairs were more aesthetically pleasing than previous power chairs.[83] These attributes would earn the line a Red Dot Award at Design Innovations '95, an international design contest in Essen, Germany.[84] At year's end, Mixon was pleased with the Storm Series sales but still had concerns about competitor Sunrise Medical's Quickie wheelchair.[85]

As had been the case with Everest & Jennings, Invacare and Sunrise enjoyed a healthy rivalry, particularly between Sunrise's Quickie line and Invacare's Action line. At one trade show in particular, Lou Slangen, senior vice president of sales and marketing, recalled buttons that read, "Why settle for a Quickie when you can get real Action?"[86] And, as the E&J rivalry had done, Sunrise also served to stir up Invacare's competitive juices.

Although being the best at providing innovative products and serving customers was always a top priority, Invacare never took itself too seriously to have fun—especially at the competition's expense.

Slangen recalled one meeting in which employees were "flogging each other about something that was screwed up.... One of the guys said, 'Can you imagine if Sunrise saw us here like this?' I said, 'But could you imagine that we could take a peek at how Sunrise talks about us?' " In answer to that question, the company created a video spoof titled "The Fly on the Wall." In it, Mixon plays a dancing fly at an imaginary Sunrise board meeting.[87]

The SensO$_2$

Invacare anticipated that the SensO$_2$ oxygen-sensing device, another significant new product for Invacare in 1994, would buoy respiratory product sales.[88] Adapted from electric car technology,[89] the SensO$_2$ was designed for use with Mobilaire oxygen concentrators. Because it could accurately measure how much oxygen a patient was receiving and sound an alarm if the level fell below a preset limit, the new product helped to reduce maintenance problems and saved home care providers from having to make unnecessary service calls.

In the fall of 1994, Enterprise Development Inc., a nonprofit organization affiliated with Case Western Reserve University in Cleveland, presented Invacare's $SensO_2$ team—J. B. Richey; Ted Wakefield, vice president, electronics; Greg Michaels, director, respiratory engineering; and Homayoun Birangi, David Nutall, and David Polacsek, project engineers—with one of its "EDI Innovation Awards" for creative new products. The $SensO_2$, which had a long life and did not require recalibration, helped to double Invacare's domestic sales of oxygen concentrators.[90]

EDI presented another Innovation Award for Invacare's new microAir Turn-Q automatic turning mattress, which helped prevent bedsores and pulmonary complications in bedridden patients by turning them as much as forty degrees side to side on a predetermined schedule.[91]

Over the next year, sales of home care products, which included oxygen concentrators, would grow 19.4 percent, and sales of rehabilitation prod-

Above: Today's wheelchair athletes can choose from a wide variety of sports. These Invacare-sponsored athletes are playing rugby in Top End wheelchairs.

Left: Team Invacare member Laurent Giammartini competes at a tennis match. Invacare continued to expand its sports sponsorships in 1994, adding several major events, including the International Paralympic Committee World Championships in Berlin and the U.S. Junior National Wheelchair Championships. The company would be endorsed by more than 150 athletes and celebrities.

ucts, such as prescription chairs, seating products, and superlight and sports wheelchairs, would grow 9.4 percent.

Giving Back

Invacare continued giving back to the community. In 1994, the company expanded its event sponsorships to include the U.S. Junior National Wheelchair Championships, the International Paralympic Committee World Championships in Berlin, the Far East and South Pacific Games in Beijing, the French National Women's Wheelchair Basketball Team, the Disabled National Athletic Team of the People's Republic of China (PRC), and twelve Easter Seals wheelchair sports camps.[92] The PRC team won twenty-three medals at the Far East and South Pacific Games in Top End wheelchairs[93] and used them exclusively. These chairs were also used in the 1996 Paralympics, held in Atlanta.[94]

In 1994, the company made further commitments to sponsor the Paralyzed Veterans of America National Wheelchair Games, the Ms. Wheelchair America pageant, the Cleveland Ballet Dancing Wheels, and the World Team Tennis Cup in Holland. In addition, Invacare fielded Team Action, a group of thirty top male and female wheelchair road racers, and several rugby teams.[95]

It also presented the first Invacare Award for Excellence in the Arts and one thousand dollars to Mary Verdi-Fletcher, founder of Cleveland Ballet

Dancing Wheels. "We created the award for individuals like Mary, who dedicate their lives to changing prejudices about people with disabilities," Mixon said.[96]

Augmenting International Operations

During 1994, Invacare's strategy of "reaching out" included making several international acquisitions. In August, Invacare acquired Rehadap S.A., a Spanish distributor of wheelchairs and other rehab products. In November, the company augmented its growing Canadian division with the purchase of Genus Medical, a manufacturer and distributor of motorized scooters and powered seating systems used on power wheelchairs. Although Invacare had not been in the power tilt and recline business, this purchase gave it a chance to "attack the number one player in the market at that time," said Lou Tabickman. "I think it was one of the turning points

Mary Verdi-Fletcher, Invacare endorsee and principal dancer and founder of Invacare-sponsored Cleveland Ballet Dancing Wheels, now Ballet Dancing Wheels, dances in her Action wheelchair with Sabatino Verlezza.

PROTECTING SENSITIVE TISSUES

WHEN INVACARE ACQUIRED MOBILITE in the early 1980s, it moved into a new market—home care beds—with a new set of challenges. Disabled and ill people who spend prolonged periods of time in bed are prone to decubitus ulcers—also know as bedsores and pressure sores.

These skin ulcers develop because of inactivity and unrelenting pressure on one part of the body. They are most often found where the skin comes into contact with bedding, typically occurring on heels, ankles, knees, buttocks, spine, hips, elbows, and any other place where the weight of the body rests. Once they have developed, bedsores progress into open ulcers and are prone to infection. At their very worst, bedsores can spread into muscle and bone tissue, requiring surgery and hospitalization to check their growth. In rare cases where infection continues unabated, bedsores can even cause death.

In the early 1980s, bedsores were prevented by in-bed exercises and by regularly rotating patients who could not move themselves. By the 1990s, however, Invacare's successful bed operation was working on newer bed designs that could help prevent the ulcers. These beds rotated automatically on a schedule, thus distributing weight and preventing bedsores. Before long, this kind of technology began to appear in wheelchairs in the form of sophisticated padding materials.

Today wheelchair users can choose from a variety of cushions, including foam, gel, air flotation, and urethane honeycomb, all of which allow for even pressure distribution during prolonged contact. In addition, tilt-and-recline technology on wheelchairs mimics the rotation of beds such as Invacare's microAir Turn-Q to help prevent bedsores from forming in the first place.

that really gave us a full line in our power wheelchair products."[97]

In December, the company added Beram AB of Gothenburg, Sweden, a distributor of wheelchairs and other rehab products. Both Rehadap and Beram had been independent Invacare distributors. The company expected these purchases to expand market share in Spain and Sweden.[98]

More acquisitions were always on the way. Said Mixon, "Invacare is always talking to ten or twelve companies, and we're looking for several different types of acquisitions"[99] that would add operations similar to Poirier or Top End. Acquisitions had to meet one of three criteria: the target company could increase Invacare's share in an existing market; it could provide a presence in a new international market; or it would bring with it a new product that could be sold through Invacare's existing sales organization.[100]

With several new acquisitions to bring into the fold, the company's continuing growth necessi-

tated further reorganization at the executive level. Gerry Blouch was named chief operating officer (COO) and would report directly to Mixon.[101] In turn, the Rehab business units would report to Blouch in his new role as COO.[102] Lou Slangen, who had been president of the rehab division and vice president of sales and marketing, was named corporate senior vice president of sales and marketing. In this role, Slangen would be responsible for the Home Care, Canada, GSI, and International units.[103] Benoit Juranville, who joined Invacare with the Poirier acquisition, was named president of Invacare Europe.[104] In addition, domestic operations were reorganized into stand-alone business units.[105]

At management's annual meeting in November, Mixon said he wanted to continue spending time in Washington and "to be able to roam the company worldwide to visit our people [and] customers [and] keep my oil can out."[106] With the continual repositioning of management, Mixon was becoming free to do so.

Invacare introduced thirty-five new products in 1995, innovation that would be fueled by strategic acquisitions made later that year. These included PinDot Products of Illinois, which would augment Invacare's rapidly growing seating division. Here, Invacare products are on display at a 1995 Medtrade show, the home health care industry's largest trade show.

CHAPTER NINE

GAINING MARKET LEADERSHIP

1995–1997

We want to make Invacare the category brand in home health care just like Kleenex is with tissues.

—Louis F. J. Slangen, senior vice president,
sales and marketing

IN 1995 ALONE, INVACARE unveiled thirty-five new products at the Medtrade show, including the Action A-T adult wheelchair. The Action A-T offered tilt-in-space seating that helped improve posture and provide pressure relief. The company also introduced three new Avanti-brand seating products.[1]

Staying true to its expansionist philosophy, Invacare also continued to seek out acquisitions that would fill gaps in its market share, augmenting the One Stop Shopping program it had unveiled in the early 1980s.

In the first part of 1995, Invacare negotiated the purchase of three companies, the first of which was PinDot Products, a Northbrook, Illinois, company that designed, manufactured, and distributed seating products. PinDot president Michael Silverman and several other key PinDot execs stayed on in what was rapidly becoming a substantial Therapeutic Support Surfaces business unit.[2]

At the end of May, Invacare bought Patient Solutions, a San Francisco firm that made ambulatory fusion pumps.[3] With sales between $1 million and $2 million, Patient Solutions gave Invacare a new product line valuable to durable medical equipment home care providers who were moving into home infusion therapy.[4]

Less than a month later, Invacare paid $5.1 million in cash for Bencraft, a Birmingham, England, firm that made manual and power wheelchairs and seating systems. At the time of the purchase, Bencraft had annual sales of $10 million.[5]

A Sharp Sales Strategy

The gradual broadening of the product line was part of a greater strategy. Mixon wanted his salespeople to be able to both open new accounts and capture business from the competition. In Mixon's mind, however, it was existing customers that Invacare really should set its sights on. "I figure if you do a better job, create a better product, deliver it faster and more innovatively, offer better services, and have a better sales force—just keep improving—you distance yourself from the competition," he said.[6]

A company that offered the widest array of products across a large distribution network would logically have the most success. To facilitate the speedy delivery of this large inventory, Invacare instituted a more efficient, automatic shipping/billing system and structured pricing. "That was a huge milestone in the customer service arena," said Judy Kovacs, vice president of customer service at the time.[7]

In 1996, Invacare began to build a more cohesive brand image by consolidating brands and creating a new logo, shown here.

The wares offered by a typical Invacare territory business manager (TBM) included everything from a $25 bed part to a $10,000 power wheelchair. Because of this tremendous flexibility, Invacare's home care providers would spend less time talking to salespeople and more time talking to their own customers. They could also benefit from volume purchasing. As a result, said Ed Wissig, former chief executive officer of American Home Patient, a home medical products provider, Invacare is "easier to deal with [than Sunrise] because they bundle their operations. Negotiating is easier, and you maximize your margins better."[8] This constant push to create new sales reflected Invacare's intense, sales-driven culture.[9]

Although Invacare was clearly the industry leader in much more than the wheelchair market by the spring of 1996, Mixon intended to press on even harder. "I'm really asking each of you to stand about three inches taller in 1996 to put in that extra effort required to go from our current position of 'industry leader' to a position of 'market dominance,'" he told his sales force.[10]

Surprisingly, the competition didn't follow Invacare's lead for many years, possibly because it believed that no sales rep could ever be knowledgeable enough to provide service for a whole line of wheelchairs, patient aids, beds, and respiratory products. In 1995, however, Sunrise announced plans to change its sales approach to one more akin to Invacare's. *Sales & Marketing Management* spoke to a Sunrise sales manager, who first said that, "In a sense it is a concession to Invacare," but then added, "I wouldn't say it's a concession to Invacare as much as it is a concession to the customer."[11]

Of course, it's one thing to change an organizational chart to match the competition; quite another to capture the competitor's essence. But then, even Invacare saw beyond the hype. "It's just a rivalry; the customer is number one," said territory business manager Curt Simonds. "The Sunrise part is just a game we play."[12]

Expanding the Australasian Market Share

Still critical to its growing domination of the competition was Invacare's acquisition strategy, which resulted in five more purchases before the year's end. In late June, the company acquired the

first of two companies it would buy in Auckland, New Zealand, on which to build a base in the Asia/Pacific region.

In the years since the mid-1980s Taiwanese invasion of the wheelchair market, Invacare still faced Asian competition. By the new millennium, Taiwan and China would both be putting out "a very good product," said Lou Tabickman, president of Invacare's European operations. "In fact, we buy a lot of our components in China that we assemble in our own wheelchairs."[13] Remaining successful in the face of another Asian onslaught would depend on Invacare's ability to continue offering attractive, low-cost wheelchairs that provide functional value—something Invacare has become very good at, said Dale Nash, then director of standard manual wheelchairs.[14]

affluent Japan, Sparrow said that Asia's more economically developed countries, such as China, would gradually become more "quality aware" as their populations aged.[16]

To supplement its existing electric control manufacturer—Dynamic Controls—Invacare purchased Thompson Rehab, a manufacturer and distributor of manual and power wheelchairs with annual sales of $4 million, from Salmond Smith Biolab.[17] Invacare next added Group Pharmaceutical (GP Healthcare), already a distributor of Invacare products in New Zealand, to its holdings.[18]

Before 1995 was over, three more companies in three countries were added. Paratec AG of Basel, Switzerland, was purchased from Rainier Kuschall for a mixture of cash and stock. The "Top End" of Europe, Paratec sold wheelchairs for active users under the Kuschall name. The company would

The Australasian market, comprised mainly of small companies, was fragmented, in part because import licensing in Australia and New Zealand had been eased in the mid-1980s, decimating domestic manufacturing in both countries, said Ken Sparrow, managing director of Invacare's Australasian operation. As a result, many companies were importing from Asia and selling directly to the customer. With a proliferation of products lacking branding, the door was wide open for Invacare to "present a proper brand." "That's Invacare's future place in the sun," said Sparrow.[15]

A solid presence in the Australasian market would give Invacare an opportunity to build a strong base from which to expand into the Asian market in the new millennium. And, although the market for quality chairs seemed limited to more

Above: The Dynamic Controls office in Christchurch, New Zealand. Dynamic, one of Invacare's early Australasian purchases, would serve as a foundation for continued growth in that marketplace in the new millennium.

Center: To expand its presence in the Australasian market, Invacare supplemented its 1993 purchase of Dynamic Controls, a New Zealand manufacturer of wheelchair controllers, with the purchase of Thompson Rehab, a wheelchair manufacturer and distributor. Here Dynamic employees program a power wheelchair unit.

distribute Paratec's products through the company's European network.[19] The purchase would prove to be somewhat knotty, however, as Kuschall had already licensed the name for use by a U.S. competitor, said Tom Miklich. "We had the unique situation of building the brand in Europe, but not owning the brand in the U.S. or Australasia," he said.[20]

The company also added Medical Equipment Repair Service (MERS) of Sarasota, Florida, which sold repair and replacement parts for oxygen concentrators and other respiratory equipment in addition to its repair service.[21] Invacare already operated its own parts unit, Canyon Products, and would fold MERS into an expanded aftermarket parts unit. Finally, Special Health Systems, a Canadian designer and manufacturer of seating and positioning systems for wheelchairs, was acquired for cash.[22]

With PinDot and Special Health Systems added to its own Avanti products, Invacare had created a line of seating and positioning products to challenge market leader Jay Medical, a unit of Sunrise. "Invacare has decided it wants to be a player in the seating market," Michelle Ummels, Invacare's former marketing manager for seating, who joined the company from Special Health Systems, told a trade magazine. "We want to be the seating company of choice."[23]

Mixon believed the company could grow the seating business as it piggybacked seating and marketed products with its Action line of rehab wheelchairs.[24] Sophisticated gels and foams allowed seating makers to market products that could significantly reduce the pressure sores that often plagued wheelchair users. Equally important, managed care providers were finding they could sometimes avoid expensive treatment for tissue damage by paying for these systems.[25]

Building the Brand

With its growing family of products, Invacare began to feel the need for a more cohesive brand image and unveiled a plan that would ultimately consolidate the company's acquisitions under three key names. Bennett Rubin was named vice president of marketing and marketing services and was asked to undertake this task and to create a new logo. The problems, recalled Lou Slangen, senior vice president of sales and marketing, were

that product awareness was low in the general public's mind and that there was no category brand preference.

If a shopper goes into Wal-Mart in December, 60 percent of them have made up their mind about what men's electric shaver they will buy. It's Norelco. In the case of home care medical equipment [and] home health care products, there is no brand preference. The only way we can achieve that, of course, is by putting all the money and all the resources and everything we have behind one brand. We can't put it behind eighteen brands. There's not enough money for that. So we had to first consolidate all of these brands, which we had forty of at one point.[26]

It was determined that for 1996 and beyond, all seating products would carry the PinDot name; sports and other wheelchairs would be sold under the Action name; and the remaining home health care and respiratory equipment would bear the Invacare name.[27] In addition, these brand names would be used solely for products sold to home medical equipment providers, Invacare's primary sales outlet until January 1996, and different brand names would be used for products sold through retail outlets.[28]

This strategy of splitting its branding between the dealer network and retail outlets signaled a careful change in Invacare's approach to its market. Up until 1996, Invacare had sold primarily through home health care providers. However, the business was changing, and consumers were purchasing home medical equipment products like Invacare's in drugstores and other retail outlets. Around $50 million worth of home medical equipment was being sold through retail outlets, and that market was expected to grow to $500 million in five years.[29] To support this new branding strategy, the company published its first corporate identity and brand guidelines manual under the direction of Susan Elder, who was manager of corporate communications at the time.

This information, coupled with the results of a May 1995 survey of home care providers, convinced Invacare that it was now acceptable to sell through retail outlets. In a survey of more than one thousand of its ten thousand home care providers,

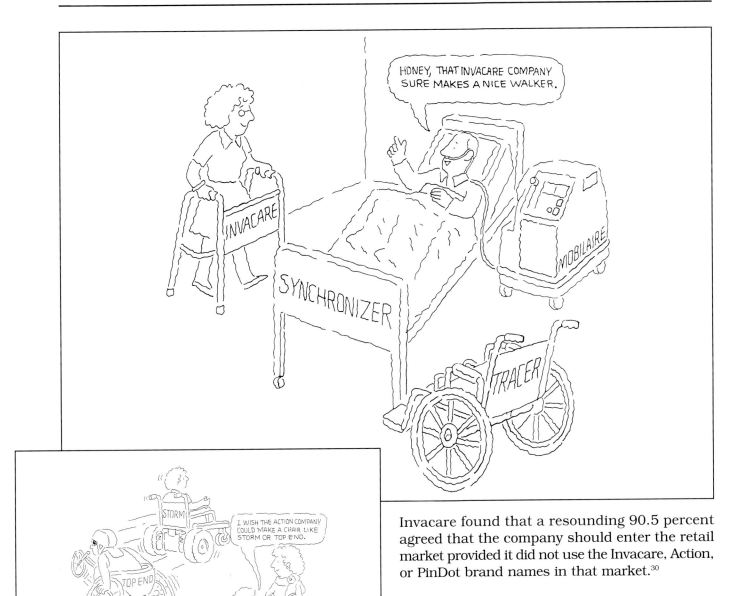

In the late 1990s, Invacare began to pare down its multiple brands in earnest in an effort to increase consumer awareness of its ever broadening product line. Consumers surrounded by Invacare products, as shown in these cartoons, did not recognize them as such because the company didn't have a cohesive branding strategy.

Invacare found that a resounding 90.5 percent agreed that the company should enter the retail market provided it did not use the Invacare, Action, or PinDot brand names in that market.[30]

The Retail Connection

The early part of 1996 was marked by additional acquisitions that would help Invacare in the retail marketplace. During the International Housewares Show in Chicago in January, the company announced that it had purchased Frohock-Stewart of Northboro, Massachusetts. It generated $10 million annually selling bath benches, wall grab bars, and other bath-safety products through retail outlets such as Home Depot. Invacare planned to combine its existing line of walkers, canes, and standard wheelchairs and beds with the Frohock-Stewart line.[31] Even with the results of its provider survey, however, Invacare did not enter this new territory without some trepidation.

ERNIE "THE ATTORNEY" MANSOUR

ERNEST P. MANSOUR, AN ATTORNEY who specializes in corporate law and litigation, has worked with Invacare since the early days of Mal Mixon's tenure. A principal with the forty-six-year-old Cleveland law firm Mansour, Gavin, Gerlack & Manos Company, L.P.A., Mansour has handled all of Invacare's litigation. "Each time over the years Mal has had a problem ... we've been able to get into it and get a result that was satisfactory," said Mansour.[1]

Mansour, Mixon, and Francis Joseph "Joe" Callahan were also partners in MCM Capital Corporation, a company they created to invest in small- and medium-size Cleveland-area businesses. Mansour's son, Mark Mansour, an accountant, is president of the company.

The firm's affiliation with Invacare began when Mansour was retained in the early 1980s to litigate a discrimination case filed after Invacare won a Veterans Administration wheelchair contract. Invacare was subsequently audited by the Office of Federal Contract Compliance (OFCC) as a matter of form. The claim alleged that the company had discriminated against African-Americans and females over a three-year period prior to the Mixon-led acquisition by not hiring them to work in the company's shipping and plating departments. When it looked as if Invacare would have to disburse back pay for those interviewees who were allegedly discriminated against, the company had two choices: sign an agreement with the government and pay a fee, or litigate.[2]

Callahan referred Mixon to Ernie Mansour. "Mansour said, 'I'll take the case, and I guarantee you won't pay a nickel.'" As it turned out, Invacare agreed to seek out those named in the case and to offer them a job if they were qualified and a position was available. But the company did not have to expend any money.[3] "Our investigation showed this [case] was completely without merit. [We] went ahead and litigated it and won the case," Mansour recalled.[4]

"My main concern is the reaction of the HME (home medical equipment) customer," Mixon told *HomeCare* magazine. "That's why we asked them what they would do. But we couldn't ignore the long-term effect of not entering the channel. The mass market would have developed with or without us."[32]

Through Frohock-Stewart, Invacare would sell its products under a new brand name—Aurora. "We wanted to select a name that clearly communicates that our products are lifestyle-oriented rather than exclusively health-related purchases," Invacare vice president at the time and Frohock-Stewart general manager Bennett Rubin told a trade magazine. "The Aurora name, which signifies a 'rebirth,' conveys a classy, elegant image and neutralizes the stigma that may be associated with buying health care products."[33]

At the time, said Miklich, Invacare did not want to compete with the Invacare brand in the dealer channel.[34] However, the company would soon change its mind about supporting multiple brands.

The move into retailing was challenging for reasons beyond the dealer market. For a long time, home care providers had not only provided information about and support for their products—a service

The year 1996 found Invacare selling items such as canes through retailers such as Home Depot and Wal-Mart—though under a different brand name, Aurora, so as not to compete with its own home care providers. The move was prompted by the purchase of Frohock-Stewart, maker of bath-safety products, which Invacare merged with its walker, cane, and standard wheelchair lines.

Mansour's services would again be needed as Invacare pitted itself against wheelchair giant Everest & Jennings (E&J). Said Mansour:

I think one of the more significant events of Invacare was the fact that, when Mal bought the company, it basically had one product—the standard wheelchair. He developed the plan to go after what they call the prescription wheelchair market, the power wheelchair.... At that time, his largest competitor dominated the market, and they were obviously concerned that Invacare was attempting to get in that market.[5]

As Invacare took on E&J, Mansour once again proved his value. "We had fairly strong evidence that Everest & Jennings was trying to choke us out of the market, which is an antitrust violation," Mansour recalled.[6] Invacare would also bring two patent lawsuits

against the company, and a beleaguered E&J would eventually settle all three suits for $1 million, thus setting the stage for Invacare's rise to the top. "I think that that was one of the key elements in Mal's bringing the company to where it is today. He broke their stranglehold on power chairs," said Mansour.[7]

Mansour and his team would also guide the company through several unsuccessful unionization attempts by the UAW and the USWA (1990 and 1998), as well as union issues in Mexico at the Invamex plant and labor problems at the Bridgend, Wales, plant. "It was the Steelworkers' bastion," said Mansour of the USWA unionization attempts in heavily unionized Lorain County. "They've come after Invacare to unionize time and again, and they've been rejected time and again."[8]

that would be absent in such places as Home Depot—they had also accepted third-party payments, such as those from Medicare. Obviously, most large retailers were unwilling to perform this service. Yet, according to Lou Slangen, senior vice president of sales and marketing, opportunities remained because the consumer was beginning to demand HME products.[35] Mixon told *Dow Jones Newswire* that he expected Invacare would begin offering everything from wheelchairs to canes in 350 Wal-Mart stores by the end of the year.[36]

Acquisitions Continue

As Invacare began its first push into retailing, it remained focused on its dealer business. In mid-1996, Invacare announced the purchase of Healthtech Products of St. Louis. Healthtech manufactured beds and furniture for nursing homes and other institutional users. It had sales of $28 million in 1995.[37] "With Healthtech, we will have a formidable product line that will address patients who have the same needs as home care patients, namely older people and people with disabilities, but whose care is provided in an institutional setting," Mixon said.[38] A few months later, Healthtech was renamed Invacare Health Care Furnishings.[39]

Shortly afterward, Invacare purchased Fabriorto Lda, of Oborto, Portugal, which manufactured and distributed manual and power wheelchairs, beds, and walking aids.[40] The purchase added another piece to Invacare's European operation, which included France, Germany, Spain, Switzerland, and the United Kingdom.

This purchase was soon followed by Product Research Corporation (PRC) of Beltsville, Maryland, which supplied repair and replacement parts for home medical equipment. The company generated

$8 million in annual sales. Mixon expected that PRC would expand the parts group that included Canyon and MERS, giving Invacare "the geographic and product-line diversity required to maintain and enhance its position as the market-share leader in aftermarket parts for home medical equipment."[41]

Finally, Invacare purchased Roller Chair Pty., of Adelaide, Australia, the leading Australian maker of power wheelchairs with $3 million in annual sales, swelling Invacare's Australasia unit, which already included Dynamic Controls, GP Healthcare, and Thompson Rehab.[42]

Still, Invacare's ever-growing international acquisitions created a new challenge for the company. Said Michael Devlin, former director of health care professional marketing and a native of Ireland:

Europe has some challenges that we just don't have in the United States. We can make one product and sell it anywhere in America. They make a product in France, and every country has got their own ... specifications for the product. So they have challenges that we don't face. As a result of that, the European technology has tended to stay there, and the United States technology has tended to stay in the United States.[43]

A New Home Base

With more to manage, the company's corporate staff had grown to eighty and was running out of office space in the busy wheelchair manufacturing plant on Cleveland Street in Elyria. In order to keep pace, it was necessary to run two shifts at the plant. "We had two shifts operating at full tilt, but when the orders really surged at the end of the quarter, we would get buried and just couldn't satisfy the demand," remembered Dave Piersma, former director of distribution for Invacare, who employed a new warehouse management system to improve the department's overall efficiency.[44]

Invacare had long anticipated the need for a new facility and had even included a new headquarters in its never implemented 1991 construction program. But now, after more than six months of study, the company decided to build a new, $5 million headquarters building next to its plant on Taylor Street. Plans called for a two-story, fifty-thousand-square-foot building that could be expanded to accommodate as many as 140 workers.[45]

At first, it looked like the senior staff would head east, into rented space in either downtown Cleveland or a suburban site near Cleveland

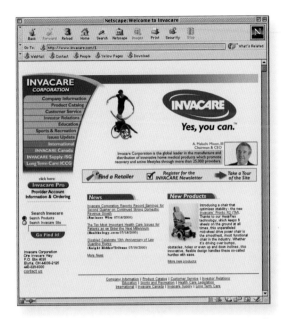

Above: The company undertook a virtual construction project in 1996: the building of its first Web site. Today, the company's Web site at www.invacare.com looks like this.

Opposite: Five years after Invacare first contemplated moving into new digs, the company began work on its much needed new $5 million headquarters. The address, One Invacare Way, is a play on Invacare always striving to be number one and to do it the "Invacare way".

Hopkins International Airport.[46] Mixon had wanted to raise the company's profile and be near hotels and restaurants for the convenience of visitors and clients.[47] In the end, however, he decided he wanted to remain within walking distance of the company's key manufacturing facilities.

"I sincerely thought at one point that we were going to Cleveland," he said. "The more we looked at it, the more sense it made to keep the head with the body."[48] He would later say that he thought the company "was not mature enough" to move top execs too far from its major manufacturing facilities.[49] The city of Elyria agreed to a tax-abatement plan that would save Invacare $580,000 in property taxes over ten years.[50]

Invacare's construction efforts also went beyond the brick-and-mortar variety. In June 1996, Invacare launched a Web site, said Susan Elder, who in addition to her role as manager of corporate communica-

tions, was also the company's first "Web Master." It included product information, company and wheelchair sports news, and customer service information, as well as an "issues update" section that answered questions about Medicare and Medicaid reimbursement and analyzed legislative issues.[51]

The Strategy Continues

By the end of 1996, the company had completed eight acquisitions that added annual sales of about $40 million.[52] In addition, near the end of the year, Gerry Blouch was named president and was elected to the board of directors, making him responsible for all company operations worldwide. Mixon remained active as Invacare's chairman and CEO.

Under Blouch, Invacare expected to continue its acquisition strategy—mostly in response to a changing industry. "The pressure on single-product companies to consolidate with bigger, financially strong, broad product line companies led to the number of acquisitions we were able to close this year," Susan Elder, the company's manager of corporate communications, told *Crain's Cleveland Business*.[53] Consolidation at both the manufacturer's level and the provider's level had increased.

The company had made those acquisitions that allowed it to expand regionally and to strengthen its product line—thus enabling Invacare to become an industry consolidator, reasoned Blouch. The trend, however, seemed to tend toward those acquisitions that eliminated competitors and added new technologies. "There clearly is an opportunity to consolidate not only among the majors, but new applications or synergistic technologies that support the products we have today," said Dave Johnson, vice president, operations and logistics.[54]

Although Invacare didn't have a lot of holes in its product lines, said Blouch, "Certainly on the radar screen there are candidates out there in a category where we're not a major player that give us the opportunity to buy share and become more dominant." However, as Invacare understood from its Everest & Jennings–dominated early years, that task is made much more difficult when a smaller number of competitors hold a greater percentage of the market share.[55]

For the next year, Invacare had no intention of letting up. Already it appeared that the move

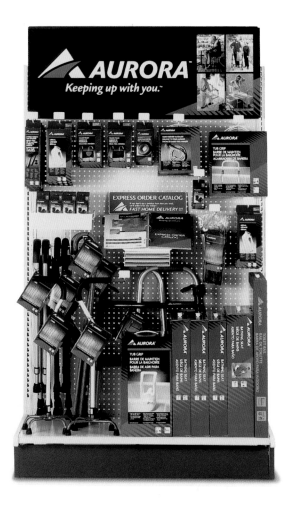

The brand name "Aurora" was chosen because it signified a "rebirth" and helped to neutralize the stigma many consumers felt when purchasing home health care products. This display, designed to help retailers display Aurora goods, shows the wide variety of products available under that brand name.

into retail was paying off. By the end of the first quarter of 1997, the Aurora product line—from canes to four-hundred-dollar wheelchairs—was now available in stores operated by Wal-Mart, Sears, J. C. Penney, and other large retailers. Mixon was estimating that retail sales, which were between $15 million and $20 million that first year, would hit $100 million in five to seven years.[56]

Retail selling was an expensive proposition, however. The company spent $1 million developing the Aurora product line. Part of that development entailed creating a strong name and learning about packaging and displays that would help the prod-

ucts to "sell themselves." Invacare also had to learn how to keep its broad product line on store shelves; the company eventually put together a retail catalog to fill in the inevitable blanks.[57]

Hostile Takeover Attempt

In 1997, still seeking more companies to fill out its product line, Invacare launched a takeover attempt of Healthdyne Technologies. On January 2, Invacare sent a letter to Healthdyne's board of directors with an offer of $12.50 a share, or $163 million. The letter also pointed out that Invacare already owned 4.9 percent of Healthdyne's stock,[58] which had been selling for just under $9 a share when Invacare made its offer.

Healthdyne appeared to be an excellent fit for Invacare's respiratory products line. "We were genuinely interested in them and thought they were a strong strategic fit," said Blouch.[59] Nearly half of Healthdyne's $120 million in revenue came from infant apnea monitors and adult sleep disorder products. Based in Marietta, Georgia, Healthdyne also made a line of respiratory products that would augment Invacare's existing line of oxygen concentrators, compressors, and nebulizers. "Healthdyne makes 80 percent of what Invacare doesn't," Mixon later told a reporter from a trade magazine. "The purchase will help Invacare to truly become a one-stop-shopping home care company."[60]

Healthdyne's board balked at the first offer, saying that the company could not respond until after its February board meeting.[61] Over the next few days, however, Healthdyne's stock began to drift higher, and Invacare decided to go public with its offer.[62] Almost immediately, Healthdyne responded publicly, saying it believed the offer was about 20 percent too low.[63]

The stock market agreed. Although Healthdyne stock had been trading at just under $9 a share at the time of Invacare's initial offer, it was soon trading at nearly $13 a share.[64] Over the next several months, the two companies fought a war of words and dollars. Invacare raised its offer first to $13, then to $13.50. Analysts predicted that it would take anywhere from $15 a share to $18 a share to snag the Georgia company.[65]

By this point, however, the bid for Healthdyne had become a hostile takeover attempt—never an easy battle to win. Healthdyne turned down all of the bids and mounted a vigorous defense that included legislative and courtroom attacks. In the Georgia legislature, it lobbied for a bill to change the way directors were elected. The new law would have allowed a shift to staggered election of directors, so that all directors would no longer have to stand for reelection every year.[66] Helping Invacare lobby the Georgia legislature were two lawyers with strong political backgrounds. One was Griffin Bell, United States attorney general under President Jimmy Carter, and the other was former Georgia governor George Busbee.[67] Both were lawyers with the large Atlanta firm of King & Spalding, which had been Healthdyne's law firm for sixteen years.[68]

The Georgia legislature declined to change the state's corporate law, which at the time made the annual election of directors the default practice. Invacare, by this time, through its tender offer, controlled 23 percent of Healthdyne stock and hoped to elect new directors at the next Healthdyne annual meeting.

When the legislative battle failed, Healthdyne and Invacare turned to the courts. Invacare first filed a shareholder suit in federal court to require Healthdyne to hold its annual meeting.[69] In June, Invacare raised its offer to $15 a share, $190 million in all. Said Mixon: "This substantial increase—made in the interest of bringing this unnecessarily drawn-out process to an end—represents our best and final offer for Healthdyne.... We do not intend to raise our price again."[70] However, securities analysts were still doubtful that the offer was high enough to pry enough shares of Healthdyne loose. One, Matthew Dodds, III, of Dillon, Read & Company, said the new bid "is still too low, but it does make things more interesting."[71] Healthdyne called the offer "grossly inadequate."[72] The company's stock rose to nearly $17 a share.[73]

The two companies continued to talk, but in August Invacare called off the takeover and

sold its Healthdyne stock. "We continue to be interested in acquiring Healthdyne, but we cannot wait around idly," Mixon told the press.[74]

Healthdyne was later bought by Respironics of Pittsburgh, which paid $370 million.[75] Respironics made competing products to combat sleep disorders.[76]

In 1997, Mixon and Blouch were disappointed when Invacare's bid for Healthdyne Technologies turned into a hostile takeover attempt. Healthdyne, which primarily manufactured sleep apnea and other sleep disorder products, would have been a good fit.

Healthdyne was worth more to Respironics than to Invacare, one analyst said, because it gave the combined company a stronger and possibly more profitable position in selling respiratory products and enabled Respironics to enter the asthma products market.[77]

In the end, however, the businesses did not integrate well, and Respironics' stock eventually "tanked." It was disappointing to the company, said Blouch, to have had a vision that in hindsight still looked "right" and strategically correct, and to lose for the wrong reasons. "I think we lost it more because of ego and pride than we did because it didn't make good business sense. I'm absolutely certain that the Healthdyne shareholders would have been far better off today if they had merged with Invacare."[78] On the other hand, said Blouch, "The hostile buyer, I don't think, would be well served by alienating the people that have created the value."[79]

Moving beyond Healthdyne

Though Healthdyne didn't make it into the Invacare family, the company looked to build its own sleep therapy business and continued to grow in other directions. In the company newsletter, Mixon laid out his plan:

We remain as committed as ever to offer a line of diagnostic and therapeutic devices for sleep disorders.

In addition to our need for a comprehensive product line, we also are working to correct a misconception in the marketplace. Although Invacare has the leading market share in the manufacture and distribution of oxygen concentrators, there are many HME providers who still do not recognize Invacare as a dominant respiratory company. A wider range of respiratory and monitoring products that delivers on our One Stop Shopping promise will change that perception.[80]

Expanding its share in the respiratory market with sleep apnea products and nebulizers would take some time. Even though the company would remain number one in the concentrator market in the coming years and would grow to number two in the nebulizer compressor market, it still had much room for market share growth. "We only have 10 percent of the market right now, total, if you look at the total respiratory marketplace," said Darrel Lowery, vice president, supply chain management.[81]

Outside of the respiratory sector, Invacare soon added Silcraft Corporation, a Traverse City, Michigan, company with forty employees and annual sales of $6 million. The company made and distributed bathtubs, barrier-free showers, and patient lifts, with which Invacare planned to augment its line of

Opposite: Expansion in the nursing home market was prompted by the purchase of Silcraft, which produced bathtubs, barrier-free showers, and patient lifts, including these products manufactured at its Michigan facility.

Left: The purchase of Suburban Ostomy Supply Company in late 1997 gave Invacare's diversification strategy a boost with the addition of seven thousand new products, such as soft goods.

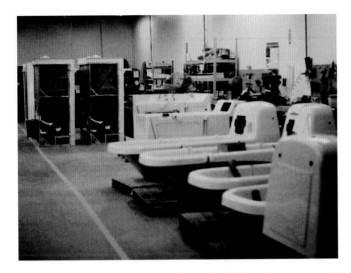

nursing home goods. "We bought Silcraft to expand the product line in the nursing home market to try to start positioning ourselves as one-stop shopping for nursing homes," explained Tom Buckley, former senior vice president of marketing.[82] Invacare planned to market the Silcraft line through its Health Care Furnishings division. The existing management would continue to operate in Traverse City.[83]

In October, Invacare paid cash for the stock of Allied Medical Supply Corporation of Ashland, Virginia. Allied, which expected to have sales of $10 million in 1997, was a distributor of wound-care products and other disposable and soft goods.[84]

Finally, as the holidays approached, Invacare announced another acquisition, this one the largest in its history. In December 1997, Invacare purchased Suburban Ostomy Supply Company of Holliston, Massachusetts, paying more than $131 million for the company.[85] Suburban Ostomy was a wholesaler of seven thousand disposable medical products that sold to twenty-three thousand home medical equipment suppliers, pharmacies, home health agencies, and other health care chains and managed care organizations.[86] Mixon believed that disposable medical supplies could represent as much as 20 percent of the revenue of their home care providers.[87] He later told shareholders:

Over the last five years, Invacare has successfully added new product lines through both internal development and acquisition in order to become the preferred supplier to the non-acute industry. In particular, in 1998 with the addition of Suburban Ostomy, we have now instituted Total One Stop Shopping,

the industry's broadest product line and an even more compelling reason to buy from Invacare.[88]

However, because Suburban, prior to Invacare's purchase, had made several acquisitions of companies that serviced home health agencies and also sold directly to consumers, the benefits of this purchase would be some time in coming, said Tom Miklich, CFO. "They didn't really understand those businesses," he said of Suburban's pre-Invacare purchases. "Right after we bought them, the Balanced Budget Act got passed. That hurt the home-health-agency business. So, we probably overpaid for Suburban, and we had to dispose of those two businesses."[89]

Invacare wasn't the only health care company looking to expand, although it was arguably the most successful. Industry consolidation continued as Graham-Field Health Products purchased Fuqua Industries. Fuqua included several home health companies, including Lumex, a wheelchair and hospital-bed maker, and Basic American, which made patient-room furnishings. A year earlier Graham-Field had acquired Everest & Jennings, meaning that Graham-Field now approached the size of industry leaders Sunrise Medical and Invacare.[90]

On the Rise

Invacare didn't need the additional competition to stay focused. Mal Mixon still believed in aggressive growth, both internally and externally. To this end, Invacare announced plans to expand its plant on Taylor Street in Elyria. The company planned to move its power chair manufacturing from Cleveland Street in Elyria and its Frohock-Stewart operation from Northboro, Massachusetts, into the expanded facility.[91] It won a small tax abatement for the project from the city of Elyria and agreed that it would add forty workers in the near future and thirty more over the next ten years. In the process, 130 associates moved from Cleveland Street to Taylor Street. In addition, during 1997 the operation of Healthtech (now Invacare Continuous Care Group) was consolidated into existing Invacare facilities to cut costs.[92] Healthtech, at one time part of a business owned by Everest & Jennings, had been purchased as an entrée to selling wheelchairs and respiratory equipment to nursing homes.[93]

Above: To further increase efficiency, Invacare would eventually separate its combination bed/respiratory plant in Sanford, Florida, by building a new respiratory plant in the same city.

Inset: Workers assemble beds at Invacare's manufacturing plant in Sanford, Florida.

The company also moved its Florida-based respiratory unit across town into a new one-hundred-thousand-square-foot Sanford facility.[94] Remarkably, Invacare made the move in just one day. "You can't have any service issues with your customers," said Darrel Lowery, who was the director of respiratory manufacturing at the time of the move. "Invacare can't go out and say, 'Sorry, we're moving our facility. We're going to be down for a couple of weeks.' "[95]

Previously, Invacare had been manufacturing its concentrators at a combination bed/respiratory plant, a modus operandi that "didn't work," said Blouch.[96] In keeping with Invacare's relentless pursuit of efficiency, bed production stayed where it was and respiratory got its own facility.

One to Watch

Even in the midst of its rough Healthdyne battle, Invacare was attracting attention because of

its phenomenal growth. *Financial World* magazine named Invacare to its list of one hundred top growth companies, ranking it seventy-eighth. The company earned the honor because of its strong record of sales and earnings growth over the previous five years and its increase in return on equity—an important measurement of management's use of shareholders' money.[97]

Then, in the spring, *Better Investing*, the magazine of the National Association of Investment Clubs, named Invacare to its "Top 100 for 1997" list, a measure of the number of investment clubs that own the stock and the amount of stock they own. Invacare was number sixty-eight on the list, meaning that 617 clubs owned 252,887 shares of Invacare stock.[98]

Winning in the Capital

Invacare was winning on other important fronts as well. That same year, the company won—if only on paper—a hard-fought legislative battle: the passage of the Consumer Choice Initiative as part of the Balanced Budget Act (BBA) of 1997. The BBA allowed Medicare beneficiaries to purchase home medical equipment with added features, even if the price of the equipment was higher than the Medicare reimbursement. "That's going to work out much better for people who make quality products," said

EASTER SEALS AND INVACARE

EASTER SEALS AND ITS CORPORATE PARTner, Invacare Corporation, share a common goal in their work with disabled children and adults: to provide products and services that make life better for these individuals. The two organizations also have Elyria, Ohio, in common, for it was in Elyria in 1885 that Winslow Lamartine Fay first founded the Fay Manufacturing Company—the company from which Invacare would develop. And it was in 1919 in Elyria that Easter Seals first began its philanthropic mission in its first incarnation as the Ohio Society for Crippled Children.

"Maybe that's why this match came about. We share a core vision of improving the quality of life for people with disabilities, and both organizations care deeply about the rights and empowerment of people with disabilities," said Mal Mixon in 1993, when the two organizations first teamed up to offer summer sports and recreation camps for people with disabilities.[1]

"Invacare Days" sports clinics offer campers the opportunity to have fun while learning sports such as wheelchair tennis, basketball, softball, and rugby, taught by Invacare-sponsored athletes like Rick Cooper, consumer marketing manager for Invacare, and Scott Law, Invacare endorsee. The camps not only introduce participants to a variety of sports and positive role models but also help campers build self-esteem and self-confidence.

"Invacare's commitment to Easter Seals' camping programs through its 'Invacare Days' clinics has brought wonderful new experiences to our campers and has made a world of difference in the lives of children and young adults with disabilities across the country," said James E. Williams Jr., president and CEO of Easter Seals. "It is a privilege to count Invacare and its team of wheelchair athletes among our supporters."[2]

Invacare and Easter Seals further expanded their relationship in 1994, when Invacare began providing both products and sponsorship to Easter Seals. "We provide a significant amount of products to various lending programs across the country so that people with disabilities who need products on a short- to medium-term basis and do not qualify for Medicare or Medicaid can go to Easter Seals and borrow them," said Susan Elder, director of marketing communications for Invacare and company liaison to National Easter Seals/former board member of Northwest Ohio Easter Seals. "We donate many types of home health care products from wheelchairs to beds to walkers, canes, crutches, and more." Through Invacare's donations, Easter Seals has provided needed equipment to hundreds of individuals. From 1994 to 2000, Elder estimated that Invacare had made donations of money, equipment, and in-kind services totaling $1 million or more.[3]

In addition to its "Invacare Days," Invacare also sponsors the Invacare 12-Hour Relay for Easter Seals, during which employees put together teams that walk, run, or roll in wheelchairs for twelve hours consecutively to raise money for local Easter Seals programs.

In the mid-1980s, Invacare joined forces with another Easter Seals corporate partner, ENESCO, maker of Precious Moments figurines, to promote a special figurine of a boy in a wheelchair. The figurine was made available to Invacare providers for a small donation, the proceeds of which benefited Easter Seals. "I still get requests every now and then from individuals wanting to know if we have the Precious Moments figurines," said Elder of the successful fundraiser.[4]

Invacare was again recognized by Easter Seals during its annual EDI (Equality, Dignity, and Independence) Awards for a 1998 ad campaign.

If all you want in
a chair is a place to sit,
buy a couch.

If you want a life, get
an Action wheelchair.
They're handcrafted
one chair at a time
from the same
high-performance
technology that's
made our Top End
chairs the choice of
champions everywhere.
They can take it. And
dish it out. Action
Superlites. Built for
life. Built for you.

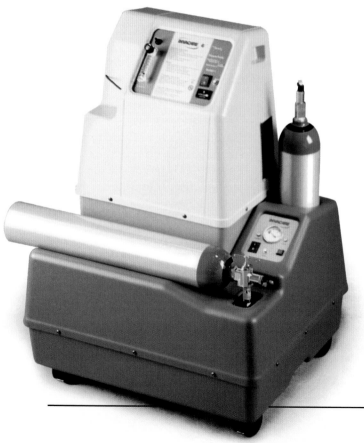

Above: In 1996, Invacare increased its brand visibility
with a new series of ads. This ad from an earlier campaign
demonstrates one in a series of strong, targeted print
pieces directed at wheelchair consumers.

Left: The Invacare Venture HomeFill complete home oxygen
system works in conjunction with a specially adapted
Invacare six-liter oxygen concentrator, allowing patients
to fill their own high-pressure oxygen cylinders.

Pat Nalley, retired vice president of sales for Invacare.
It "should be an incentive to make the best—not a
disincentive."[99] The act would also benefit Medicare
recipients, who could now reach into their own pockets to pay for the extras. Final rules are expected to
be published in May of 2001.

Invacare was recognized for its part in the passage of the Consumer Choice Initiative. "The industry owes a debt of gratitude to Invacare, and to its
president, Mal Mixon, who over the course of the
past seven years has spearheaded lobbying efforts

In one of several collaborative efforts with the National Easter Seals Society, Invacare partnered with ENESCO Corporation, which produced this 1996 Precious Moments figurine entitled "Give Ability a Chance" and donated the proceeds from the sale to Easter Seals. *(Photo courtesy ENESCO.)*

to gain Medicare beneficiaries their freedom of choice," said *HomeCare* magazine.[100]

It was an incomplete victory, however, as the BBA also cut payments for home oxygen services to three-quarters of prior levels and froze other fee schedules, eliminating cost-of-living increases.[101] Fortunately, Invacare was prepared to help offset the reduction in reimbursement for oxygen prod-

ucts. Almost immediately after the new law went into effect, Invacare introduced the Invacare Venture HomeFill complete home oxygen system, which was designed under the leadership of J. B. Richey. The HomeFill had a concentrator to draw oxygen from the air and a multistage pump that allowed patients to fill the high-pressure tanks they used away from home.[102] The innovation saved money not only for consumers but also for home care providers, who previously had to make a trip to deliver new tanks and pick up old ones.[103]

This product earned Invacare another EDI Innovation Award from Enterprise Development Inc. at Case Western Reserve University. The citation recognized the work of Richey and research and development manager Gerry Goertzen. The award noted that at the end of 1997, "Demand for the product exceeded supply."[104]

This honor was followed by one from National Easter Seals, which awarded Invacare and its advertising agency, Cleveland-based Bill Brokaw Advertising, with another of the society's "Equality, Dignity, and Independence (EDI) Awards," for "communications which boost the independence of people with disabilities."[105]

For Mixon, who had long felt that Invacare existed to fulfill a need for its customers, these were high words of praise and proof positive that the Invacare brand was growing in the right direction. What it chiefly needed, however, was further consolidation.

Invacare switched from the Nasdaq to the New York Stock Exchange (NYSE) on June 25, 2000, and marked the day with a celebration at the exchange, which included decorating the building's facade with the company's logo and banners of its sponsored athletes.

CHAPTER TEN

BUILDING A TRUSTED BRAND

1998–PRESENT

A product has features; a brand makes a promise.

—Louis F. J. Slangen, Invacare, 2000

ALTHOUGH 1997 WAS A GOOD year for Invacare on many levels, it fell somewhat shy of Mixon's aggressive projections. On one hand, sales had increased 5.5 percent to $653.4 million and income had increased almost 4 percent to $40.4 million[1]—the highest the company had ever reported.[2] But, as Mixon told employees in his annual briefing, estimates were partially off target because of a dramatic decline in sales to Apria Healthcare Group, a home health care dealer with annual sales of $1 billion.[3]

Apria had 350 outlets in fifty states, making it one of the largest companies in the business.[4] According to Mixon, Apria, which was created through the merger of Abbey Home Medical and Homedco, was having problems with the consolidation. The result was a decline in orders from $50 million to $20 million.[5]

Gerry Blouch, Invacare's president and chief operating officer, noted that Invacare's European business was also down, due to weaker currencies, insufficient cost cutting, and strong competition in Germany. Domestically, the liquid oxygen, infusion therapy, and retail businesses were falling short. Brightening the picture, Blouch reported, sales of wheelchairs, particularly power chairs in the United States and Kuschall chairs in Europe, were rising, and Invacare Canada reported record sales.[6]

The Vision

Mixon next unveiled a three-year strategic plan that would carry Invacare into the new millennium. First, Invacare would exit what Mixon called "nonstrategic businesses that were losing money." For example, he said, the liquid oxygen business was not profitable. In the future, Invacare would outsource liquid oxygen manufacturing.

Secondly, Invacare would hasten the consolidation of its manufacturing facilities. Recent acquisitions had left Invacare with too much redundant manufacturing capacity. This had to be rationalized and leveraged for Invacare to reap the rewards of its new size and capabilities. Mixon also wanted to accelerate the company's development of sophisticated ordering and customer service systems.[7]

Finally, Mixon announced that Invacare would continue to strengthen its brand name. In the future, he said, the company would convert its products to fewer brands and establish these as market leaders. In the end, Mixon announced a single strategic

At the dawn of the new millennium, Invacare worked to strengthen its brand recognition with a series of television direct-response campaigns for a variety of products, such as these scooters.

This impressive display at the 1998 Medtrade show demonstrated the breadth of Invacare's ever growing home health care and rehabilitative product lines.

vision: Invacare would become "the global leader in supplying durable and consumer products to the nonacute market."[8]

Shortly after making this speech, Mixon announced one of these guided initiatives. Already a leader in home care beds, Invacare would make inroads into the burgeoning sleep disorder therapy business, Mixon told the annual meeting of shareholders.[9]

If everything worked according to plan, Mixon expected sales to grow between 24 percent and 30 percent annually. As in the past, the company would rely partly on acquisitions, expecting fully half of this growth to come from acquisitions and the other half to be internal. Earnings would follow this ambitious upward climb, ranging from 17 percent to 20 percent growth annually.[10]

Taking Care of Home Care Providers

With the new goals in place, Invacare moved aggressively to further bolster its position with an even larger number of home care dealers. As the company had recently discovered, a reduction in orders from a single company the size of Apria could seriously damage its business. Hoping to avoid a repeat, Invacare looked to position itself as a primary or single-source supplier for a wide range of home health care products.

In January, it inked a deal with Apria extending an existing contract. Invacare had been Apria's single-source vendor for home care beds, oxygen concentrators, patient aids, standard wheelchairs, and other products, and its shared primary vendor of rehab products. The contract was expanded to make Invacare Apria's single source for lift-out chairs and shared primary vendor for low-air-loss therapy and compressed oxygen.[11]

Little more than a week later, it announced a deal to supply home care products to another giant home care provider, RoTech Medical, which had 699 locations in forty states.[12] Under the two-year agreement, Invacare would supply RoTech with 90 percent of its home care beds, standard wheelchairs, oxygen concentrators, and patient aids.[13]

In March, true to Mixon's earlier predictions, Invacare agreed to distribute ResMed Continuous Positive Airway Pressure (CPAP) devices for three years. ResMed's Sullivan-brand products are used to treat sleep apnea and other sleep disorders. Invacare would market the CPAP devices through its sales network to home care providers while ResMed would continue to sell through its own sales reps.[14] Invacare's entry into that niche had come late, and consequently the company was playing

catch-up. Said Darrel Lowery, vice president of respiratory products at the time,

We will to be a key player. We don't think we're going to gain number one market share overnight, but we're going to lay out some plans long-term so people will know that Invacare is definitely one of the top [manufacturers of sleep products] in the United States.[15]

At the same time Invacare was strengthening its relationships with home care providers, it was expanding its own role as a distributor. The company had long wanted to cover the entire home care medical equipment market, so it was only logical to expand on what was now known as Total One Stop Shopping—even if it meant selling someone else's products. Earlier that year, Invacare had won exclusive distribution rights to the Ferno Recline-A-Bath, a bathing system for institutional use that included an integral whirlpool. The new product, manufactured by Ferno-Washington, of Wilmington, Delaware, would be sold as a complement to Invacare's Silcraft line.[16]

The Best Employer

During this time, Invacare was targeted by the United Steelworkers of America (USWA) in a unionization attempt. This was not the first time. In 1990, the big union had tried to organize employees but was never able to gain sufficient support to hold an election. It took eight years before the USWA was ready to try again.

This latest attempt to unionize Invacare had nothing to do with its treatment of workers and everything to do with geography. Invacare's neighbors in industrial Lorain County included Ford Motor Company, U.S. Steel, and other automotive company suppliers. It was a heavily unionized area with a long tradition of union activity. Plus, the company was "one of the largest employers in Lorain County," said Larry Steward, former vice president of human resources.

Historically, you've had steel mills and auto companies—very heavy industry kinds of things ... represented by unions. Most of those industries are now under siege and aren't doing well. They're losing members left and right. So here's this plum employer sitting right here in Lorain County.[17]

Invacare, however, was not an easy target for unionization. When the union charged that Invacare's wages and benefits weren't competitive, Mixon simply pointed out that the company's average wage increase in 1998 of 4.5 percent was higher than the 2.7 percent awarded to union employees, according to the Bureau of Labor Statistics.

Furthermore, Invacare was known for its excellent worker relations—which extended all the way

ACQUISITIONS AT A GLANCE

1979
- Invacare, by Mal Mixon and his investor group.

1981
- Easley Medical Products, home care bed manufacturer (Sanford, Florida). These beds would carry the Mobilite name.

- Prime Aire, maker of oxygen concentrators (Hartford, Connecticut).

- Ortomed Aids, manufacturer of home health and rehabilitation products (Shannon, Ireland). Ortomed was founded as a joint venture with Denis O'Brien, a business executive.

1982
- American Oxygen, start-up manufacturer of industrial oxygen concentrators. Invacare acquired a majority interest.

- Lam Craft, manufacturer of laminated nursing home furniture and other institutional "case goods."

1984
- Carters (J&A), wheelchair maker (Bridgend, Wales) and Rajowalt/Carters Inc., maker of splints and other equipment for bone repair (Atwood, Indiana).

- Gunter Meier, small German wheelchair firm. Invacare bought an 85 percent interest in the company.

1989
- Invacare SARL in France, to act as a distribution company.

1991
- Canadian Wheelchair Manufacturing, wheelchair maker (Mississauga, Ontario).

- Canadian Posture & Seating Centre (CPSC), maker of seating products (Kitchener, Ontario).

1992
- Poirier S.A., France's largest wheelchair and lightweight wheelchair maker (Tours).

- Hovis Medical, (Mississauga, Ontario) which would become Invacare's Canadian sales representative and later unite with Canadian Wheelchair Manufacturing and CPSC to form the company's Canadian unit.

- Perry Oxygen Systems, maker of liquid oxygen products (Port St. Lucie, Florida).

1993
- Top End Wheelchair Sports, maker of sport wheelchairs (Pinellas Park, Florida). Top End would be merged with Invacare's Action line to form Top End by Action.

- Dynamic Controls, maker of electric controllers (Christchurch, New Zealand). Invacare had been buying its controllers from the company since the early 1980s.

- Geomarine Systems Inc. (GSI), maker of mattress systems (New York).

1994
- Rehadap, Spanish distributor of wheelchairs and other rehabilitation products.

- Genus Medical, Canadian manufacturer and distributor of motorized scooters and powered seating systems for power wheelchairs.

- Beram, distributor of wheelchairs and other rehabilitation products (Gothenburg, Sweden).

1995
- PinDot Products, designer, manufacturer, and distributor of seating products (Northbrook, Illinois).

- Patient Solutions, maker of ambulatory infusion pumps (San Francisco, California).

- Bencraft, maker of manual and powered wheelchairs and seating systems (Birmingham, England).

- Thompson Rehab, New Zealand–based manufacturer and distributor of manual and power wheelchairs.

- Group Pharmaceutical (GP Healthcare), New Zealand–based distributor of Invacare products.

- Paratec, a sports wheelchair maker (Basel, Switzerland).

- Medical Equipment Repair Service (MERS), seller of repair and replacement parts for oxygen concentrators and other respiratory equipment (Sarasota, Florida).

- Special Health Systems, a Canadian-based designer and manufacturer of seating and positioning systems for wheelchairs.

1996
- Frohock-Stewart, maker of home health care products such as bath benches (Northboro, Massachusetts).

- Healthtech Products, maker of beds and furniture for nursing homes and other institutions (St. Louis, Missouri). Healthtech would later be renamed Invacare Health Care Furnishings and Invacare Continuing Care Group.

- Fabriorto, manufacturer and distributor of manual and power wheelchairs, beds, and walking aids (Oborto, Portugal).

- Product Research, supplier of repair and replacement parts for home medical equipment (Beltsville, Maryland).

- Roller Chair, maker of power wheelchairs (Adelaide, Australia).

1997
- Silcraft, maker of bathtubs, barrier-free showers, and patient lifts (Traverse City, Michigan).

- Allied Medical Supply, maker and distributor of soft goods (Ashland, Virginia).

- Suburban Ostomy Supply, wholesaler of disposable medical products (Holliston, Massachusetts), renamed Invacare Supply Group in 2000.

2000
- Scandinavian Mobility International (SMI), one of Europe's largest manufacturers and distributors of bed systems and mobility aids for home care and institutional markets.

to the executive offices. "Most of my adult life and net worth are wrapped up in Invacare," Mixon wrote to employees.

> *I live, eat, and breathe Invacare. I take immense pride in the great company we have built together.... We are far from perfect, but we listen to our team members and pledge to continue to improve life at Invacare for everyone.*
>
> *But only by remaining competitive with a team that wants to win, can we remain the best employer in Lorain County.*[18]

Employees, said Steward, understood that "over the years, we've been very successful because of our ability to be flexible, and I think that once we all sat down and talked about that issue face to face, people understood that it was in our mutual best interests for our long-term growth to remain as is."[19] Invacare felt strongly that unionizing would hamper its ability to accommodate customers, who relied on the company's ability to provide them with the products they absolutely needed.[20]

Once again, the union was turned away. And once again, the union didn't give up. Little more than a year later, in late August, the United Steelworkers of America filed a petition for an election with the National Labor Relations Board. An election was scheduled for October 7.[21] Unlike the other attempts to organize, which were killed early, this organizing effort was successful enough in gathering signatures to bring the issue to a vote.[22] Out of 1,500 associates, 985 were targeted for the vote.[23]

Just days before the vote, however, two nonprofit groups, the Employers Resource Council, an employers' group serving northeastern Ohio, and Enterprise Development Inc., an economic development group, named Invacare among the ninety-nine best employers to work for in the region. They recognized Invacare's policies and programs in benefits and compensation, safety, health, diversity, recruitment and selection, training and education, and community involvement.[24]

In the end, the vote was 712 to 214 against unionizing. One worker interviewed after the vote succinctly summed up her coworkers' attitudes. "They've been good to us," said the associate. "I've never had a gripe. And I've never known anyone here to have a problem who man-agement hasn't tried to make happy again."[25]

It was also, said long-time employee and human resources generalist Jim Dowdell, a safe place to work. "Our people are important to us and we don't want them getting hurt," he said.[26]

The bottom line, said Gil Haury, retired director of the company's corporate test lab, is that Invacare is a good place to work. "People are very friendly, and everybody gets along very well. Everybody is focused on having the highest-reliability product for the value of the customer. There's no argument from anybody on that's what we want to get done."[27]

The unionization attempts did serve their purpose, however. "It's a good wake-up call for the company that we need to always keep on our guard and make sure we've got our ear to the ground and listen to associates, improve the environment, and do the best we can to be competitive in the industry," said Dave Johnson, vice president, operations and logistics.[28]

"I think it all gets back to this sort of Invacare work ethic where we never settle for second best in anything, whether it's technology, or the sales force, or our marketing efforts or anything," said Susan Elder, director of marketing communications. "There probably aren't too many companies that lead their industry and are as hard on themselves as Invacare

Above: Making Invacare a safe place to work has always been a priority for the company, said Jim Dowdell. Safety and job satisfaction may be two reasons that Invacare, located in heavily unionized Lorain County, has not been unionized.

Right: Susan Elder, director of marketing communications, said that the company's success lay in the fact that Invacare never settled for second best in technology, sales, or any other aspect of the business.

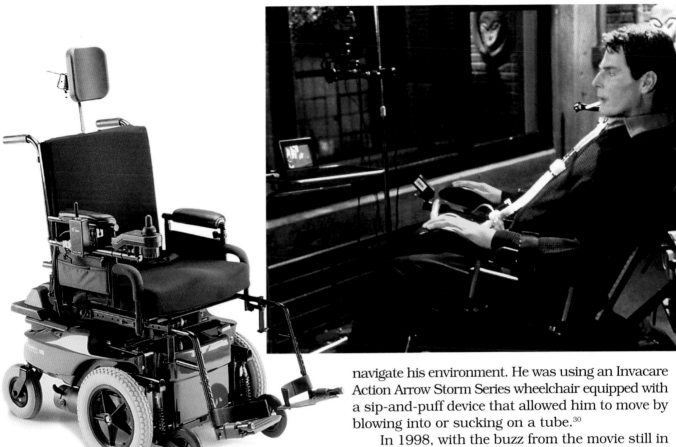

is, but it fosters a real environment of a lot of change and pushing real hard to improve constantly and continually—and it's just a lot of fun."[29]

Invacare Innovates:
The Gearless-Brushless Wheelchair Motor

When Mal Mixon predicted that half of the company's growth would come from internal development, he already knew that Invacare had an ace in the hole. The company's products included some of the most innovative on the market, keeping Invacare on the very cutting edge of home care and wheelchair technology. In fact, an Invacare wheelchair even became a minor celebrity in the 1998 made-for-TV movie "Rear Window," starring paralyzed actor Christopher Reeve. Although the movie, a remake of Alfred Hitchcock's classic motion picture starring the immensely popular activist actor, did not win overwhelming critical praise, reviewers were amazed by the technology that allowed Reeve to

navigate his environment. He was using an Invacare Action Arrow Storm Series wheelchair equipped with a sip-and-puff device that allowed him to move by blowing into or sucking on a tube.[30]

In 1998, with the buzz from the movie still in the press, Invacare introduced a product that *HomeCare* magazine said had the potential to revolutionize the wheelchair industry. It was a power wheelchair featuring a revolutionary gearless-brushless motor developed by J. B. Richey in conjunction with a Colorado-based company called Unique Mobility.[31] This superior motor would be available on the Arrow, Ranger X, and Storm Series of power wheelchairs.[32] The advantages of the gearless-brushless motor ran deep. Not only was it quiet and more efficient than existing systems, but the motor was less prone to wear, and it was easier to drive.[33] "I told Mal, 'Eventually, all wheelchairs

Above left: The Invacare Action Ranger II MWD power-tilt-system wheelchair is easily maneuverable.

Above right: Christopher Reeve used his own Invacare Action Arrow Storm Series power chair in the 1998 television remake of Alfred Hitchcock's thriller *Rear Window*. (© *ABC Photography Archives*.)

will be gearless and brushless. It's just the way things will go,'" predicted Richey.[34]

"You've got to be constantly pushing the edge of the envelope on enhancing what you do, how you do it, and how you support your customers with technology," emphasized Blouch. "If you're not doing that, you're dead."[35]

In the next year, Invacare would introduce its Solo "tilt-in-space chair," which helps prevent decubitus ulcers.[36] In the past, tilting often caused a chair to be unstable. To correct the problem, engineers made the wheelbase longer, which prevented tipping but restricted mobility. In engineering the Solo, Invacare improved the product without sacrificing mobility. "It's been a combination of manufacturing, marketing, design engineering, and thinking outside the box," said Neal Curran, vice president of engineering and product development, of the success of the company's most recent wheelchair innovations.[37]

Creating a Name

Generating internal growth was but one part of Mixon's three-year plan. Another important element was the creation of an Invacare brand name. Two years after Mixon's 1997 vision speech, Invacare still sold products under a host of brand names.[38]

In the beginning of 1999, however, Invacare began to pare down its portfolio in earnest, with the ultimate goal of having all products carry only the Invacare brand name. Thus the company's rehab wheelchair product line, Action, became a product name, and PinDot, its seating and positioning brand, became part of the Action series. During the transition, the Aurora name would be used for mass merchandising and the Suburban Ostomy name for distributed, disposable soft-goods products.[39] "Ultimately, however, the goal will be to have just the name Invacare on our cartons, said Lou Slangen, senior vice president, sales and marketing.[40]

"Up to this point in time," Mixon told a reporter, "as we grew, we put our resources primarily in product development, distribution, building our manufacturing facilities and making sure that we could

Neal Curran, vice president of engineering and product development, helped to fuel the company's most recent wheelchair innovations.

GETTING RID OF THE GRIND

THE DEVELOPMENT OF THE POWER wheelchair has been a godsend for individuals whose disabilities prevented them from operating a manual chair. Prior to 1999, however, power-chair users had to accept a trade-off in the inherent negatives associated with conventional geared motors.

That all changed with the introduction of the veritable stealth motor by Invacare in 1999: J. B. Richey's ingenious gearless-brushless motor. Richey developed the motor over a five-year period in conjunction with Unique Mobility, a magnet motor manufacturer based in Golden, Colorado.

Considered the wave of the future, the gearless-brushless wheelchair motor is a cleaner, quieter, and more durable motor than its noisy predecessors. Although the technology is relatively new to the wheelchair industry, it's actually been used in everyday equipment such as photocopiers and washing machines for more than a quarter of a century.

meet the demands of our customers. We have a great reputation within the sales channel, meaning that our provider-customers know who we are, but consumers really don't know Invacare."[41]

Actually, Mixon wanted to reach more than the users of his products. He saw the brand as something that also would stick in the minds of the people whom the consumers relied on. "More and more the (purchasing) decision is made by the caregiver," he told another reporter. "So if your grandmother or mother needs a wheelchair, I want you to know about the Invacare brand because you're the one who will be choosing it."[42] Moreover, said Slangen, it was about raising awareness, comfort levels, and familiarity—to bring Invacare to the level of a category brand.

When you think of baby powder, you think of Johnson & Johnson. When you think of home health care products, you think of Invacare. That's

Bottom: The right wheelchair can be a liberator, allowing the consumer to pursue an active lifestyle. Here tennis players check out the competition during a match at the Invacare-sponsored Florida International Wheelchair Tennis Championship, held in Boca Raton in April 2000.

Inset: World women's tennis champion Daniela DiToro of Australia takes a break during the championship. She is using an Invacare Top End T3 Tennis Elite wheelchair.

THE MEANING OF INVACARE

FOR INVACARE, THE END OF THE 1990s brought a renewed focus as the company strived to hone its image with one brand. In 1998, the company embellished its existing logo by placing it onto an elliptical medallion. In a brochure titled "The Meaning of Invacare," the company explained its name and new logo.

Our name

The Invacare name combines two important features of our can-do personality—innovation and health care. When you combine the power of innovation and care, the result is Invacare.

Innova**t**ion + Health **Care = Invacare**

Our colors

The Invacare logo appears in white on a strongly contrasting blue field, displaying strength and determination with a sense of well-being and calm. The white logotype is straightforward and honest, conveying clarity of purpose. Blue is a cool color that implies truth, responsibility, and trust. This color scheme conveys a confident, trustworthy company.

Our logo

The Invacare logo combines the equity of the name with a pair of arcs that express vitality, energy, and an encompassing embrace. These elements are contained in an elliptical medallion that signifies excellence and accomplishment. Altogether, this logo conveys the global vision and achievement appropriate for the world's leading manufacturer and distributor of nonacute health care products.

Our tag line

Our tag line, "Yes, you can," conveys the promise of the Invacare brand name and expresses our can-do personality. It is positive and upbeat and expresses our commitment to providers, health care professionals, consumers, and associates to help them accomplish whatever is important to them.

the journey we're on, and there, of course, [is] the whole issue as society is changing. Now that they are more accepted, [home health care product users] have the perception that "I can go on with my life."[43]

To help the company begin its brand journey, Invacare created a new logo that was built upon the existing version that featured the Invacare name in blue against a white field, braced above and below by a pair of blue arcs. Now the colors would be reversed. The field would be blue and "Invacare" and the two arcs would be white. The logo was further enhanced as a raised, three-dimensional medallion that could be affixed to products. The medallion, chosen for its intimation of excellence and accomplishment, would have the arcs and name in silver.[44] "In its new format, the Invacare logo would symbolize the global vision of the world's leading manufacturer and distributor of nonacute home health care products," said Elder, who introduced the new logo.[45]

Invacare also added a new, upbeat tag line—"Yes, you can"—that epitomized the company's "can-do" attitude. And Mixon, the helmsman who had urged the company forward to success and who was well recognized within the industry, became Invacare's spokesperson for this new campaign. "The most visible person in the home health care industry is Mal. So one of the things our [ad] agency came up with is that we make Mal the spokesperson in all of our trade advertising," said Slangen.[46]

THE E. P. NALLEY AWARD

MENTOR TO MAL MIXON LONG BEfore joining Invacare in 1980 as an international manager, E. P. "Pat" Nalley endures at the company through the E. P. Nalley Award of Sales Excellence. Established in 1991 upon Nalley's retirement, it honors those employees who live up to Nalley's exacting standards for consistent gain and performance and never accept a "No," as well as being

- Aggressive
- Competitive
- Enthusiastic about their job, their company, and life
- Willing to "bust through the roadblocks" and "bleed Invacare blue" and
- Willing to stand up for the company and their associates

To be nominated for the award, candidates must have been with Invacare for eight years or more and must have met or bested their sales goal in the year they are nominated by their regional manager. Past winners include

- 1991 Gil Cash
- 1993 Gary Brown
- 1995 Ken Mikuls
- 1997 Alan Archer
- 1998 Mark Hill
- 1999 Dean Olejniczak
- 2000 Tom McGrenery

Tom McGrenery, territory business manager, was the 2000 recipient of the E. P. Nalley Award of Sales Excellence. He is shown with Mike Parsons, vice president of North American sales (left), and Pat Nalley (right).

In 1996, it was a natural decision to make Mal Mixon, long recognized by the industry for his leadership, Invacare's spokesperson for a new series of ads, including these.

In an earlier brochure titled "The Meaning of Invacare," Mixon recounted the company's early years, when a can-do attitude was all it had to grow on:

In 1979 when I assumed leadership of Invacare, I was faced with a constant string of challenges. "Where are you going to get the money?" "How are you going to do that?" Over and over, I encountered discouraging voices telling me "You can't do it." But somewhere inside me, a stronger voice said, "Yes, you can."

That's how much I believed in the people at Invacare. That's how strongly I believed that this company could make a difference.[47]

The new tag line emphasized that, with Invacare, consumers, health-care professionals and providers now had choices and the means to make their goals a reality. Slangen summarized the campaign:

It's all "Yes, you can." Yes, you can go on with your life, for the consumer. For a provider, it is yes, you can run your business with Invacare products and programs. For a health care professional, it is yes, you can take care of your clients with Invacare products.[48]

Moreover, the campaign was intended to help remove the stigma many consumers still felt when purchasing home health care products, such as scooters and wheelchairs—no matter how much they really needed them. "A lot of people first have to go through the psychological move of accepting the fact that they've got to want the scooter," said Slangen.[49] Paraplegic author Gary Karp agreed in his book *No Pity*.

Choosing a wheelchair is not an especially pleasant process, particularly if you are facing it for the first time.... But the right wheelchair is a liberator, not a prison. When you choose the right chair, your quality of life increases dramatically.[50]

Part of the hurdle is psychological, but the other part is societal. Fortunately, attitudes are beginning to shift, gradually chipping away at the well-worn stigma, allowing those with disabilities to look beyond the psychological paralysis some face in having to use a wheelchair, scooter, or other health aid, and to move forward with their lives in the "Yes, you can" fashion.[51]

Invacare next initiated television and print advertising campaigns as part of its multimillion-dollar Marketing Advantage Partnership (MAP) program aimed at increasing both product and brand awareness. The company's initial ten-market television campaign, called Direct Response Television (DRTV), would feature a series of spots that targeted seniors and focused on scooters and power chairs.

In keeping with Invacare's practice of taking care of its providers, the ads were run in markets in which participating Invacare providers received all of the leads generated from the consumers calling in to request product information. Invacare's MAP program also gave another nod to its provider network. Through its cooperative advertising program, providers could place ads themselves and Invacare would shoulder part of the cost.[52]

In addition, Invacare upgraded its Web site (www.invacare.com). By 2000, the company would have five sites—live or in various stages of development, one for each of the company's business units: its corporate site; The Aftermarket Group (TAG); Invacare Continuous Care Group (ICCG); Invacare Supply Group (ISG, previously Suburban Ostomy); and Invacare Canada. "The challenge is to make sure that we are using the most cost-effective technology to meet Invacare's needs and remain strongly competitive in our market space," said Dave Pessel, former chief information officer (CIO).[53]

As Invacare's name recognition began to mount, Mixon dryly observed to a reporter that "it's very expensive to build a brand."[54] Slangen told another reporter that Invacare spent about $3 million in 1999 on the new advertising and planned to spend another $5 million in 2000.[55] In total, the company reported advertising expenditures of $17.4 million in 1999, compared with $13.4 million in 1998 and $10.4 million in 1997.[56]

The reward for these expenditures was evident, said Slangen, when a provider survey indicated that "even in products where we do not have the number one market share, people perceive Invacare as the number one brand."[57] In fact, one of Invacare's ad programs won an award at the Easter Seals 10th annual Equality, Dignity, and Independence (EDI) Awards. The ad, prepared by Bill Brokaw Advertising of Cleveland, received honors in the print category.[58]

DELIVERING EFFICIENCY

IN AN EFFORT TO FURTHER SUPPORT ITS home-care providers, Invacare Supply Group (ISG—formerly Suburban Ostomy, which Invacare purchased in 1997) in 2000 began offering Home Delivery Plus. This service enables Invacare, which has been managing direct-to-patient home deliveries for more than a decade, to help home care providers sell supplies and meet patient needs while making a profit. Helping its home care providers maximize potential with existing customers and cut costs has always been an Invacare goal. And, in an age when profitability has become difficult, Invacare says, "Don't get out, get smart," said Mike Perry, vice president of distributed products, who joined the company in 1981.

"We've been doing home delivery for a lot of years, but based on what's going on in the supply end of the home health care providers business, there's a need for the home health care dealer to be more efficient in the way he operates," he said. "Home Delivery Plus allows us to cost-effectively handle the transaction of the supply product directly to the patient on behalf of the provider and in the provider's name. We save them between $1 and $2 per transaction, and we save them the approximately 20 percent per year associated with inventory costs."

Invacare handles the storing, picking, packing, and shipping of items; there are 15,000 to choose from, and Invacare, shipping from seven distribution centers, can cover 95 percent of the U.S. population in 48 hours and 55 percent in 24 hours. The company also uses an innovative Disease Management Marketing Program to suggest helpful companion products with each order on a personalized card that includes the provider's information. Invacare has further evolved the program to give the provider all the documentation needed for billing based on HCFA requirements.

In addition to on-line ordering capability, Invacare also offers special information on the Home Delivery Plus service at the company's Web site, www.invacare.com.

"It's marketing for the dealer—and it's paying for itself," said Perry.

Home Delivery Plus is yet another way the company is taking care of home care providers, said Mike Perry, vice president of distributed products for Invacare.

By year's end, Invacare's newly constructed Elyria headquarters received the American Institute of Architects Ohio Design Award. Designed by Van Dijk Pace Architects of Westlake, Ohio, the building was honored as a "deceptively clever project that makes a distinctive architecture out of what could have been a limiting constraint of adherence to a strict economy of means."[59]

In many ways, the new building was symbolic of Invacare's rise. It was bold and unique and had been created from the ground up.

Raising Its Business Profile:
The NYSE and Scandinavian

In conjunction with the advertising campaign, Invacare moved to strengthen its standing in the business community. A long-time member of the Nasdaq stock exchange, Invacare announced in 2000 that it planned to switch to the New York Stock Exchange (NYSE). To accommodate the move, Invacare's ticker symbol was changed from IVCR to IVC. Mixon and his daughter, Elizabeth Ewig, rang the bell to open trading on June 25, 2000, and on Wall Street, in front of the Exchange, the company sponsored a wheelchair basketball demonstration by the Dallas Wheelchair Mavericks, the

National Wheelchair Basketball Association champions, and a concert by Van Gogh, the world's only wheelchair rock 'n' roll band.[60]

Just days after its debut on the NYSE, Invacare launched another acquisition attempt, this time aiming at Scandinavian Mobility International A/S (SMI), a leading maker of wheelchairs and patient beds in northern Europe. Unfortunately, Invacare was not the only company interested in Scandinavian and had to bid against an existing offer from Nordic Capital. Invacare's initial offer of $131.3 million was 25 percent higher than Nordic's,[61] leading the European company to counter. Invacare then came back with an offer of $146 million and clinched the deal.[62]

Scandinavian was an important acquisition for Invacare, nearly doubling the size of the company's European operations.[63] It made Invacare the largest manufacturer of home medical products in Europe and enabled Invacare to consolidate some of its European manufacturing facilities.[64]

"I think it was strategically a great acquisition for us to make because whereas Invacare was strong in the central European countries and the southern

Above: Mixon and friends celebrate the listing of Invacare as IVC on the NYSE. Shown, left to right, are Ernie and Lois Mansour; Christine Vadini; William Johnston, NYSE president; Mal Mixon; his daughter, Elizabeth, and her husband, Alex Ewig; Tom Miklich (hidden); Mixon's wife, Barbara; and Susan Elder, director of marketing communications for Invacare.

Below: Members of the Dallas Wheelchair Mavericks of the National Wheelchair Basketball Association pose with Mixon and William Johnston, NYSE president. The Mavericks were on hand to perform at Invacare's June 25, 2000, opening on the NYSE.

Above: Left to right, NYSE president William Johnston, Mal Mixon, and Tom Miklich, Invacare CFO, at opening day on Wall Street.

Below: Invacare-sponsored Van Gogh, the world's only wheelchair rock 'n' roll band, helped the company to celebrate its stock exchange move with a concert performance.

countries, Scandinavian Mobility was strong in the Nordic countries. So, from a geographic perspective, it was a good marriage because we were basically a wheelchair company in Europe," said Kathy Leneghan, corporate controller and former finance director for Invacare's European operations.

We'd do patient aids as well as concentrators, but Scandinavian Mobility had a full bed range, which we did not have in Europe. We had it domestically, but not in Europe, and they also had wheelchairs—both power and manual—but they were in different segments in the market. So, there wasn't a lot of redundancy from a product perspective with the consolidation.[65]

Essentially, Invacare in Europe at the time was in the same position that it had held in the United States in the early 1980s. Internally, however, the SMI acquisition didn't affect the U.S. operation very much. The North American and the European operations tended to function autonomously. The one trick was to make sure the company could "get those synergies, get the efficiencies in the operation, rationalize the product line and bring these people more into the Invacare mold," said Lou Tabickman, president, European operations.[66]

In spite of the necessary differences, Invacare wanted to begin establishing a common work culture, said Larry Steward, former vice president, human resources—one "that is Invacare."[67]

Whenever we make acquisitions, we really try to bring those acquisitions into the Invacare fold because we think that we've been highly successful in terms of how we've been able to manage our businesses here in the States as an example, and we think that our culture is one that helps us be as successful as possible. So we're a very meat and potatoes, hard-driving kind of company that's focused always on being the best, being number one in whatever product line we're engaged in, and we're trying to get all of our associates worldwide to think and act in that way.[68]

New Goals for the Future

Just past the millennium, Invacare was in an interesting position. In some ways, its history

WORLDWIDE VISION

TO DESIGN, MANUFACTURE, AND DELIVer the best value in medical products which promote recovery and active lifestyles for people requiring home and other nonacute health care.

VALUES

Customers
Serving the customer is our principal reason for being in business. Our customers include providers, health care professionals and consumers. We are committed to consistently exceeding their needs and expectations.

People
People are Invacare's most valuable resource. Our culture empowers and rewards people as part of a team that enjoys competition and winning.

Innovation
We will be the market leader in product and service innovation, resulting in improved ways to manage our growing business.

Quality
We are committed to applying Six Sigma quality management discipline to everything we do, from how we design and manufacture products to how we serve our customers. Through continuous improvement, we seek to achieve world-class quality.

Citizenship
We conduct our business worldwide in a legally, ethically, socially, and environmentally responsible manner. We accept leadership responsibility in all communities where we live and work.

Shareholder Value
Maximizing shareholder value while observing Company values will discipline our actions.

GOALS

People
- Develop and maintain outstanding associate relations in all operations by putting people first.
- Become a model for equal opportunity employment in hiring and promotion practices.
- Become a preferred employer for people with disabilities.
- Develop outstanding leaders who manage with a strong sense of urgency, decisiveness, compassion, responsibility, and accountability.

Financial
- Sustain annual internal sales growth of 50 percent above the industry growth rate.
- Achieve total revenues of $2 billion by the year 2005.
- Consistently achieve annual earnings per share growth of 15 percent.
- Target debt-to-total capital to be 40 percent.
- Exceed inventory turns of ten by the year 2005.
- Develop and implement annual RONAE targets for each business group company-wide.

Strategy

- Design, manufacture, and deliver innovative, technologically superior products to meet customer needs.
- Offer the industry's broadest product line to home care providers and nonacute institutional providers.
- Achieve a leading market share position in each major product category in which we participate.
- Focus sales and marketing on the nonacute care market.
- Build an Invacare brand preference with consumers for our products through creative pull-marketing communications and public relations programs.
- Influence providers to present Invacare as the preferred brand through superior customer service, innovative provider support programs, and aggressive product line extension.
- Build a strong referral base among health care professionals who influence the purchase of our products.
- Develop the best electronic data interchange (EDI) programs for our customers.
- Hire the best people, our greatest resource, and empower them to seek continuous improvement throughout all facets of the business.
- Establish authority for action at the lowest possible organization level, with clear accountability for specific goals and objectives which complement the Company's strategies.
- Recognize and reward associates for achievement of specific, measurable objectives and superior financial performance.
- Advocate political and societal change to mainstream and gain employment for people with disabilities. Maintain a high profile in wheelchair sports activities.
- Drive Six-Sigma quality management throughout the organization and, at a minimum, maintain ISO 9000 status in all facilities.
- Leverage our expertise in the design, manufacture, and distribution of superior goods for the the nonacute marketplace into all major developed markets worldwide.

stretched back almost 150 years—yet in other important ways, the company was only twenty-one years old, for that was when Mal Mixon led the leveraged buyout of the tiny wheelchair manufacturer from Johnson & Johnson and began a two-decade-long growth strategy that turned Invacare into not only the largest wheelchair manufacturer in the world but the largest home health care medical products company as well. By 1999, it was clear that Invacare would very soon surpass an important milestone: $1 billion in annual sales. And, when an aging population and the continued downward pressure on medical costs were taken into account, it appeared likely that Invacare's future growth would be unlimited. In fact, after taking more than a century to earn its first billion, the company's new goal was to reach $2 billion by 2005.

"I think it's a nice milestone," said Mixon. "In the first 21 years of my running the company, it's grown from $19 [million] to $1 billion." In that time Invacare had worked to build a better product, to deliver it faster, to make it affordable through financing programs, and to expand its product line to offer One Stop Shopping. Beyond selling customers a product and delivering it on time, Invacare sought to create a partnership. "We want home care providers to say, 'Invacare not only makes and delivers the best products in the industry, they help me get business— they create business for me,' " Mixon emphasized.[69]

Invacare, said Dan T. Moore, III, board member and one of the original Invacare investors, had finally arrived.

Is it a complicated product? Not particularly. Do we have an innovative sales organization? Absolutely. It would be almost impossible for someone to replicate that.[70]

Now that the company had established itself and could afford to do so, it was time to build a single brand that would be recognized and trusted by consumers worldwide. In 2000 and beyond, all products from soft goods to power wheelchairs would bear the Invacare logo. "We don't believe any of our other competitors have the financial resources to do this," said Mixon. "So it's certainly a major part of our future."[71]

As part of this goal, Invacare in 2000 began work on an extensive new Web site that would not only educate consumers about various medical conditions through content provided by the world-renowned Cleveland Clinic, but also suggest applicable Invacare products and link consumers directly to providers.

The revamped site will also provide personalized content for providers, clinicians, and investors.

"When somebody visits our Web site, they'll be called by name and will be shown pages, based on their profile, that we think they'll be interested in seeing," said Steve Neese, vice president of e-commerce. "Most Web sites out there in the medical devices industry are just basically static pages of information. So we're moving to this dynamic model. The idea is that people get exactly what they want."[72]

In addition to its e-commerce initiatives, Invacare sought to build name and product recognition on an international level: Invacare's millennial goal was to enter all major developed markets worldwide. "When we purchased Invacare, it was selling only in the United States," Mixon recalled.[73] Although Invacare today is a significant player with number-one market share in the United States, Europe, and Canada, the company hope to see further expansion and solidification of its position as the premier designer, manufacturer, and deliverer of home health care products worldwide.

In the past, a combination of shrewd acquisitions and integration, as well as innovative product engineering under the direction of J. B. Richey and Neal Curran, had fueled the company's devel-

Above: In 2000 and beyond, Invacare is taking technology to the next level by creating dynamically driven Web pages that offer custom content tailored to each individual Web-site visitor, said Steve Neese, vice president of e-commerce.

Right: Providing the customer with a high-quality product in a timely manner is one efficiency measure that has always served Invacare well, according to John Dmytriw, senior operations director.

opment. Both strategies would continue to form the basis of Invacare's growth model, but the company would now place a special emphasis on aggressive product development. To fund this program, Invacare would cut costs and then funnel the savings into a three- to five-year initiative geared to foster the development of more innovative products and technologies.

"We want to go back to what we really think made us great, and that is innovative product development," said Mixon.[74] To fund this project in the face of continued government reimbursement issues, Invacare would employ the cost-cutting strategies that had served it so well during the early, tumultuous years when the company struggled for efficiency. "The way we keep it simple for all of us is to continually focus on the same three themes, namely, quality, delivery, and cost," said John Dmytriw, senior operations director.

We always want to make the product with the highest possible quality to keep our returns down, to keep our customers satisfied, because if you don't have a good quality product, it doesn't matter what it costs. We're always pushing for faster delivery of our products because people want them as fast as they can get them. As for cost, we have emphasized flexible automation with computerized controls to minimize tooling costs and maximize efficiency.[75]

In 2000, Invacare was spending a little less than 2 percent of sales on product development, a figure it hoped to triple by 2005. "If we could go from $20 million to $60 million in product development over the next five years, I guarantee you that we'd be a force to be reckoned with because nobody else can really do that," said Mixon.[76]

At the center of this new vision was Mal Mixon, both the guiding force behind the market strategy and the business mind behind the acquisitions. Honored at the end of 1999 by *HME News* as one of the ten most powerful people in the home medical equipment industry, Mixon had been called "a charging buffalo" and a man with "energy and vision" who is not hesitant to take on big challenges.[77] Mixon was all these things and more.

Thanks to his persistence and determination, Invacare had grown significantly, changing the face of the home health care industry and guiding government legislation along the way. This was just the sort of legacy that Mixon hoped to create for Invacare, long after the company passed the $1 billion mark in 2000.

Looking back over the company's phenomenal growth and success, Invacare could truly be called an American entrepreneurial success story, one that literally started with nothing.

"It's about innovation and intelligent risk taking and good people getting it done. We've always been driven by excellence, by being the best. Second best is something that never enters our mind. When I pass the baton of leadership in a few years, I am confident the groundwork has been laid to create a major corporation over the next twenty years. I am confident that Invacare will someday be a *Fortune 500* company."[78]

With Invacare's new objective of reaching $2 billion in sales by 2005, Mixon's goal seemed more attainable than ever. To reach it, the company would work to increase sales by 10 to 12 percent per year, and earnings by 13 to 15 percent. "We believe our "Yes, you can" approach to doing business will allow us to achieve continued growth and further shareholder value," said Mixon in 2001.

It was an approach that had served the company well for more than two decades. The "Yes, you can" philosophy is one that forms the very fabric of the Invacare story. A story, said a characteristically optimistic Mixon, that is just beginning.

NOTES TO SOURCES

Chapter One

1. Rory A. Cooper, Elaine Trefler, and Douglas A. Hobson, "Wheelchairs and Seating: Issues and practice," s.v. "Technology and Disability," on-line database available from Elsevier Science Ireland Ltd. (1996), n.p., n.d., 4.

2. Herman Kamenetz, M.D., *The Wheelchair Book: Mobility for the Disabled* (Springfield, Illinois: Charles C. Thomas, 1969), 5.

3. Cooper, Trefler, and Hobson, "Wheelchairs and Seating: Issues and practice," 6.

4. Marisa Bartolucci, "Making a chair able by design," *Metropolis*, November 1992, 29.

5. Neal Curran, interviewed by Jeffrey L. Rodengen and Anthony L. Wall, tape recording, 28 March, 2000, Write Stuff Enterprises.

6. *Encyclopaedia Britannica*, 15th ed., s.v. "wheel."

7. Kamenetz, *The Wheelchair Book*, 5.

8. Ibid., 7.

9. Ibid., 8.

10. Ibid.

11. Ibid., 10.

12. Ibid., 11.

13. Ibid., 14.

14. Ibid.

15. Bartolucci, "Making a chair able by design," 29.

16. Pamela Tudor-Craig, "Times and Tides (history of invalid chairs)," *History Today*, January 1998, 2.

17. A. Bennett Wilson Jr., *How to Select and Use a Manual Wheelchair* (Topping, Virginia: Rehabilitation Press, 1992), 4.

18. "Commemorative Stamp" [column], *PN/Paraplegia News*, September 1988, 59.

19. Kamenetz, *The Wheelchair Book*, 14.

20. Bartolucci, "Making a chair able by design," 30.

21. Tudor-Craig, "Times and Tides (history of invalid chairs)," 3.
22. *Encyclopaedia Britannica*, 15th ed., s.v. "bath chair."
23. Kamenetz, *The Wheelchair Book*, 20.
24. Ibid.
25. Herman Kamenetz, M.D., "Wheelchairs and Other Indoor Vehicles for the Disabled," *Orthotics Etcetera*, n.d., 445.
26. Ibid.
27. Theda Skocpol, *Protecting Soldiers and Mothers: The Political Origins of Social Policy in the United States* (Cambridge: Belknap Press, 1992), 104.
28. Joseph P. Shapiro, *No Pity: People with Disabilities Forging a New Civil Rights Movement* (New York: Random House, 1993), 213–214.
29. Ibid.
30. Kamenetz, "Wheelchairs and Other Indoor Vehicles," 446.
31. Bartolucci, "Making a chair able by design," 32.
32. Kamenetz, "Wheelchairs and other Indoor Vehicles," 446.
33. "Commemorative Stamp" [column], 59.
34. Shapiro, *No Pity: People with Disabilities*, 5.
35. Ibid.
36. "The Old Order," *PN/Paraplegia News*, May 1997, 45.
37. Ibid.
38. Shapiro, *No Pity: People with Disabilities*, 215.
39. Wilson, *How to Select and Use a Manual Wheelchair*, 4.
40. "The Old Order," 45.
41. Ibid.
42. Ibid.
43. Bartolucci, " Making a chair able by design," 32.
44. *Encyclopaedia Britannica*, 15th ed., s.v. "poliomyelitis."
45. Cooper, Trefler, and Hobson, "Wheelchairs and Seating: Issues and practice," 5.
46. Ibid.
47. Ibid.
48. Ibid.
49. Bartolucci, "Making a chair able by design," 33.
50. Cooper, Trefler, and Hobson, "Wheelchairs and Seating: Issues and practice," 5.
51. Ibid.
52. Ibid.
53. Bartolucci, "Making a chair able by design," 33.
54. Ibid.
55. Cooper, Trefler, and Hobson, "Wheelchairs and Seating: Issues and practice," 5.
56. Bartolucci, "Making a chair able by design," 33.
57. Cooper, Trefler, and Hobson, "Wheelchairs and Seating: Issues and practice," 5.
58. Gary Karp, *Choosing a Wheelchair* (Cambridge: O'Reilly & Associates, 1998), 4.
59. Cooper, Trefler, and Hobson, "Wheelchairs and Seating: Issues and practice," 5.
60. Karp, *Choosing a Wheelchair*, 4.

61. Bartolucci, "Making a chair able by design," 34.

62. Cooper, Trefler, and Hobson, "Wheelchairs and Seating: Issues and practice," 6.

63. Shapiro, *No Pity: People with Disabilities*, 211.

64. Ibid.

65. Ibid., 212.

66. Ibid., 212–213.

67. Cooper, Trefler, and Hobson, "Wheelchairs and Seating: Issues and practice," 6.

68. Ibid.

69. Rory A. Cooper, "A perspective on the ultralight wheelchair revolution," s.v. "Technology and Disability," on-line database available from Elsevier Science Ireland Ltd. (1996), n.p., n.d., 383.

70. Ibid.

71. Cooper, Trefler, and Hobson, "Wheelchairs and Seating: Issues and practice," 6.

72. Ibid., 5.

73. Ibid.

74. A. Bennett Wilson Jr., *Wheelchairs: A Prescription Guide*, (Charlottesville: Rehabilitation Press, 1986), 2.

75. Ibid.

76. Ibid.

77. Curran, interview.

78. Roger Rosenblatt, "Christopher Reeve is preparing to walk again. What prospects can doctors really offer victims of spinal-cord injury?" *Time*, 26 August 1999.

79. U.S. Patent Office Web site.

80. *Medical Industry Today*, 10 June 1997.

81. "Golden, Colo.-Based Company to Make Motor for Performance Wheelchair," *The Denver Post*, 18 November 1998.

82. Ibid.

83. J. B. Richey, interviewed by David L. Patten, Jeffrey L. Rodengen, and Anthony L. Wall, 28 March 2000, Write Stuff Enterprises.

84. Ibid.

Chapter Two

1. *Interchange* (A newsletter for members and friends of The Marmon Group), January 1984, 2.

2. Ibid.

3. *Encyclopedia Britannica*, 15th ed., s.v. "bicycle."

4. *Interchange*, January 1984, 2.

5. *Elyria City Directory*, 1889, 8.

6. *Interchange*, January 1984, 2.

7. "Elyria 175: Commemorating the 175th anniversary of the settlement of the city of Elyria and the 125th anniversary of the city hall," 1992, 64.

8. Otmar Sackerlotzky, interviewed by Anthony L. Wall, tape recording, 28 March 2000, Write Stuff Enterprises.

9. *Interchange*, January 1984, 2.

10. Ibid.

11. Ibid.

12. Ibid., 3.

13. Ibid.

14. Ibid.

15. *Elyria City Directory*, 1903, 179.

16. *Elyria Republican*, 21 July 1904.

17. Articles of Incorporation of The

Worthington Company,
19 February 1907, 1.

18. The Worthington
Company Catalog,
n.d., 4.

19. Ibid.

20. *Interchange*,
January 1984, 4.

21. The Worthington
Company Board of
Directors meeting
minutes, n.p.,
20 February 1908, 2.

22. *Interchange*,
January 1984, 4.

23. The Worthington
Company Board of
Directors meeting
minutes, n.p.,
27 October 1909, 2.

24. Ibid.

25. Ibid., 1.

26. Articles of
Incorporation of The
Colson Company,
15 January 1918.

27. *Interchange*,
January 1984, 4.

28. Ibid.

29. Ibid.

30. "Record Year for
Colson Co.,"
Finance & Industry,
21 May 1927, 19.

31. Ibid.

32. *(Elyria)*
Chronicle-Telegram,
6 December 1929.

33. *Interchange*,
January 1984, 4.

34. Ibid.

35. *(Elyria)*
Chronicle-Telegram,
26 February 1960.

36. *Interchange*,
January 1984, 4.

37. *(Elyria)*
Chronicle-Telegram,
1 February 1958.

38. Nyal Yost,
interviewed by Jon
VanZile, tape recording,
10 February 2000,
Write Stuff Enterprises.

39. Ron Thomas,
interviewed by
Anthony L. Wall,
28 March 2000,
Write Stuff Enterprises.

40. Ibid.

41. *(Elyria)*
Chronicle-Telegram,
1 February 1958.

42. Ibid.

43. Ibid.

44. Ibid.

45. Yost, interview.

46. *(Cleveland) Plain Dealer*,
20 December 1968.

47. Ibid.

48. Lou Hyster,
interviewed by
Heather G. Cohn,
tape recording,
11 January 2001,
Write Stuff Enterprises.

49. *(Elyria)*
Chronicle-Telegram,
12 April 1970.

50. Yost, interview.

51. Cleveland Chamber of
Commerce Industrial
Department Reference
file, n.d. [1960].

52. W. Courtland Shea,
n.p., April 1980, 2.

53. Tom Lorenz,
"Here's Looking
Through You,"
Cleveland Magazine,
October 1976, 62.

54. "The History of
Nuclear Medicine"
[on-line database]
(Reston, Virginia
[cited 2000]); available
from the Society of
Nuclear Medicine at
www.snm.org.

55. "Rising health care
market is the target
for firm here,"
(Cleveland) Plain Dealer,
18 May 1975.

56. John E. Bryan,
"Boston Capital
Corp. Sets Purchase
of Ohio-Nuclear,"
(Cleveland) Plain Dealer,
19 May 1970.

57. "Boston Capital
Changes Name,
Elects New Chief
and Moves

to Cleveland," *Wall Street Journal*, 3 June 1971.

58. Bryan, "Boston Capital Corp. Sets Purchase. 19 May 1970.

59. "Rising health care market is the target," 18 May 1995.

60. W. F. Bynum and Roy Porter, eds., *Companion Encyclopedia of the History of Medicine* (London: Routledge, 1993), 843-844; and Briget Travers, ed., "World of Invention" (Detroit: Gale Research Inc., 1994), 167.

61. Lorenz, "Here's Looking Through You."

62. Ibid.

63. Richey, interview.

64. "Technicare Corp.," *(Cleveland) Plain Dealer*, 3 August 1973.

65. "Rising health care market is the target," 18 May 1995.

66. Ibid.

67. Ibid.

68. Bynum and Porter, *Companion Encyclopedia of the History of Medicine*, 844.

69. Lorenz, "Here's Looking Through You."

70. Ibid.

71. "Rising health care market is the target," 18 May 1995.

72. *Technicare Annual Report*, 1978, 8.

73. Richey, interview.

74. Ibid.

75. Ibid.

76. "Dover Corp. Purchases Technicare Subsidiary," *Wall Street Journal*, 2 September 1977, 18.

77. Technicare 1978 Annual Report, iii.

78. Jim Dowdell, interviewed by Anthony L. Wall, tape recording, 5 June 2000, Write Stuff Enterprises.

Chapter Two Sidebar: Everest & Jennings

1. *Universal-Traveler*, n.d., Everest & Jennings publication.

2. Kamenetz, *The Wheelchair Book*.

3. *Universal-Traveler*.

4. Everest & Jennings Web site, www.everest-jennings.com.

5. *Universal-Traveler*.

6. Everest & Jennings Web site.

7. *Universal-Traveler*.

8. Ibid.

9. "The Mobility of Franklin Delano Roosevelt,", paper produced by Everest & Jennings, 1998, 4.

10. Everest & Jennings Web site.

11. *Universal-Traveler*.

12. Everest & Jennings Web site.

13. "Wheelchair maker looking for way back to the top," *Los Angeles Times*, 3 March 1987.

14. "The perils of being too successful," *Forbes*, 9 February 1987, 88.

15. Everest & Jennings Web site.

16. Everest & Jennings Web site.

17. Sunrise Medical Inc. Web site, www.sunrisemedical.com.

18. "Everest & Jennings closing plant; laying off 50 workers," *St. Louis Business Journal*, 20, no. 36 (1999): 12.

Chapter Three

1. Yost, interview.

2. A. Malachi Mixon, III, interviewed by David A. Patten, Jeffrey L. Rodengen, and Anthony L. Wall, tape recording, 30 March 2000, Write Stuff Enterprises.

3. A. Malachi Mixon, III, interviewed by Heather G. Cohn and Anthony L. Wall, tape recording, 7 September 2000, Write Stuff Enterprises.

4. Richey, interview.

5. A. Malachi Mixon, III, "Invacare Corporation: Always Pursuing Excellence—Every Day in Every Way" (speech delivered at a meeting of the Newcomen Society of the United States, 3 December 1996), 8.

6. Mixon, interview, 7 September 2000.

7. Jeffrey Bendix, *Cleveland Enterprise*, spring 1991, 26.

8. Mixon, "Invacare Corporation: Always Pursuing Excellence," 9.

9. Mixon, interview, 7 September 2000.

10. Ibid.

11. Mixon, interview, 30 March 2000.

12. Mixon, interview, 7 September 2000.

13. Mixon, interview, 30 March 2000.

14. Mixon, interview, 7 September 2000.

15. Dan T. Moore, III, interviewed by Heather G. Cohn, tape recording, 18 September 2000, Write Stuff Enterprises.

16. Mixon, interview, 7 September 2000.

17. Ibid.

18. Ibid.

19. Ibid.

20. Mixon, "Invacare Corporation: Always Pursuing Excellence," 8–9.

21. Moore, interview.

22. Mixon, "Invacare Corporation: Always Pursuing Excellence," 8–9.

23. William M. Jones, interviewed by Heather G. Cohn, tape recording, 11 September 2000, Write Stuff Enterprises.

24. Ibid.

25. Moore, interview.

26. Francis Joseph Callahan Jr., *Shoot for the Pin: The Memoirs of Francis Joseph Callahan, Jr.* (Naples, Florida: Presstige Printing, 1999), 222.

27. Mixon, interview, 7 September 2000.

28. Bendix, *Cleveland Enterprise*, Spring 1991, 26.

29. Ibid.

30. Mixon, "Invacare Corporation: Always Pursuing Excellence," 9.

31. Dale LaPorte, interviewed by Heather G. Cohn, tape recording, 1 September 2000, Write Stuff Enterprises.

32. Mixon, interview.

33. Richey, interview.

34. Mixon, interview.

35. Thomas W. Gerdel, "Area investors purchase Invacare from Technicare," *(Cleveland) Plain Dealer*, 4 January 1980, 11B.

36. Mixon, interview, 7 September 2000.

37. Ibid.

38. Moore, interview.

39. Yost, interview.

40. Mike Parsons, interviewed by Anthony L. Wall, tape recording, 14 April 2000, Write Stuff Enterprises.
41. Mixon, "Invacare Corporation: Always Pursuing Excellence," 11.
42. Moore, interview.
43. Yost, interview.
44. Debbie Warden, interviewed by Heather G. Cohn, tape recording, 5 January 2001, Write Stuff Enterprises.
45. Edith Powers, interviewed by Anthony L. Wall, tape recording, 12 September 2000, Write Stuff Enterprises.

Chapter Three Sidebar: Mal Mixon: Invacare's Original Yes, You Can

1. Charles Butler, "Mal Bonding," *Sales & Marketing Management*, July 1995, 66.
2. Betsy Yerak, "Serial Entrepreneur," *(Cleveland) Plain Dealer*, 14 September 1997, H1.
3. Ibid.
4. Butler, "Mal Bonding," 66.
5. Ibid.
6. Dyan Machan, "Nam returnees make good," *Forbes*, 11 July 1988, 135.
7. Ibid.
8. Butler, "Mal Bonding," 66.
9. Dan Shingler. "It's the Midas touch," *Crain's Cleveland Business*, 21 October 1991, 17.
10. Ibid.
11. Ibid.
12. Dan Shingler, "Sweeping IPO profit at Royal," *Crain's Cleveland Business*, 29 July 1991, 1.
13. Jennifer A. Scott, "Money Games: To Invacare Corp.'s Mal Mixon and his close circle of friends, venture capitalism is a hobby that more than pays for itself," *Small Business News— Cleveland*, June 1996.
14. Kristen Baird, "MCM Capital's Buyout Bandwagon Carries $50MM," *Crain's Cleveland Business*, 2 March 1998, 4.
15. Francis Joseph Callahan Jr., *Shoot for the Pin*, 227.
16. Case Western Reserve University, press release, 20 February 1992.
17. Invacare Corp., press release, 31 July 1996.
18. "Business Hall of Fame," *Inside Business*, July 1996, 124.
19. "Invacare CEO honored," *(Cleveland) Plain Dealer*, 14 November 1995, 10C.

Chapter Four

1. Hymie Pogir, interviewed by Anthony L. Wall, tape recording, 28 March 2000, Write Stuff Enterprises.
2. Ibid.

3. E. Patrick Nalley, interviewed by Heather G. Cohn, tape recording, 19 June 2000, Write Stuff Enterprises.

4. Betty Medsger, "The most captive consumers," *Progressive*, March 1979, 34-39.

5. Nalley, interview.

6. Medsger, "The most captive consumers," 34–39.

7. Everest & Jennings International, 1980 Annual Report, 21.

8. Yost, interview.

9. Gil Haury, interviewed by Anthony L. Wall, tape recording, 9 February 2000, Write Stuff Enterprises.

10. Mixon, "Invacare Corporation: Always Pursuing Excellence," 10.

11. Mixon, interview.

12. Ibid.

13. Parsons, interview.

14. Ibid.

15. Haury, interview.

16. Ibid.

17. Invacare Corp., 1980 Annual Report, 3.

18. Yost, interview.

19. Ibid.

20. Gerald B. Blouch, interviewed by Jeffrey L. Rodengen, tape recording, 28 March 2000, Write Stuff Enterprises.

21. Thomas Wiegand, interviewed by Jeffrey L. Rodengen, tape recording, 28 March 2000, Write Stuff Enterprises.

22. Mixon, interview, 30 March 2000.

23. Ibid.

24. Invacare Corp., 1980 Annual Report, 3.

25. "Invacare Corp. to make medical items in Ireland, " *The Cleveland Press*, 7 May 1981.

26. Invacare Corp., 1980 Annual Report, 2.

27. Nalley, interview.

28. Ibid.

29. Ibid.

30. Ibid.

31. Mixon, "Invacare Corporation: Always Pursuing Excellence," 12.

32. Nalley, interview.

33. Ibid.

34. Ibid.

35. Ibid.

36. Mixon, interview, 30 March 2000.

37. Nalley, interview.

38. Parsons, interview.

39. Ibid.

40. Ibid.

41. Karp, *Choosing a Wheelchair*, 40.

42. Haury, interview.

43. Thomas W. Gerdel, "Wheelchair firm sues competition on price cutting," *(Cleveland) Plain Dealer*, 1 April 1982.

44. Libbie Lockard, interviewed by Anthony L. Wall, tape recording, 30 May 2000, Write Stuff Enterprises.

45. Richey, interview.

46. Ron Thomas, interview.

47. Richey, interview.

48. Donald Sabath, "Invacare of Elyria has high hopes for its new wheelchair," *(Cleveland) Plain Dealer*, 11 July 1981.

49. Richey, interview.

50. Sackerlotzky, interview.

51. Gerdel, "Wheelchair firm sues competition."

52. Amy Richards, "Invacare rolls up wheelchair sales in

flat market,"
(Elyria)
Chronicle-Telegram,
15 December 1982.

53. "Executive Scene,"
(Cleveland) Plain Dealer,
5 May 1982.

54. Mixon, interview,
30 March 2000.

55. Jan Lovelace,
interviewed by
Anthony L. Wall,
tape recording,
30 March 2000,
Write Stuff Enterprises.

56. Mixon, interview,
30 March 2000.

57. Lockard, interview.

58. Pauline Thoma,
"Joined Hands:
Lorain County
unites against
economic slump,"
(Cleveland) Plain Dealer,
26 May 1987,
C1.

59. Amy Richards,
"Invacare gets
state $$ boost,"
(Elyria)
Chronicle-Telegram,
n.d. [1982], 1.

60. Amy Richards,
"Invacare seeks
space at Bendix,"
(Elyria)
Chronicle-Telegram,
20 August 1983.

61. "Two new Invacare
divisions created for
four products,"
(Cleveland) Plain Dealer,
27 February 1983.

Chapter Five

1. Amy Richards,
"Invacare going public,
plans major buy,"
(Elyria)
Chronicle-Telegram,
19 March 1984.

2. Howard Swindell, "Going
Public?"
Crain's Cleveland
Business,
12 August 1985, T-4.

3. "Invacare Corp.—
History,"
in Gale Business
Resources
[database on-line;
cited 20 January 2000],
2 of 5.
Available from
http://www.galenet.com.

4. Swindell, "Going Public?"
T-4.

5. Catherine L. Kissling,
"Invacare stock offer
weak, but Mixon
keeps hopes high,"
Crain's Cleveland
Business,
27 August 1984,
3.

6. Swindell, "Going Public?"
T-4.

7. Prospectus, Invacare
Corp., 11 May 1984,
23.

8. William Mehlman,
"For Invacare There
May Be Nowhere Else
To Go But Up,"
Insiders' Chronicle,
8 July 1985, 9.

9. 1984 Second Quarter
Report, Invacare Corp.

10. Prospectus,
Invacare Corp.,
11 May 1984, 17.

11. "Invacare opens
plants in Florida,
Connecticut,"
Crain's Cleveland
Business,
26 November 1984,
15.

12. 1984 Second Quarter
Report, Invacare Corp.

13. Parsons, interview.

14. Prospectus,
Invacare Corp.,
11 May 1984, 16.

15. Ibid., 53.

16. Diasonics Inc.,
press release,
2 May 1984.

17. Robin Reeves,
"Health care company
in 18m takeover,"
Financial Times
(London), 9.

18. Prospectus, Invacare Corp., 11 May 1984, 17.
19. Richey, interview.
20. Ibid.
21. Ibid.
22. Ibid.
23. Invacare Corp., 1984 Annual Report.
24. Parsons, interview.
25. Pogir, interview.
26. Nalley, interview.
27. Parsons, interview.
28. Nalley, interview.
29. Mixon, interview, 30 March 2000.
30. "Invacare Says Charge Will Result in Loss for 4th Period, Year," *Wall Street Journal*, 28 December 1984, 24.
31. Sackerlotzky, interview.
32. Ibid.
33. Ibid.
34. *Merriam-Webster's Collegiate Dictionary*, 10th ed., s.v. "zeolite."
35. Parsons, interview, 14 April 2000.
36. Lou Tabickman, interviewed by Anthony L. Wall, tape recording, 9 May 2000, Write Stuff Enterprises.
37. Yost, interview.

38. Invacare Corp., 1984 Annual Report, 10.
39. Richey, interview.
40. A. Malachi Mixon, III, Quarterly report to shareholders, 13 August 1986.
41. A. Malachi Mixon, III, "Annual Meeting Remarks," 13 May 1986.
42. Ibid.
43. Ibid.
44. Mehlman, "For Invacare There May Be Nowhere Else," 9.
45. Ibid., 1.
46. Catherine L. Kissling, "Invacare pushing to reduce costs, get edge on rivals," *Crain's Cleveland Business*, 19 May 1986, 3.
47. Mixon, "Annual Meeting Remarks," 23 May 1985.
48. Kissling, "Invacare pushing to reduce costs," 3.
49. Launzy Z. Sims, III, "New health care products aid Invacare in hopes of waking up sleepy market," *Crain's Cleveland Business*,

5 August 1985, 2.
50. Mixon, interview, 30 March 2000.
51. Swindell, "Going Public?" T-4.
52. Lovelace, interview.
53. Swindell, "Going Public?" T-4.
54. Mixon, interview, 30 March 2000.
55. Lovelace, interview.
56. Catherine L. Kissling, "Invacare going high-tech?" *Crain's Cleveland Business*, 3 July 1984, 2.
57. Kissling, "Invacare stock offer weak," 3.
58. Swindell, "Going Public?" T-4.
59. Douglas A. Fox, "Invacare Corp.," *McDonald & Co. Securities*, 1 December 1987, 3.
60. Kissling, "Invacare pushing to reduce costs," 3.
61. Invacare Corp., press release, 18 March 1986.
62. A. Malachi Mixon, III, Quarterly report to shareholders, 13 March 1986.

63. "Invacare Corp. Says It Broke Even in the First Quarter," *The Wall Street Journal*, 13 May 1986.

64. Catherine L. Kissling. "Return of healthy balance sheet has Wall St. noticing Invacare," *Crain's Cleveland Business*, 6 October 1986, 47.

65. Ibid.

Chapter Six

1. Kissling. "Invacare pushing to reduce costs," 3.

2. Thomas, interview.

3. Kissling, "Invacare pushing to reduce costs," 3.

4. Lockard, interview.

5. "Light wheelchairs promote activities," *Design News*, 21 October 1985, 53.

6. Thomas, interview.

7. "Light wheelchairs promote activities," 53.

8. Internet research, n.p., n.d.

9. Thomas W. Gerdel, "Elyria firm wins patent suit," *(Cleveland)* *Plain Dealer*, 13 March 1987, 16B.

10. Mixon, interview, 30 March 2000.

11. Lockard, interview.

12. Mixon, remarks to annual meeting, 13 May 1986.

13. Ibid.

14. "Invacare creates rehab marketing team," *Paraplegia News*, October 1985, 78.

15. Mixon, Remarks to annual meeting, 13 May 1986.

16. Kissling, "Invacare pushing to reduce costs," 3.

17. Invacare Corp., press release, 29 April 1987.

18. Parsons, interview.

19. Lockard, interview.

20. Thomas, interview.

21. Invacare Corp., press release, 29 April 1987.

22. "Invacare Corp. to Acquire Huntco in Cash-Stock Pact," *Wall Street Journal*, 30 April 1987.

23. A. Malachi Mixon, III, remarks to annual meeting, 28 May 1987.

24. "Invacare to close 2 Ohio plants," *(Cleveland)* *Plain Dealer*, 23 January 1987, B12.

25. Thomas W. Gerdel, "Invacare will flex its new muscle, " *(Cleveland) Plain Dealer*, 29 May 1987, 12B.

26. "New Invacare logo," *Paraplegia News*, August 1987, 32.

27. Delinda Karle, "Invacare, thanks to FTC, to hunt smaller game," *(Cleveland) Plain Dealer*, 17 August 1987, 9B.

28. "Business Brief: Invacare Corp," *Wall Street Journal*, 10 August 1987.

29. Karle, "Invacare, thanks to FTC, to hunt smaller game," 9B.

30. Ibid.

31. Ibid.

32. Blouch, interview.

33. "Innovations," *Paraplegia News*, June 1988, 42.

34. Gregory Stricharchuk, "Fast Track: Focus on Business Basics Spells Success for Invacare—

Wheelchair Concern Catered to Dealers and Its Sales Have Soared," *Wall Street Journal,* 21 December 1990, B2.

35. A. Malachi Mixon, III, annual meeting remarks, 25 May 1988.

36. Gregory Stricharchuk, "Invacare Expects to Post Big Jump in Net on Quarterly Sales Gain of About 18%," *Wall Street Journal,* 31 October 1988, 9B.

37. Invacare Corp., 1988 Annual Report, 7.

38. Invacare Corp., "Invacare Corp. financial results," 4 August 1988.

39. Mixon, annual meeting remarks, 25 May 1988.

40. Invacare Corp., press release, 11 March 1987.

41. Mixon, annual meeting remarks, 25 May 1988.

42. A. Malachi Mixon, III, news release, 7 August 1989.

43. Stricharchuk, "Invacare Expects to Post Big Jump," 9B.

44. Parsons, interview.

45. Sackerlotzky, interview.

46. Mixon, annual meeting remarks, 25 May 1988.

47. Tabickman, interview.

48. Stricharchuk, "Invacare Expects to Post Big Jump," 9B.

49. Ibid.

50. Invacare Corp., press release, 9 May 1988.

51. Parsons, interview.

52. Sackerlotzky, interview.

53. Invacare Corp., press release, 9 March 1989.

54. A. Malachi Mixon, III, annual meeting remarks, 26 May 1989.

55. Parsons, interview.

56. Mixon, annual meeting remarks, 26 May 1989.

57. "Inside Industry," *Paraplegia News,* April 1989: 48.

58. Mixon, annual meeting remarks, 26 May 1989.

59. A. Malachi Mixon, III, remarks to employees, 13 December 1988.

60. Darrel Lowery, interviewed by Anthony L. Wall, tape recording, 28 March 2000, Write Stuff Enterprises.

61. Mixon, remarks to employees, 13 December 1988.

Chapter Seven

1. "Invacare Corp.—History," in Gale Business Resources @ www.galenet.com.

2. Jon Barnes, "Industry leader Invacare seen as good buy," *Crain's Cleveland Business,* 2 January 1989, 23.

3. Delinda Karle, "Invacare expecting boost in business," *(Cleveland) Plain Dealer,* 24 May 1990, 7C; James F. Peltz, "Wheelchair Maker Tries to Regain Profits," *Los Angeles Times,* 3 April 1990, 9A.

4. Parsons, interview.

5. "Invacare Corp.," *Paraplegia News,* July 1989, 60.

6. A. Malachi Mixon, III, news release, 7 August 1989.

7. Judy Kovacs, interviewed by Anthony L. Wall,

tape recording,
15 May 2000,
Write Stuff Enterprises.

8. "Governor Meets with
Rival Union Factions,
Businessmen,"
Associated Press,
17 August 1989.

9. Ibid.

10. "Mexicans Open
Strike—Hit Border
Plants,"
Journal of Commerce,
17 August 1989,
4A.

11. "Invacare restructures
domestic operations,"
*(Elyria)
Chronicle-Telegram,*
21 September 1989,
C4.

12. Louis F. J. Slangen,
interviewed by
Jeffrey L. Rodengen,
tape recording,
28 March 2000,
Write Stuff Enterprises.

13. Rebecca Yerak.
"Invacare's potential
attracts new CFO,"
(Cleveland) Plain Dealer,
3 July 1990,
4C.

14. Ibid.

15. "Invacare Appoints
Chief Financial Officer,"
Invacare Corp., press
release, 31 May 1990.

16. A. Malachi Mixon, III,
annual meeting
remarks, 23 May 1990.

17. Ibid.

18. David Williams,
interviewed by
Heather G. Cohn,
tape recording,
12 March 2001,
Write Stuff Enterprises.

19. Ibid.

20. Ibid.

21. Mixon, annual meeting
remarks, 23 May 1990.

22. Ibid.

23. James F. Peltz,
"Wheelchair Maker
Tries to Regain Profits,"
Los Angeles Times,
3 April 1990: 9A.

24. Karle, "Invacare
expecting boost in
business," 7C.

25. Gregory Stricharchuk,
"Fast Track: Focus
on Business Basics,"
B2.

26. Mixon, annual meeting
remarks, 23 May 1990.

27. Parsons, interview.

28. Stricharchuk,
"Fast Track: Focus
on Business Basics,"
B2.

29. "Invacare—Focusing
on Active Wheelchair
Users—Creates
New Division,"

Invacare Corp.
press release,
12 November 1990.

30. Ibid.

31. Ibid.

32. Stricharchuk,
"Fast Track: Focus
on Business Basics,"
B2.

33. Slangen, interview.

34. David Prizinsky,
"European '92
standards will put
firms to test,"
*Crain's Cleveland
Business,*
14 January 1991,
7.

35. Ibid.

36. Sackerlotzky, interview.

37. Ibid.

38. Elizabeth Ehrlich,
"The quality
management
checkpoint,"
International Business,
May 1993, 56.

39. Ibid.

40. Ibid.

41. Ibid.

42. Michael Devlin,
interviewed by
Anthony L. Wall,
tape recording,
8 April 2000,
Write Stuff Enterprises.

43. 1992 Invacare
Annual Report, 2.

44. A. Malachi Mixon, III, remarks to shareholders, 24 May 1993.
45. Haury, interview.
46. Tom Buckley, interviewed by Anthony L. Wall, tape recording, 15 May 2000, Write Stuff Enterprises.
47. Marcus Gleisser, "Invacare altering shareholder rights plan," (Cleveland) Plain Dealer, 3 April 1991, 2G.
48. Amy Richards, "Stock split seen for Invacare this year," (Elyria) Chronicle-Telegram, 25 May 1991, 1.
49. Invacare Corp., press release, 12 November 1990.
50. Barbara Mooney, "Invacare ads focus on consumer market," Crain's Cleveland Business, 8 July 1991, 6.
51. Buckley, interview.
52. Prospectus, Invacare Corp., 23 May 1991, 6.

53. A. Malachi Mixon, III, annual meeting remarks, 24 May 1991.
54. Sana Swiolop, "The Importance of lobbying; in medical devices, some regulation is inevitable," Financial World, 21 August 1990, 58.
55. Stephen Phillips, "Mr. Mixon Goes to Washington," (Cleveland) Plain Dealer, 29 December 1991, 1E.
56. Chris Thompson, "Cities courting Invacare to win head-quarters," Crain's Cleveland Business, 12 August 1991, 1.
57. Barbara Kingsley, "Cities cooperate to retain company," (Cleveland) Plain Dealer, 8 September 1991, 2B.
58. A. Malachi Mixon, III, remarks at 1991 annual meeting, 27 May 1992.
59. "Invacare buys Canadian concern," Wall Street Journal, 11 October 1991, B8F.

60. Invacare Corp., press release, 4 November 1991.
61. Ibid.
62. Dale Nash, interviewed by Anthony L. Wall, tape recording, 15 May 2000, Write Stuff Enterprises.
63. Ibid.
64. Ibid.
65. 1991 Invacare Annual Report, 1.
66. Invacare Corp., press release, 20 February 1992.

Chapter Seven Sidebar: Wheelchair Racing

1. Against the Wind: The Racing the Wind Web site [based on a show for WILL-TV], available @ www.will.uiuc.edu/WILL.
2. Ibid.
3. Ibid.
4. Ibid.
5. WBZ News 4 100th.com, A celebration of the Boston Marathon, 1996.
6. Los Angeles Times [from on-line source], Nov. 24, 1985, Part 10, 2.

7. WBZ News 4 100th.com, A celebration of the Boston Marathon, 1996.

8. *New Mobility*, August 1996, 34.

9. *Technology and Disability*, n.d. (1996), 384.

10. Ibid.

11. *New Mobility*, August 1996, 34.

12. Ibid.

13. *Technology and Disability*, n.d. (1996), 384.

14. *St. Petersburg Times*, 1 February 1987, 1C.

15. *New Mobility*, August 1996, 34.

16. Ibid.

17. Invacare Corp. Web site [cited 1999], available @ www.invacare.com.

18. *New Mobility*, August 1996, 34.

19. *Los Angeles Times*, 24 November 1985, Part 10, 2.

20. Against the Wind: The Racing the Wind Web site.

Chapter Eight

1. Wiegand, interview.

2. Invacare Corp., press release, 20 February 1992.

3. Bill Corcoran, interviewed by Anthony L. Wall, tape recording, 28 March 2000, Write Stuff Enterprises.

4. Ibid.

5. Invacare Corp., press release, 20 February 1992.

6. Invacare Corp., press release, 27 July 1992.

7. Thomas R. Miklich, interviewed by Anthony L. Wall, tape recording, 15 May 2000, Write Stuff Enterprises.

8. Sackerlotzky, interview.

9. Invacare Corp., 1993 Annual Report, 26.

10. Invacare Corp., "Partnering with Invacare," 1996.

11. Blouch, interview.

12. Invacare Corp., press release, 1 April 1992.

13. Invacare Corp., 1992 Annual Report, 16.

14. Miklich, interview, 15 May 2000.

15. Invacare Corp., 1993 Annual Report, 13.

16. Ibid., 6.

17. Invacare Corp., 1987 Annual Report, 29; Invacare Corp., 1992 Annual Report, 30.

18. Invacare Corp., 1992 Annual Report, 2.

19. Invacare Corp., press release, 29 April 1993.

20, Invacare Corp., press release, 22 October 1992.

21. Ralph Winter. "Invacare Says Solid Growth Likely in '92; Share Net and Sales to Echo Earlier Increases; Chief Cites Disabilities Act," *Wall Street Journal*, 30 April 1992.

22. Invacare Corp., 1992 Annual Report, 10.

23. Ibid., 9.

24. A. Malachi Mixon, III, remarks to shareholders, 24 May 1993.

25. Ibid.

26. Invacare Corp., press release, 7 August 1992.

27. Invacare Corp.,
1993 Annual Report,
13.
28. Ibid.
29. Invacare Corp.,
press release,
7 August 1992.
30. "Entrepreneur award
winners picked,"
*Crain's Cleveland
Business*,
29 June 1992,
2.
31. "200 Best Small
Companies in America,"
Forbes,
9 November 1992.
32. Ibid.
33. "250 Companies
on the Move,"
Business Week (special
enterprise issue), 1993.
34. Invacare Corp.,
1993 Annual Report, 4.
35. David Price,
"Elyria firm to score
in health reform,"
*(Elyria)
Chronicle-Telegram*,
27 October 1993.
36. "Business Briefs,"
Wall Street Journal,
5 March 1993
(corrected 10 March
1993, A2).
37. Invacare Corp.,
press release,
4 March 1993.

38. Ibid.
39. Alice Graves,
"Wheelchair makers
race toward Top End,"
n.d., n.p.
40. Invacare Corp.,
1993 Annual Report, 9.
41. Miklich, interview.
42. "Invacare Acquires
Low Air Loss Therapy
Manufacturer GSI,"
PR Newswire
(Financial News,
Elyria, Ohio),
13 July 1993.
43. Invacare Corp.,
1993 Annual Report, 7.
44. Sackerlotzky, interview.
45. A. Malachi Mixon, III,
Remarks to shareholders,
24 May 1993.
46. Louis F. J. Slangen,
interviewed by
Anthony L. Wall,
tape recording, 7
September 2000,
Write Stuff Enterprises.
47. Invacare Corp., 1993
Annual Report, 13.
48. A. Malachi Mixon, III,
remarks to
shareholders,
23 May 1992.
49. Ibid.
50. Ibid.
51. Invacare Corp.,
1993 Annual Report,
5.

52. Raquel Santiago,
"Invacare Corp.,"
*Crain's Cleveland
Business*,
23 May 1994,
S-17.
53. Invacare Corp.,
press release,
19 November 1993.
54. Corcoran, interview,
28 March 2000.
55. Stephen Hudak,
"Taking his views
to the top,"
(Cleveland) Plain Dealer,
26 June 1994, 8B.
56. Ralph Winter,
"Invacare Expects
to Keep Rolling
During 2nd Half;
New Products,
Rising Share
of Market to
Boost Net
for Wheelchair Maker,"
Wall Street Journal,
8 September 1995.
57. Blouch, interview.
58. Hudak,
"Taking his views
to the top," 8B.
59. Ibid.
60. Invacare Corp.,
press release,
19 November 1993.
61. Thomas W. Gerdel,
"Invacare refines
racing chair,"

(Cleveland) Plain Dealer,
30 December 1993, 1F.

62. Ibid.

63. Karp, *Life on Wheels,*
497.

64. WBZ News 4
100th.com, A
celebration of the
Boston Marathon,
1996.

65. Devlin, interview.

66. Stephen Phillips,
"Invacare specialist
knows racing
ups, downs,"
(Cleveland) Plain Dealer,
27 March 1994,
2G.

67. Thomas, interview.

68. Ibid.

69. Ibid.

70. Ibid.

71. Thomas W. Gerdel,
"Invacare refines
racing chair,"
(Cleveland) Plain Dealer,
30 December 1993,
1F.

72. Phillips, "Invacare
specialist knows racing
ups, downs," 2G.

73. Invacare Corp.,
1994 annual report,
7.

74. Ibid.

75. Conversation with
Susan Elder.

76. Ibid.

77. Invacare Corp.,
press release,
17 November 1993.

78. "Inside Industry,"
Paraplegia News,
March 1994, 72.

79. Invacare Corp.,
press release,
18 November 1993.

80. Invacare Corp.,
1994 Annual Report,
5.

81. J. B. Richey,
interviewed by
Jeffrey L. Rodengen,
tape recording,
15 February 2000,
Write Stuff Enterprises.

82. A. Malachi Mixon III,
Remarks to
shareholders,
23 May 1994.

83. Curran, interview.

84. "Inside Industry,"
Paraplegia News,
June 1995, 104.

85. A. Malachi Mixon, III,
"Presentation to
Management,"
24 November 1994.

86. Slangen, interview.

87. Ibid.

88. Invacare Corp.,
1994 Annual Report, 2.

89. A. Malachi Mixon, III,
Remarks to
shareholders,
23 May 1994.

90. "EDI Innovation
Awards,"
Cleveland Enterprise,
fall 1994, 15.

91. Ibid., 14.

92. Invacare Corp.,
1994 Annual Report, 7.

93. Ibid., 2.

94. "Frontlines,"
Corporate Cleveland,
March 1994, 8.

95. Invacare Corp.,
1994 Annual Report, 7.

96. "Arts Award,"
Paraplegia News,
November 1994,
82.

97. Tabickman, interview.

98. Invacare Corp., 1994
annual report, 6.

99. "Nellcor, Respironics,
Healthdyne, in Market
for Acquisitions,
Firms Tell Robertson,
Stephens Conference;
Sunrise Medical,
Invacare Also Looking,"
The Gray Sheet,
5 December 1994,
10.

100. Ibid.

101. Invacare Corp.,
1994 Annual Report, 7.

102. A. Malachi Mixon, III,
"Presentation to
Management
(Invacare Corp.),"
24 November 1994.

103. Ibid.
104. Invacare Corp., 1994 Annual Report, 8.
105. Ibid.
106. Mixon, "Presentation to Management," 24 November 1994.

Chapter Eight Sidebar: Team Invacare

1. Against the Wind: The Racing the Wind Web site (based on a show for WILL-TV), n.d., available @ www.will.uiuc.edu/WILL.
2. Invacare Corp. Web, n.d., available @ www.invacare.com.
3. Ibid.

Chapter Eight Sidebar: Top End

1. Invacare Corp. Web site, n.d., available @ www.invacare.com.
2. *San Diego Union Tribune*, 6 November 1987, D-2.
3. Invacare Corp. Web site, n.d., available @ www.invacare.com.
4. *Technology and Disability*, 1996, 386.
5. Invacare Corp. Web, n.d., available @ www.invacare.com.

6. Ibid.
7. Ibid.
8. Ibid.
9. Ibid.
10. Ibid.

Chapter Nine

1. "Invacare adding 35 new products to home care line," *Drug Topics*, 12 December 1994, 72.
2. Invacare Corp., press release, 5 May 1995.
3. "Invacare Corp. Acquisition," *Wall Street Journal*, 26 May 1995, A8.
4. "In Brief," *The Gray Sheet*, 26 June 1995, 27.
5. "Invacare Acquires Wheelchair Maker for $5 Million," *Medical Industry Today*, 13 June 1995.
6. Mixon, interview, 30 March 2000.
7. Kovacs, interview.
8. Butler, "Mal Bonding," 66.
9. Ibid.
10. A. Malachi Mixon, III, CEO briefing, 11 April 1996.

11. Butler, "Mal Bonding," 66.
12. Ibid.
13. Tabickman, interview.
14. Nash, interview.
15. Ken Sparrow, interviewed by Anthony L. Wall, tape recording, 10 May 2000, Write Stuff Enterprises.
16. Ibid.
17. "Invacare buys New Zealand wheel chair manufacturer," *(Elyria) Chronicle-Telegram*, 5 July 1995.
18. Invacare Corp., 1995 Annual Report, 6.
19. "Mergers & Acquisitions," *Medical Industry Today*, 20 September 1995.
20. Miklich, interview.
21. "Mergers & Acquisitions," *Medical Industry Today*, 12 October 1995.
22. "Invacare pays cash for Ontario company," *(Cleveland) Plain Dealer*, 28 November 1995, 4C.
23. Jack Beaudoin, "Incremental growth, innovation forecast," *HME News*, July 1996.

24. A. Malachi Mixon, III, CEO briefing, 8 April 1997.
25. Beaudoin, "Incremental growth, innovation forecast."
26. Slangen, interview, 28 March 2000.
27. "Invacare launches new brand strategy," *(Lorain) Morning Journal*, 5 December 1995.
28. Invacare Corp., 1995 Annual Report, inside front cover.
29. "Invacare to Enter Retail Market with Frohock-Stewart Buy," *HomeCare*, February 1996.
30. Invacare Corp., press release, 14 January 1996.
31. "Health for the masses: Medical-goods company courts an emerging market," *HFN: The Weekly Newspaper for the Home Furnishing Network*, 29 January 1996, 39.
32. "Invacare to Enter Retail Market with Frohock-Stewart Buy."
33. "A new name in health products," *HFN: The Weekly Newspaper for the Home Furnishing Network*, 20 May 1996, 72.
34. Miklich, interview.
35. Eric Gruenenwald, "Does Size Matter?" *HomeCare*, October 1996, 63.
36. Ralph Winter, "Invacare Sees '96 Up 20% Over Yr-Ago. At $1.28/Shr," Dow Jones Newswire, 5 December 1996.
37. "Mergers & Acquisitions," *Medical Industry Today*, 20 March 1996.
38. Marcus Gleisser, "Invacare gains entry into institutional market," *(Cleveland) Plain Dealer*, 15 February 1996, 3C.
39. Invacare Corp., press release, 2 May 1996.
40. "Invacare Corp.—Gabriorto Lda," *In Vivo: The Business and Medicine Report*, March 1996.
41. "Acquires third parts company..." *HME News*, August 1996.
42. "...and rolls into Australia," *HME News*, August 1996.
43. Devlin, interview.
44. Dave Piersma, interviewed by Jeffrey L. Rodengen, tape recording, 28 March 2000, Write Stuff Enterprises.
45. Madalyn Dinnerstein, "Invacare offices staying," *(Elyria) Chronicle-Telegram*, 6 August 1996, A1.
46. Stan Bullard, "Invacare narrows new HQ search," *Crain's Cleveland Business*, 10 June 1996, 1.
47. Dinnerstein, "Invacare offices staying."
48. Jeff Stacklin, "Mixon: It made more sense to keep HQ here," *(Elyria) Chronicle-Telegram*, 7 August 1996, A1.
49. John Reynolds, "Invacare tax break clears first hurdle,"

(Lorain) Morning Journal, 28 August 1996.

50. Jane Trager, "The Invacare deal: Not as sweet as the one in '91," *(Elyria) Chronicle-Telegram,* 28 August 1996, A2.

51. "Invacare weaves way to the Web," *(Elyria) Chronicle-Telegram,* 1 1 June 1996, A4.

52. Mixon, CEO briefing, 11 April 1996.

53. Dan Shingler, "Companies dish out a deluge of deals," *Crain's Cleveland Business,* 1 January 1996, 10.

54. Corcoran, interview.

55. Blouch, interview.

56. Raquel Santiago, "Invacare sees growth in retail sales," *Crain's Cleveland Business,* 3 March 1997, 3.

57. Ibid.

58. Steven Lipin and Matt Murray, "Invacare makes $163 million offer to acquire Healthdyne Technologies," *Wall Street Journal,* 13 January 1997, B6.

59. Blouch, interview.

60. Christopher Gray, "Invacare, a home-care equipment maker and distributor, is planning to acquire Healthdyne Technologies, a maker of home-care medical devices," *Modern Healthcare,* 5 May 1997, 50.

61. Michael E. Kanell, "Ohio Company Bidding for Marietta, Ga.-Based Healthdyne," Knight-Ridder/Tribune Business News, 13 January 1997, 113B1006.

62. Ibid.

63. "Invacare Would Expand Respiratory Offerings with Proposed Healthdyne Technologies Acquisition," *The Gray Sheet,* 13 January 1997, 3.

64. Lipin and Murray, "Invacare makes $163 million offer," B6.

65. "Healthdyne Bid Rejected for Antitakeover Provision," *Wall Street Journal,* 26 March 1997, B10.

66. Monica Langeley and Steven Lipin, "Georgia Senate Passes Bill to Thwart Hostile Bids," *Wall Street Journal,* 24 March 1997, A2.

67. Andy Miller, "Invacare lobbies hard against bill blocking bid for Healthdyne," *Atlanta Journal and Constitution,* 27 March 1997, G1.

68. Michael E. Kanell, "Healthdyne Founder Doesn't Trust Invacare to Preserve Georgia Operations," *Atlanta Journal and Constitution,* 28 March 1997.

69. Gray, "Invacare, a home-care equipment maker," 50.

70. Michael E. Kanell, "Invacare increases Healthdyne bid,"

Atlanta Journal and Constitution, 5 June 1997, E1.

71. Ibid.

72. "Healthdyne Technologies Inc.: New Invacare Tender Offer Called Grossly Inadequate," *Wall Street Journal*, 12 June 1997, B4.

73. "CACI International and Telesprectrum plunge following warnings of weak quarterly results," *Wall Street Journal*, 24 June 1997, C7.

74. "Update," *Modern Healthcare*, 11 August 1997, 44.

75. "Rivals to Combine, Settle Patent Dispute," *Medical Industry Today*, 12 November 1997.

76. "Respironics' $370 mil. Healthdyne merger would create combined 238-rep sales force," *The Gray Sheet*, 17 November 1997, 3.

77. Ibid.

78. Blouch, interview.

79. Ibid.

80. "Message from Mal ..." *Innovator*, summer 1997, 1.

81. Lowery, interview.

82. Buckley, interview.

83. Invacare Corp., press release, 6 May 1997.

84. "Invacare Buys Allied Medical," *Wall Street Journal*, 8 October 1997, A15.

85. Robert F. Dixon, "Suburban Ostomy sold; firm remains in Holliston," *(Framingham, Mass.) Middlesex News*, 18 December 1997.

86. Invacare Corp., press release, 23 January 1998.

87. Ibid.

88. A. Malachi Mixon, III, remarks at the annual meeting of shareholders, 28 May 1998.

89. Miklich, interview.

90. James Bernstein, "Graham-Field to Acquire Rival," *(Long Island) Newsday*, 9 September 1997.

91. Invacare Corp., press release, 4 March 1997.

92 Invacare Corp., 1997 Annual Report, 3.

93. Buckley, interview.

94. Lowery, interview.

95. Ibid.

96. Blouch, interview.

97. Invacare Corp., press release, 18 February 1997.

98. Invacare Corp., press release, 21 May 1997.

99. Nalley, interview.

100. Denise Novoselski, "Tomorrow's Promise," *HomeCare*, September 1997.

101. Invacare Corp., 1997 Annual Report, 7.

102. A. Malachi Mixon, III, Letter to dealers, 7 October 1997.

103. Richey, interview, 28 March 2000.

104. "The 1998 EDI Innovation Awards," *Cleveland Enterprise*, spring 1988, 20.

105. Carol Marie Cropper, "Easter Seal Society Selects Recipients," *New York Times*, 6 October 1997, D12.

Chapter Nine Sidebar: Ernie "The Attorney" Mansour

1. Ernest P. Mansour, interviewed by Anthony

L. Wall, tape recording,
11 September 2000,
Write Stuff Enterprises.

2. Mixon, interview,
7 September 2000.

3. Ibid.

4. Mansour, interview.

5. Ibid.

6. Ibid.

7. Ibid.

8. Ibid.

**Chapter Nine Sidebar:
Easter Seals**

1. "Invacare and Easter
Seals Announce
Partnership," PR
Newswire (domestic
news; Chicago),
24 August 1993.

2. James E. Williams,
statement
[in lieu of interview],
September 2000,
Write Stuff Enterprises.

3. Susan Elder,
interviewed by
Anthony L. Wall,
tape recording,
12 September 2000,
Write Stuff Enterprises.

4. Ibid.

Chapter Ten

1. Invacare Corp., 1997
Annual Report.

2. Mixon, remarks to
shareholders,
28 May 1998.

3. A. Malachi Mixon, III,
CEO briefing,
8 May 1998.

4. Invacare Corp.,
press release,
19 January 1998.

5. Mixon, CEO
briefing,
8 May 1998.

6. Gerald B. Blouch, CEO
briefing,
8 May 1998.

7. Mixon, CEO briefing,
8 May 1998.

8. Ibid.

9. A. Malachi Mixon, III,
remarks to shareholders,
28 May 1998.

10. Mixon, CEO briefing,
8 May 1998.

11. Invacare Corp.,
press release,
19 January 1998.

12. "Invacare Signs
Supply Deal with
RoTech Medical,"
Medical Industry Today,
27 January 1998.

13. Invacare Corp.,
press release,
26 January 1998.

14. Invacare Corp.,
press release,
27 March 1998.

15. Lowery, interview.

16. Invacare Corp.,
press release,
19 February 1998.

17. Larry Steward,
interviewed by
Anthony L. Wall,
tape recording,
28 March 2000,
Write Stuff
Enterprises.

18. Jane Trager,
"Mixon rips union
in letter to workers,"
*(Elyria)
Chronicle-Telegram*,
28 August 1998.

19. Steward, interview.

20. Thomas, interview.

21. Chrissy Kadleck and
Dan Harkins,
"Steelworkers
schedule Invacare
organizing vote,"
*(Elyria)
Chronicle-Telegram*,
14 September 1999.

22. Raquel Santiago,
"Invacare workers
to vote on joining
steelworkers,"
*Crain's Cleveland
Business*,
27 September 1999,
3.

23. Ibid.

24. Invacare Corp.,
press release, 29
September 1999,

25. Chrissy Kadleck, "Invacare workers vote down union," (Elyria) Chronicle-Telegram, 8 October 1999, A1.

26. Dowdell, interview.

27. Haury, interview.

28. Corcoran, interview.

29. Conversation by Susan Elder.

30. Stuart Drown, "Elyria's Invacare Corp. is able to post higher revenues, market share," Akron Beacon Journal, 27 June 1999.

31. Miklich, interview.

32. Invacare Corp., press release, 18 November 1998.

33. John Eaton, "Unique motor debuts on performance wheelchair," Denver Post, 18 November 1998, C3.

34. Richey, interview.

35. Blouch, interview, 28 March 2000.

36. Haury, interview.

37. Curran, interview.

38. Chrissy Kadleck, "Mixon Hopes to Keep Invacare Rolling," (Elyria) Chronicle-Telegram, 8 August 1999, A1.

39. Raquel Santiago, "Invacare introducing new brand plan," Crain's Cleveland Business, 19 July 1999, 1.

40. Slangen, interview, 28 March 2000.

41. "CEO Interview—A. Malachi Mixon," Wall Street Transcript, 6 March 2000.

42. Weld Royal, "A Brand new pitch," Industry Week, 6 March 2000, 41.

43. Slangen, interview, 28 April 2000.

44. Invacare Corp., "Corporate and Brand Identity Guidelines," 1999.

45. "The Meaning of Invacare" [brochure, Form No. 98-56], Invacare Corporation, 1998.

46. Slangen, interview, 28 March 2000.

47. "The Meaning of Invacare."

48. Slangen, interview, 28 March 2000.

49. Ibid.

50. Karp, Choosing a Wheelchair, 1.

51. Slangen, interview, 28 March 2000.

52. Kadleck, "Mixon Hopes to Keep Invacare Rolling," A1.

53. Dave Pessel, interviewed by Anthony L. Wall, tape recording, 30 May 2000, Write Stuff Enterprises.

54. Santiago, "Invacare introducing new brand plan," 1.

55. Adrian Michaels, "Invacare to raise direct marketing efforts," Financial Times (London), 11 November 1999, 23.

56. Invacare Corp., 1999 Annual Report, 24.

57. Slangen, interview, 28 March 2000.

58. Stuart Elliott, "Easter Seal Society Presents Awards," New York Times, 25 October 1999, C22.

59. Invacare Corp., press release, 8 December 1999.

60. "Invacare moves to NYSE Friday," (Elyria) Chronicle-Telegram,

24 June 1999;
Invacare Corp.,
press release.
25 June 1999.

61. Invacare Corp.,
press release.
1 July 1999.

62. Invacare Corp.,
press release.
31 August 1999.

63. Tabickman, interview.

64. Invacare Corp.,
press release,
5 October 1999.

65. Kathy Leneghan,
interviewed by
Heather G. Cohn,
tape recording,

11 January 2001,
Write Stuff Enterprises.

66. Tabickman, interview.

67. Steward, interview.

68. Ibid.

69. Mixon, interview,
7 September 2000.

70. Moore, interview.

71. Mixon, interview,
7 September 2000.

72. Steven Neese,
interviewed by
Anthony L. Wall,
tape recording,
5 June 2000,
Write Stuff Enterprises.

73. Mixon, interview,
7 September 2000.

74. Ibid.

75. John Dmytriw,
interviewed by
Heather G. Cohn,
tape recording,
5 January 2001,
Write Stuff Enterprises.

76. Mixon, interview,
7 September 2000.

77. "Marching Orders:
Ten people who set
the beat for the
HME industry,"
HME News,
November 1999,
55.

78. Mixon, interview,
30 March 2000.

INDEX